A SHORT HISTORY OF WRITING INSTRUCTION

FROM ANCIENT GREECE TO TWENTIETH-CENTURY AMERICA

EDITED BY
JAMES J. MURPHY

Hermagoras Press
1990

Published 1990 by Hermagoras Press,
P.O. Box 1555, Davis, California 95617.

Typesetting & Camera-ready Production
by Graphic Gold, Davis, California.
Cover Illustration by Janet K. Williams.

Manufactured in the United States of America.

ISBN 0-9611800-6-4
2 3 4 5 6 7 8 9 0

TABLE OF CONTENTS

PREFACE

One of the major figures in this book, the Roman educator Quintilian, points out that writing — unlike speaking — must always be learned from a teacher since it cannot be learned by natural imitation as oral language is. In fact he uses the example of a two-year-old who can understand and speak even though the child is years away from being able to be taught even the rudiments of the written alphabet.

Writing instruction therefore plays an important role in any literate culture.

This book offers a survey of the ways in which writing has been taught in Western culture, from ancient Greece to present-day America. While there have been many studies of individual periods or specific educators, this volume provides the first systematic coverage of teaching writing over the twenty-five centuries from the ancient Sophists to today.

The modern reader, it is hoped, may find useful ideas in this account of the ebb and flow of teaching methods and philosophies over the years.

CHAPTER ONE

WRITING INSTRUCTION IN ANCIENT ATHENS AFTER 450 B.C.

KATHLEEN E. WELCH

Writing in its various physical forms—from Sumerian Cuneiform to Egyptian hieroglyphic—may be more than five thousand years old,[1] but our records of systematic instruction in composition date more precisely to Athens in the middle of the fifth century before Christ.

Instruction in language formed a center of systems of education in Athens after 450 B.C., systems that in various guises provided some structures for Western education for about 2500 years. The residue of this ancient material—part of the revolutionary thought that characterized the second half of the fifth century and the fourth century B.C.—clings to modern writing instruction in many ways that are not readily apparent. By the second half of the fifth century B.C., language instruction appears to have focussed in many schools of higher learning on rhetorical communication. In fact, *rhetorike*— the ability to make oneself believed, or the crafting of persuasion— constituted the center of much higher education for the formative period from 450 B.C. (thirty years after the birth of the Sophists Antiphon and Gorgias) until the death of Isocrates in 388 B.C., and well beyond. Writing, and instruction in writing assumed an important aspect of rhetorical education, practice, and theory—that is, an important aspect of most systems of higher education—in this intense period of intellectual movement. It also played a significant role in primary and secondary education. Before 450 B.C. writing

---

[1]See especially Christine Gaur, *A History of Writing* (London: British Library, 1984).

appears not to have been important in Greek education.[2]

TWO CHALLENGES IN WRITING THE HISTORY OF WRITING INSTRUCTION

The historicizing of rhetoric and writing instruction (or any other area) is far from being a self-evident activity, as Victor J. Vitanza, John Schilb, and other writers have demonstrated.[3] The writing of history is always a "construction." The familiar objectivist idea that historical areas or ideas are "out there" and need only be located and examined has been questioned seriously in recent theory and poses a challenge to writers who construct the past in discourse. The construction that I make here sets up the period after 450 B.C. as a center of inquiry because it comprises the schools associated with the most powerful rhetoricians and philosophers who supplied higher education: the Sophists (for example, Gorgias, Lysias, and Alcidamus); Isocrates (who can be classified as a Sophist[4] or as a member of a different category); and the Socratics (including Plato). This category also takes account of the schools from which students of higher education and others came.

The period from 450 B.C. onwards is important, even though my construction could very well have included a different period (for example, the 100 years following the deaths of Aristotle and Demosthenes in 322 B.C., when different rhetorical, social, political, and educational issues dominated; or the contrasts between Spartan education and Athenian education; or the contributions of Ionic education to Athenian systems). In addition, I could have focussed on economic issues that inevitably form educational practice. Other considerations could be studied, including socio-political and cultural

---

[2]Tony M. Lentz, *Orality and Literacy in Hellenic Greece* (Carbondale: Southern Illinois University Press, 1989).

[3]See, for example, Dominick La Capra's *Soundings in Critical Theory* (Ithaca: Cornell University Press, 1989).

[4]I follow Kathleen Freeman, *Ancilla to the Pre-Socratic Philosophers: A Complete Translation of the Fragments in Diels, Fragments der Vorsokratiker* (Cambridge, MA: Harvard University Press, 1983), W.K.C. Guthrie, *The Sophists* (Cambridge, England: Cambridge University Press, 1969), and others in separating Isocrates from the Sophists. Nonetheless, Isocrates functioned as a Sophist in much of his agenda. See Norlin's analysis of Isocrate's career as a Sophist, George Norlin, Trans., *Isocrates*, 3 volumes (Cambridge, Mass: Harvard University Press, 1932), xix. (vol. 2)

issues; the place of slavery as an educational component; or the fluctuations in the oppression of women as part of the structure of, say, Athenian society when Aristotle provided instruction in the Lyceum. The pressures of all these issues on primary and secondary education could have been examined as well. Alternatively, I could have focussed on some of the implications of the research provided by Martin Bernal as a way of beginning to reconstruct ancient Greek writing pedagogy. Bernal argues persuasively that nineteenth- and twentieth-century constructions of classical Greek culture have been based on what he calls an Aryan Model of scholarship,[5] in which, for example, Egyptian participation in the formation of ancient Greek culture was consciously excluded. However, the implications of Bernal's analysis for research in classical rhetoric and in writing instruction have not yet had time to take hold, as they may do in progressive rhetoric and composition studies and in, one hopes, other areas as well. Investigation of any of these issues as they relate to the burgeoning power of writing and of instruction in writing could open up very different aspects from the ones we may have been conditioned to expect.

Challenges in determining the ways that writing instruction figured in these early systems (including primary and secondary education as well as higher education) lie in at least two kinds of absence: 1) the absence of material. We do not possess enough written material, visual media, or other kinds of evidence to determine enough details of the writing instruction that the various schools provided; and 2) the absence of evidence in the historicizing of pedagogical practice of any kind. Nevertheless a standard, valuable source is H.I. Marrou's *A History of Education in Antiquity.* This book, first published in France in 1948, remains an important source not only for the period under discussion here but for analyses of education generally in the Homeric era, in Sparta, and in Athens before the Sophistic/Platonic intellectual revolutions. Although Marrou consigns women in education to a category called

---

[5]Martin Bernal, *Black Athena: The Afroasiatic Roots of Classical Civilization, Vol I: The Fabrication of Ancient Greece 1785-1985* (New Brunswick, NJ: Rutgers University Press, 1987), 330-402.

"the feminine,"[6] he does provide valuable insight into the education of males.

The first absence concerns the storage and transmission of material. Storing artifacts such as wooden writing boards used in a primary school requires a belief that the material is worth saving. In other words, modern attitudes toward educational archives would have to have been operating. In the extraordinarily fluid context of the era under discussion, the idea of documenting teaching practices in a way that we would now find important was not apparently a major consideration for the people running schools at the primary, secondary, or higher education levels. For the Sophists, we have to rely on fragments of their writings that lie embedded in other writers' work. These fragments are more aptly regarded as quotations, as Jonathan Barnes has done in *Early Greek Philosophy*,[7] a collection of ancient philosophical writings important to the discipline of philosophy.

Even if storage and transmission of educational material had been considered important, the materials used could not for the most part have survived. The papyri and much other material that were used in schools would have disintegrated. Perhaps more seriously than the scarcity of documentary evidence, the received, negative tradition of the Sophists as amoral teachers means that their teaching methods have not received appropriate consideration under any circumstances. This presentation, the Platonic-Aristotelian position, dominated critical response to the Sophists until the nineteenth-century resuscitation of these thinkers. The breathing in of new ways of thinking about the Sophists continues and offers one of the most dynamic areas of research in current rhetoric and composition studies. The oppressive weight of the Platonic-Aristotelian appropriation (indeed, their virulent rejection) of the Sophists' important work continues to hamper the historicizing of rhetoric and composition studies. It is a burden that historicists struggle with in training current writers in rhetoric and composition.

The second absence — the absence of historicizing of pedagogical material — derives partly from the fact that educational practice has

---

[6]H.I. Marrou, *A History of Education in Antiquity,* trans. George Lamb (Madison: University of Wisconsin Press, 1982), 463.

[7]Jonathan Barnes, *Early Greek Philosophy* (Harmondsworth, England: Penguin, 1987).

been singularly disregarded by most academics, who frequently regard such investigations as not relevant or not worthy of attention. Disregard has clung to pedagogical practice in many fields and has inhibited investigation of the ways that pedagogy creates (as well as transmits) knowledge. This chronic dismissal has led to many problems for those who, like various rhetoric and composition writers and teachers, seek to change the practices of disciplines or at least to examine the ways that these practices form knowledge. As Robert Scholes has written in *Textual Power*, we disregard educational practices at our own peril.[8] We can now analyze these early schools as institutions that have exerted differing amounts of influence on writing instruction. In addition, we can create alternative historical descriptions that show us more productive ways to construct our own institutions for the teaching of writing and its intertwined relationship to thinking.

HIGHER EDUCATION AND WRITING INSTRUCTION: AN OVERVIEW

A striking feature of higher education in the era under discussion is the remarkable similarity of teaching methods even between competing schools (for example, between Isocrates' school and Plato's or between the stationary schools of Plato and Isocrates and the moving schools of the travelling Sophists) all in effect employing the same pedagogical theory. One interpretation of the currently identifiable[9] educational groups that emerged from the explosion of discourse changes in the second half of the fifth century and the fourth century B.C. reveals that a struggle among many stances toward language, rhetoric, and power emerged. Struggles over which stance would become most powerful were common. For example, a look at some of Plato's dialogues, particularly those named after Sophists such as Protagoras and Gorgias (in addition to characters in the dialogues with the names of Sophists) indicates that he positioned himself staunchly in

---

[8]Robert Scholes, *Textual Power: Literary Theory and the Teaching of English* (New Haven: Yale University Press, 1985). See the annual volume *History of Universities* (Oxford University Press) for an example of recent attention to higher education.

[9]Marrou's *History of Education in Antiquity* lays out these similarities in convincing detail; see especially 150-175.

opposition to the Sophists intellectually and ethically. In addition, he opposed Isocrates, although he treated him with much more respect than he treated the other Sophists.

Nevertheless, the methods Plato promoted as a teacher were remarkably similar to those of the Sophists. In addition, the pedagogical methods used by Plato's teacher Socrates (based on Plato's presentation of these methods rather than on more direct evidence from Socrates, whose attitudes toward writing appear to be consistently negative) bore a striking resemblance to those of the Sophists with whom he, like his protege Plato, had large problems. In other words, many attitudes toward educational behavior in the era under discussion were remarkably alike. They all departed from the practices that dominated what Marrou calls "old education," in which more aristocratic values and taste were inculcated.[10] While the former groups had particular agendas that conflicted in various ways with one anoher (for example, Isocrates' idea of philosophy and Plato's idea of philosophy), their pedagogical methods remained remarkably alike.

The teacher's authority over a small group of pupils, the study of oral communication, small group instruction (through seminars and/or lectures), note taking, and immersion in subjects for study characterized the behavior of all these groups, as did a belief in providing a wide array of subjects for study. In addition, the hierarchical stance between teacher and students provided a powerful model for instruction in virtually all areas.

With the striking changes in literacy taking place (literacy in the sense of a shift in consciousness that includes more abstraction, in addition to literacy in the sense of a skill)[11] writing as a pedagogical device assumed more importance at the primary, secondary, and higher education levels.

THE ORIGIN OF ALPHABETS AND WRITING

When discussing the earliest known systems for the teaching of writing in the conventional Western tradition, it is useful to refer to

---

[10]Marrou, 36-45.

[11]See Walter J. Ong, *Orality and Literacy: The Technologizing of the Word* (London: Methuen, 1982) and Lentz, *Orality and Literacy in Hellenic Greece.*

the origin of alphabets and the origin of writing. Roy Harris, in *The Origin of Writing,* argues that little has been written on the origin of writing, while an enormous amount has been written on the history of writing and of scripts.[12] The distinction is an important one. On a closely related issue, Harris writes:

> One reason, indeed, why the origin of writing is such an absorbing question is that the way it has usually been treated illustrates most aptly a conceptual mistake virtually endemic in the Western intellectual tradition. Our carefully cultivated European awareness of languages as unique chronological continuities, each carrying and embodying its own cultural inheritance, has fostered from Graeco-Roman antiquity onward a recurrent tendency to suppose that basic questions concerning language can be given merely historical answers. When history fails to provide the answers, as is inevitably the case, the blame is doubly laid at history's door. In other words, the responsibility for coming up with an answer is handed over to those whose job it is to unearth fresh evidence about the past. The question of the origin of writing provides a classic example of this process. The result is total inability to see that the question is as much a question about our own understanding of language in the present as about the practices of our cultural ancestors in the remote past.[13]

Harris's recognition that we historicize ourselves as we create the history of writing remains central to any inquiry that records and explains past events. He implicitly refutes the entrenched scholarly (particularly philological) conceptualization that historical material is "out there," and need only be retrieved and presented. Those who assume this rhetorical stance appear to be made confident by the tacit idea that progress will prevail.

The conventional designation for the establishment of the

---

[12]Roy Harris, *The Origin of Writing* (London: Duckworth, 1986). 159; see Harris's annotated bibliography of the conventional treatments of the origin of writing.
[13]Harris, ix.

Greek alphabet is in the eighth century B.C.[14] A dominant version of this establishment goes like this: a workable, easy-to-learn alphabet emerged complete with vowels, a phenomenon that makes the alphabet much more flexible.[15] In the subsequent three centuries, the alphabet came to assume increasing importance in daily lives. After about three hundred years of "ordinary" use, the alphabet led many people to become more abstract in their thinking and to conceptualize differently. In modern terms, the psychology of the group changed. This abstraction led, of course, to rapid and decisive achievements in thinking. In *Orality and Literacy,* Walter J. Ong writes that "The Greek alphabet was democratizing in the sense that it was easy for everyone to learn. It was also internationalizing in that it provided a way of processing even foreign tongues. This Greek achievement in abstractly analyzing the elusive world of sound into visual equivalents...both presaged and implemented their further analytic exploits.[16]

The result was a burgeoning of literacy—a great rush of verbal, analytic achievement of the fifth century B.C. rhetoricians (the Sophists and Isocrates, and, I would argue, Plato), the dramatists (Aeschylus, Euripides, Sophocles, Aristophanes, and the others), and what have been traditionally called the "philosophers" (Socrates, Plato, Aristotle). In other words, one of the great shifts of consciousness occurred in this vibrant period. The linearity and abstractness of writing, brought on by the elegant simplicity of the Greek alphabet three hundred years before, enabled ways of

---

[14]See I.J. Gelb's standard *A Study of Writing,* rev. ed. (Chicago: University of Chicago Press, 1963) for one analysis of the alphabets and syllabaries that preceded the Greek alphabet. See also David Diringer's standard *Writing* (London: Thames and Hudson, 1962) and Denise Schmandt-Bessarat's "An Ancient Token System: The Precursor to Numerals and Writing," *Scientific American* (Nov./Dec., 1986), 32-39. Schmandt-Bessarat writes that ancient token systems led to writing and to numbers: "Both traditions, however—that of simple tokens and that of complex tokens—made powerful contributions to the world's record-keeping abilities, and to humanity's capacity for efficient, reliable communication. This story is, in essence, a study in the stages whereby human culture slowly, and then ever more quickly, mastered the art of abstraction, which stands as one of the peculiar marks of distinctive human consciousness." (39)

[15]See Harris for alternative interpretations.

[16]Ong, 90.

thinking to alter.[17] Harris puts it this way: "The careful organisation of a Socratic dialogue, let alone the organisation of connexions between one dialogue and another, is the kind of organisation which not even a Plato can undertake without at least jotting down a few notes."[18]

This unusual linguistic activity supplies the background for our immediate concern with the teaching of writing in the century after 450 B.C., the focus chosen for the treatment here, and, in fact, for many periods beyond this one. An additional issue presents itself here: how did the profound changes in everyday relationships to language (from our vantage point deep within the burgeoning power of electronic forms of discourse, or the phenomenon Ong calls "secondary orality") affect writing pedagogy?

WRITING INSTRUCTION AT THE PRIMARY SCHOOL LEVEL

Primary schools in ancient Athens taught writing as a technique, according to Marrou. He presents reading, recitation, and writing as having been taught together.[19] Partly because of these connected verbal goals, short passages or sentences were given to students by the teacher. The male students attended elementary school from the ages of seven to fourteen. I will return to this topic below under "Procedures Used in Primary School Writing Instruction."

The students under discussion are male because of cultural constructions of females as inherently inferior and consequently in need of different kinds of education appropriate to that assumed inferiority. Nonetheless, females were educated, even if they were not sent to schools. Sarah B. Pomeroy, in *Goddesses, Whores, Wives, and Slaves,* compares the enormous differences in instruction given to girls:

> Since citizen girls were not to look forward to the public careers that brought status to men, it was sufficient for them to be instructed in domestic arts by their mothers. While her male contemporary was living in his parents' house and developing

---

[17]Eric A. Havelock, *Preface to Plato* (Cambridge, MA: Harvard University Press, 1963).

[18]Harris, 25.

[19]Marrou, 154.

mental and physical skills, the adolescent girl was already married and had young children.[20]

So while a boy from a privileged social class would be completing elementary school at the age of fourteen, a girl of the same age and socioeconomic category would be married.

Eva C. Keuls describes the education of females this way in *The Reign of the Phallus: Sexual Politics in Ancient Athens:*

> Keeping women ignorant was another major component of the techniques of dominance. Women were completely cut off from any kind of formal education; that many, perhaps most, nevertheless learned how to read—by a female educational underground, one supposes—was a source of anxiety to men.[21]

Keuls provides us with the scene of the now familiar situation: the yoking of women and children by infantilizing the former group. She continues: "The aim was to keep women frozen in their development, so that they would become, as it were, perpetual children, and this attempt may often have been successful."[22] While an opening of educational opportunities for females occurred in the fourth century,[23] the education of females, including instruction in writing, remained separate and unequal to that of males. It is no surprise that we have more material on writing instruction of males than we do for females. Partly because of this situation, I will here present the instruction in writing provided males. The "underground education" of females alluded to by Keuls will remain part of the future project of the reconstruction of classical rhetoric and writing.

MATERIALS USED IN WRITING INSTRUCTION

The basic materials used for writing in the primary schools were first of all, according to Marrou, wooden boards. The boards could be single or multiple. In the latter case, the boards were held

---

[20]Sarah B. Pomeroy, *Goddesses, Whores, Wives, and Slaves* (New York: Schocken Books, 1975), 74.

[21]Eva C. Keuls, *The Reign of the Phallus: Sexual Politics in Ancient Athens* (New York: Harper & Row, 1985), 104.

[22]Keuls, 104.

[23]Marrou, 103; Pomeroy, p. 136-139.

together by hinges or string. Marrou writes:

> Each board had a waxed surface inside a hollow frame, and the pupil wrote on this with a pricker whose other end was rounded and was used as a rubber. Often boards were used that could be written on in ink. The pen was made from a reed that was split and pointed, and the ink, which was solid like our Chinese ink, was made into a powder and watered down beforehand by the master or a servant. In this case a small sponge was used as a rubber.[24]

Marrou states that papyrus was used as well but that its high price and unavailability made its use less frequent in schooling than it might otherwise have been. As an alternative to the costly papyrus, pottery fragments were brought into instructional service. These were called *ostraca;* William Smith states that *ostraca* were used as well by poor people.[25] The material used in this early period — wood, clay fragments, reeds, and so on — may well require the modern writer to make a leap of imagination in trying to understand the tactile, ordinary, experience of encoding in writing.

PROCEDURES USED IN PRIMARY SCHOOL WRITING INSTRUCTION

Marrou writes that the elementary school boy was taught the letters of the alphabet individually. Using Plato and Seneca as sources, Marrou states that probably the teacher would draw a letter "and then, before he let the child try it by himself, take his hand and make him go over it, so as to give him the 'feel' of the letter. Once the child had learned how to do it he would go on practising, repeating the same letter for a line or a page at a time."[26] The instruction proceeded from the smallest units to the larger units, from letters, to syllables, to words, to short sentences.

Further practice in writing came about when the student wrote down the words read by the teacher. Kenneth J. Freeman writes in *Schools of Hellas:*

---

[24]Marrou, 155.

[25]Marrou, 155; William Smith, *Smaller Classical Dictionary* (New York: E.P. Dutton, 1958).

[26]Marrou, 156.

As soon as the boy had acquired a certain facility in writing, he entered the dictation class. The master read out something, and the boys wrote it down. At first, of course, very simple words would be dictated, and there would not be much to write. But, later on, the boys would write at his dictation passages of the poets and other authors.[27]

This instruction was provided by a teacher called a *grammatistes,* who taught writing, reading, literature, and arithmetic.[28] (The other two parts of primary school were the study of music and lyric poetry, taught by the *kitharistes* and the study of gymnastics and games, taught by the *paidotribes,* according to Beck). In addition to the teachers, the child had a pedagogue, a family servant (or slave) who accompanied the boy and watched over him.[29] Some pedagogues at times had responsibility for helping to educate the boy as well.

Part of the intellectual revolution of the second half of the fifth century and the fourth century B.C. involved the centrality of writing. While oral traditions remained strong, writing nonetheless gained in strength. In *Orality and Literacy in Hellenic Greece,* Lentz argues that oral and written discourse competed with each other in ways that strengthened each. In his chapter "Basic Education," Lentz writes:

> The very teaching of grammar...demonstrates the tension between oral and written culture. Students do learn to write, but first they learn the system of sounds the writings will represent. The system of sound they are taught, in turn, owes its existence to the awareness of abstractions fostered by writing.[30]

The intertwining of speaking and writing had helped to bring about the large educational changes of this period.[31]

Writing issues that current compositionists would consider

---

[27]Kenneth J. Freeman, *Schools of Hellas* (New York: Teachers College Press, 1969), 87.

[28]Frederick A.B. Beck, "Education," *Oxford Classical Dictionary,* ed. N.G.L. Hammond and H.H. Scullard, 2nd ed. (Oxford: The Clarendon Press, 1972), 370.

[29]Marrou, 143-144.

[30]Lentz, 69.

[31]Lentz, 49, cites Frederick A.B. Beck, in *Album of Greek Education: The Greeks at School and Play* (Sydney: Cheiron Press, 1975) for the evidence of such things as vase depictions of student writing after 450 B.C.

important—issues related to writing and thinking—occurred at
the secondary level (a difficult category to determine) and in
higher education. Since the majority of students received only
primary education, work in writing-as-thinking probably did not
take place. Lentz writes:

> Basic education in writing, however, was apparently a useful
> tool for recording and preserving words and lists in the archaic
> tradition. Literacy as we know it was not a conception, much
> less a goal, in elementary education.[32]

We can surmise from Marrou and Lentz that writing instruction at
the earliest level in classical Greece emphasized merely technical
orthographic skills. It is important to remember that even though
literacy was not, as Lentz argues, a goal at this stage, that working
with wooden boards, papyri or *ostraca,* and reeds enacted effects
that neither the teacher or the students were aware of. Subtle
psychological changes were coming about as a result of writing,
even if these changes were not necessarily apparent to those
enacting them.

WRITING INSTRUCTION AT THE SECONDARY LEVEL

Two prominent issues stand out in ancient Athenian secondary
schooling in the era under consideration: secondary education was
exclusive (much more exclusive than elementary education was),
and it was available institutionally only to males. Socioeconomic
category and gender thus determined the availability of this stage
of instruction, in writing and in other parts of the course of study.
By this point in education, women were already enacting adult
roles, as were, presumably, males in lower socioeconomic categories.

This period of education was conducted by the *grammatikos,*
or grammarian, and centered on the intensive study of then-
classical writers, particularly Homer, whose tenacious hold over the
course of study troubled Plato.[33] "The Hellenistic age carried its
official canonization of the classics to great lengths," Marrou
writes. He continues:

---

[32]Lentz, 47-48.
[33]See Havelock's *Preface to Plato* for an analysis of Plato's objection to the
emphasis given Homeric and other poems in fourth-century education.

In spite of all Plato's efforts, the higher Hellenistic culture remained faithful to the archaic tradition and based itself on poetry, not science. As a result of this, education was not so much concerned to develop the reasoning faculty as to hand on its literary heritage of great masterpieces.[34]

Part of this education depended on the development of writing skills by the pupils. Lentz writes:

> Schools taught reading and writing along with literature, demonstrating writing's acceptance as part of the normal curriculum of the day. Music and gymnastics remained the two major parts of the Greek concept of education...[35]

As writing became more and more important in Athenian and Greek culture, its appearance in secondary schools became more important.

Beck, in *Greek Education, 450-350 B.C.*, describes secondary education as an amorphous group of studies; sometimes this period provides preparatory courses for the schools of higher education.[36] Similarly, Lentz emphasizes primary and higher education. It appears that writing instruction was conducted at a more advanced level with the same writing utensils used in primary instruction.

HIGHER EDUCATION AND WRITING: PARTICULAR VERSIONS

The higher education offered was provided by the Sophists who travelled from place to place, by Plato, Isocrates, and other philosophers or thinkers. The Sophists and Isocrates emphasized the teaching of practical as well as theoretical issues. The Sophists competed with one another and disagreed in various ways, but they resembled one another in other ways. Beck writes:

> What they had in common apart from their professionalism was their...belief in the power of knowledge to improve human character....This implies both a theory of the disciplinary value

---

[34]Marrou, 161.

[35]Lentz, 52.

[36]Frederick A.B. Beck, *Greek Education 450-350 B.C.* (New York: Barnes & Noble, 1964), see esp. 141-142.

of certain studies...and the rejection of the aristocratic theory of 'virtue' as a matter of innate gifts and divine descent.[37]

The idea that most human beings were trainable represents a significant departure from archaic traditions which had fostered an elitism based on birth. The lecture method and small group work were important teaching strategies for the Sophists.[38] A broad curriculum was promoted by most of the Sophists, who trained their students to respond knowledgably on many subjects. It seems clear that the Sophists used writing as well as speaking in their instruction; however, the exact uses of writing employed by them have not been determined.

The Sophists trained their fee-paying students for three or four years.[39] Rhetoric provided the center of study. Marrou claims that in this training "the spoken word reigned supreme."[40] Indeed the fact that the Sophists moved from place to place could mean that they privileged speaking training over writing training. However, students did, according to Freeman, take notes.[41] Given the current state of the scant evidence and the Platonic-Aristotelian denunciation of the Sophists (an attitude partly evident in Marrou's presentation), it is difficult to know the details of Sophistic uses of writing. Nevertheless, we do know that they were undergoing the same shifts in consciousness brought about by the gradually increasing power of literacy that the rest of the culture underwent.

Plato's deeply ambivalent attitude toward writing poses many problems for modern interpreters of rhetoric and writing. A common attitude is that Plato simply denounced both rhetoric and writing. This interpretation frequently derives evidence from *Gorgias,* in which a virulent attack on rhetoric is launched. However, Plato's interest in rhetoric and writing is presented in a much more complex (and favorable) way in the later dialogue *Phaedrus,* in which the power of writing is regarded with great complexity. Most persuasive of all in Plato's attitude toward writing is the fact that he not only wrote, but that he wrote carefully crafted dialogues. Plato's engagement with writing was

---

[37]Beck, *Greek Education, 450-350 B.C.,* 148.
[38]Ibid., 167.
[39]Marrou, 49.
[40]Ibid., 52.
[41]Freeman, 87.

intense and pivotal. He not only displayed his great power with the written word; he exploited it thoroughly, even in those places where he was presenting an anti-writing stance.

Plato presents his desired curriculum, which he always associates with the health of the larger culture and with the pursuit of knowledge, most elaborately in two places, *The Republic* and *Laws,* two utopian works which have been minutely studied from various perspectives. He advocated the study of reading and writing from an early age.[42] His Academy eventually incorporated rhetoric in its curriculum. Paul Friedlander compares Plato's teaching to that of the Sophists. For Socrates and Plato,

> philosophy is possible only as an exchange between two people; it is an infinite conversation renewing itself constantly out of a personal question. For this reason, genuine philosophical discourse must decide whom it is addressed to and whom not—a principle that must have determined Plato's teaching in contrast to Sophistic instruction. The written word, on the other hand, is addressed to each and everyone.[43]

Isocrates, who resembles Plato as well as the Sophists in so many ways, was committed to writing as an important way of thinking. His commitment was to prose composition, however, and not to poetry, the kind of writing that had dominated so much of the traditional curricula. Isocrates' emphasis on prose composition in his long-running school (first at Chios and then at Athens) recognized the growing power of writing in the culture and helped to establish it as an important part of study. It is easy for modern readers to disregard the power poetry exerted in this period. Like Plato, Isocrates did much to promote prose composition. This change as well can be seen as part of the growing power of literacy, since poetry had been orally dominant for so many centuries. Since he would not speak in public, he wrote all his speeches. He was thoroughly conditioned by the shift to literacy. Lentz writes:

> Isocrates, the retiring rhetorician, provided another link in the continuing interaction between oral and written modes of

---

[42]Marrou, 73.
[43]Paul Friedlander, *Plato: An Introduction,* trans. Hans Meyerhoff (New York: Pantheon, 1958), 113.

communication and thought. His voice and temperament tied him to the techniques and form of written communication, yet he nevertheless retained ties to the oral culture that placed value on the ability of a citizen to speak ...Isocrate's theory and practice offered a perfect illustration of the continuing competition between written and oral culture as the Hellenic world grew more dependent of writing.[44]

Isocrates' *Antidosis,*[45] a kind of autobiography written when he was in his eighties, reveals the emphasis he placed on writing. He trained his students in writing and speaking while providing them with a diverse curriculum (he is frequently designated the founder of the liberal arts tradition). Isocrates trained his students to think critically, to address, through their advanced and meticulous work in rhetoric, any situation that might arise. Freeman discusses Isocrates' commitment to written composition. He used his own writings and that of other Sophists as texts to train his students in writing.[46] More than Plato, the Sophists, or other thinkers of his time, Isocrates appears to have realized the centrality of writing to effective thinking. His role in the advancement of writing as a pedagogical device has not yet received adequate scholarly attention.

Writing as an educational, social, and individual force continued to exert greater power after the deaths of Plato and Isocrates. Educational opportunities were given to a broader range of people and the state participated in financing much of it. These two widening phenomena appear to have increased the teaching of writing. The Greek world was rapidly becoming more literate. Schools at all levels both reflected this fact and promoted it.

---

[44]Lentz, 135.
[45]Norlin, *Isocrates,* Vol.2, see note 4 above.
[46]Freeman, 188-189.

CHAPTER TWO

ROMAN WRITING INSTRUCTION AS DESCRIBED BY QUINTILIAN

JAMES J. MURPHY

Writing and rhetoric go hand in hand in the Roman educational program. If oral eloquence was the desired product of the schools, writing was a major means to that end.

"In writing are the roots, in writing are the foundations of eloquence." This judgment, written in A.D. 95 by Marcus Fabius Quintilianus in his *Institutio oratoria,*[1] was not unique to him. It was an idea pervasive in Roman culture over many centuries. Quintilian himself quotes Cicero as saying a century and a half earlier that the pen is "the best modeler and teacher of eloquence." Three centuries after Quintilian the young Aurelius Augustinus—a teacher of rhetoric later to be Christian bishop and one of the four Latin Fathers of the Church—describes in his *Confessions* his own efforts to teach oral and written composition to the unruly young in North Africa. The Christian encyclopedists of the sixth and seventh centuries still insist on the same point.

The Roman educational system—and indeed it was truly a "system"—had rhetorical efficiency as its primary goal. Quintilian's term for this objective is Facility *(facilitas),* or the capacity to produce appropriate and effective language in any situation. This result was to be achieved by a carefully coordinated program of reading, writing, speaking and listening. The process carried boys

---

[1]*Institutio oratoria* X.3.1. Quotations from Books One, Two and Ten will be from James J. Murphy (ed.), *Quintilian On the Teaching of Speaking and Writing: Translations from Books One, Two and Ten of the Institutio oratoria* (Southern Illinois University Press, 1987). Quotations from other books will be from *The Institutio oratoria of Quintilian,* trans. H.E. Butler. Four volumes. (Loeb Classical Library: Harvard University Press, 1921-22).

from beginning alphabet exercises at six or seven through a dozen years of interactive classroom activities designed to produce an adult capable of public improvisation under any circumstances.

Writing was an integral part of this process, inseparable from the other elements. As Quintilian notes:

> I know that it is often asked whether more is contributed by writing, by reading, or by speaking. This question we should have to examine with careful attention if in fact we could confine ourselves to any one of these activities; but in truth they are all so connected, so inseparably linked with one another, that if any one of them is neglected, we labor in vain in the other two—for our speech will never become forcible and energetic unless it acquires strength from great practice in writing; and the labor of writing, if left destitute of models from reading, passes away without effect, as having no director; while he who knows how everything ought to be said, will, if he has not his eloquence in readiness and prepared for all emergencies, merely brood, as it were, over locked-up treasure (*Institutio* X.1.1).

Since Roman writing instruction was so firmly embedded in such a complex process, then, the modern reader needs to understand all the elements of the system itself in order to appreciate the role played by writing. Consequently the following section describes the manner in which rhetorical education supplanted the "Old Education" in Rome during the first century before Christ. The next sections discuss that educational process as described in Quintilian's *Institutio oratoria* (A.D. 95). The continuity of the system in later antiquity and the early middle ages is the subject of the next section, which is followed by a brief analysis of the advantages and disadvantages of the Roman educational pattern.

THE ROMAN TRANSITION TO SYSTEMATIC RHETORICAL EDUCATION

The first century before Christ was the turning point in the Roman transition from the "Old Education" of the conservative Republic to the more systematic rhetorical program which dominated European practice for the next two millennia.

The change was from a native Latin, tutorial process to a Greek-originated "school" system. In a real sense it was a triumph of Isocratean educational principles over a familial approach which

had emphasized private tutors and apprenticeship. The historian
Cornelius Tacitus, writing later in the middle of the first Christian
century, looks back fondly on "the good old days" before there
were "professors of Rhetoric":

> "Well then, in the good old days the young man who was
> destined for the oratory of the bar, after receiving the rudiments
> of a sound training at home, and storing his mind with liberal
> culture, was taken by his father, or his relations, and placed
> under the care of some orator who held a leading position at
> Rome. The youth had to get the habit of following his patron
> about, of escorting him in public, of supporting him at all his
> appearances as a speaker, whether in the law courts or on the
> platform, hearing also his word-combats at first hand, standing by
> him in his duellings, and learning, as it were, to fight in the
> fighting-line. It was a method that secured at once for the young
> students a considerable amount of experience, great self-possession,
> and a goodly store of sound judgment: for they carried on their
> studies in the light of open day, and amid the very shock of
> battle, under conditions in which any stupid or ill-advised
> statement brings prompt retribution in the shape of the judge's
> disapproval, taunting criticism from your opponent — yes, and
> from your own supporters expressions of dissatisfaction. So it was
> a genuine and unadulterated eloquence that they were initiated in
> from the very first; and though they attached themselves to a
> single speaker, yet they got to know all the contemporary
> members of the bar in a great variety of both civil and criminal
> cases. Moreover a public meeting gave them the opportunity of
> noting marked divergences of taste, so that they could easily
> detect what commended itself in the case of each individual
> speaker, and what on the other hand failed to please."[2]

Thus there were three levels of education: home training, military
service, then apprenticeship to some prominent orator to learn the
practical ways of the world. Cicero's father, for instance, placed
him with Q. Mucius Scaevola Augur; moreover, the young boy's
advisers had earlier warned him away from the new-fangled Latin
rhetorician L. Plotius Gallus, and Cicero went off instead to Rhodes
to study Greek rhetoric there before taking up his apprenticeship.

---

[2]P. Cornelius Tacitus, *A Dialogue on Oratory,* trans. Sir William Peterson. (Loeb
Classical Library: Harvard University Press, 1946), 105-06.

If Roman education was a male-centered education, it was because the society was male-centered. Women had little status under the law, and children—even adult sons with their own careers—were regarded as subjects of their fathers in many circumstances. This was not so much a conscious social decision as it was a continuation of assumptions common to many ancient societies including the Greek and the Judaic. It is important therefore for a modern reader, even while deploring this situation, to look beyond it to assess the teaching methods actually employed.

Plutarch tells us how the elder Cato (234 - 149 B.C.) taught his own son two centuries before Christ:

> When his son was born, no duty (save perhaps some public function) was so pressing as to prevent him from being present when his wife bathed the child and wrapped it in its swaddling-clothes. His wife suckled the child with her own milk, and would often give her breast to the children of her slaves, so as to gain their affection for her son by treating them as his brothers. As soon as the boy was able to learn, Cato took him personally in charge and taught him his letters, although he owned an accomplished slave, named Chilon, who was a schoolmaster and gave lessons to many boys. But Cato, to use his own words, would not have a slave abuse his son nor perhaps pull his ears for being slow at his lessons; nor would he have his boy owe a slave so precious a gift as learning. So he made himself the boy's schoolmaster, just as he taught him the laws of Rome and bodily exercises; not merely to throw the javelin, to fight in armour or to ride, but also to use his fists in boxing, to bear heat and cold, and to swim against the currents and eddies of a river. And he tells us himself that he wrote books of history with his own hand and in large characters, so that his son might be able even at home to become acquainted with his country's past; that he was as careful to avoid all indecent conversation in his son's presence as he would have been in presence of the Vestal virgins; and that he never bathed with him. This last point seems to have been a Roman custom, for even fathers-in-law were careful not to bathe with their sons-in-law to avoid the necessity of stripping naked before them.[3]

---

[3]Quoted in Aubrey Gwynn S.J., *Roman Education from Cicero to Quintilian* (Oxford: Clarendon Press, 1926; reprinted Columbia Teachers College, n.d.), 19.

Signficantly, the resident schoolmaster Chilon is both Greek and a slave. The militant Romans had conquered Greece, so that many educated Greeks were brought back to Rome as slaves. During the republican period, then, most teachers had a very low social status since they were enslaved members of a conquered class.

Matters Greek were thus to be despised. Despite a popular visit to Rome in 168 B.C. by the grammarian and literary scholar Crates of Malos, there was general resentment against Greek philosophy and against certain Greek practices like nudity in athletics. In 161 B.C., the Roman Senate passed a decree enabling the Praetor to expel all Greek teachers of philosophy and rhetoric. Nevertheless there are scattered evidences of Greek teachers in Rome over the succeeding half century.

The first clear evidence of a Latin—as opposed to Greek— teacher of rhetoric comes from 93 B.C. In that year one L. Plotius Gallus began teaching in Latin, but was stopped almost at once. In 92 the two Censors, Cn. Domitius Aenobarbus and L. Licinius Crassus, issued the following edict which was aimed not only at Plotius Gallus but at other unnamed teachers:

> A report has been made to us that certain men have begun a new kind of teaching, and that young men are going regularly to their school; that they have taken the name of teachers of Latin rhetoric (*Latini rhetores*): and that our young men are wasting their whole days with them. Our ancestors ordained what lessons their children were to learn, and what schools they were to frequent. These new schools are contrary to our customs and ancestral traditions (*mos maiorum*), and we consider them undesirable and improper. Wherefore we have decided to publish, both to those who keep these schools and to those who are accustomed to go there, our judgement that we consider them undesirable.[4]

The tone of this decree would make it appear that the phenomenon of Latinized rhetoric was a recent and even sporadic or unusual occurrence. Yet two almost simultaneous publications, both issued shortly after the decree, show instead that there already existed a well-organized and comprehensive system of Latin rhetoric which included provisions not only for theory but for teaching.

---

[4]Quoted in Gwynn, *Roman Education,* 61.

As a matter of fact we do not know exactly how a rather generalized rhetoric from the time of Aristotle (died 322 B.C.) became a specifically-organized and standardized five-part system by about 100 B.C. We know the names of some Greek teachers, especially on the island of Rhodes, and we know about some lost treatises like that of Hermagoras of Temnos mentioned by both Cicero and Quintilian. Of the precise transition to the five-part theory of rhetoric, however, we know comparatively little.

What we do know is that a young Roman student, Marcus Tullius Cicero, wrote a rhetorical treatise about 89 B.C. titled *On Invention (De inventione).*[5] Cicero declares that rhetoric is divided into the five "parts" of Invention, Arrangement, Style, Memory, and Delivery. Cicero discusses only the first of these five, promising to write later about the other four; actually he never carried out the promise.

What we also know is that an anonymous author published a book around 86 B.C. which actually did treat all five of the parts named by Cicero. Since the book is addressed to one Caius Herennius, it has traditionally been titled the *Rhetorica ad Herennium (The Book of Rhetoric Addressed to Herennius).*[6] Its full treatment of the five parts makes the *Rhetorica ad Herennium* the first complete Latin rhetoric. It is a rigorously practical manual. The author says he will treat only what is pertinent to speaking: "That is why I have omitted to treat those topics which, for the sake of futile self-assertion, Greek writers have adopted" (I.1.1). Moreover, he uses only his own Latin examples throughout the book (as he explains in IV.6.9-10).

The remarkable correspondence between these two books would seem to indicate the prior existence of a standardized theory of rhetorical education, dating perhaps to 100 B.C. or even earlier. The adolescent Cicero is clearly reporting only what he had been taught some time earlier, while the older author of the *Ad*

---

[5]Cicero, *De inventione. De optimo genere oratorum. Topica.* Trans. H.M. Hubbell. (Loeb Classical Library: Harvard University Press, 1968). Cicero was only nineteen when he wrote the *De inventione.*

[6]Cicero, *Ad C. Herennium De ratione dicendi (Rhetorica ad Herennium),* trans. Harry Caplan. (Loeb Classical Library: Harvard University Press, 1954). Caplan's Introduction (especially xxi-xxxii) has interesting notes on the possible author of the book and its possible relation to the *De inventione* of Cicero.

Herennium not only admits the influence of "my teacher" and refers to students studying in schools (*utuntur igitur studiosi*), but specifically declares that rhetorical skill is to be attained through the three means of Precept, Imitation, and Exercise (I.1.1).

Rhetoric, then, is the "Precept" portion of the Roman educational triad. As such it is embedded in a consciously-organized program which is designed to translate the "rules" into activities which will make the students into rhetorical men. In fact the author of the *Ad Herennium* says that the five parts of rhetoric are what should be "in the orator" (*in oratorem*)—a phrase which Harry Caplan translates as "faculty." In other words, the whole apparatus aims at practical ability rather than mere knowledge. This ability is to be "in" the person, not in his books.

The striking homogeneity of Roman rhetorical theory at this early period may be seen clearly in the similar definitions of the five parts as given by Cicero and the author of the *Ad Herennium:*

Cicero	*Rhetorica ad Herennium*
Invention is the discovery of valid or seemingly valid arguments to render one's cause plausible.	Invention is the devising of matter, true or plausible, that would make the case convincing.
Arrangement is the distribution of arguments thus discovered in the proper order.	Arrangement is the ordering and distribution of the matter, making clear the place to which each thing is to be assigned.
Expression is the fitting of the proper language to the invented matter.	Style is the adaptation of suitable words and sentences to the matter devised.
Memory is the firm mental grasp of matter and words.	Memory is the firm retention in the mind of matter, words, and arrangement.
Delivery is the control of voice and body in a manner suitable to the dignity of the subject matter and the style.	Delivery is the graceful regulation of voice, countenance, and gesture.

Both books accept Aristotle's view that speeches are of three kinds: Forensic, dealing with legal accusation and defense; Deliberative or Political, dealing with public policy; and Epideictic, dealing with praise or blame.

The similarity of the two books was so great that during the middle ages and early Renaissance it was commonly assumed that Cicero was the author of both. Medieval writers called the *De inventione* Cicero's "First Rhetoric" (*Rhetorica prima*) or "Old Rhetoric" (*Rhetorica vetus*), relying on Cicero's statement that he planned to write on all five parts of rhetoric; these same writers believed that the *Rhetorica ad Herennium* was Cicero's carrying-out of this promise, terming it his "Second Rhetoric" (*Rhetorica Secundus*) or, more frequently, his "New Rhetoric" (*Rhetorica nova*). It was only in the fifteenth century that humanists like Lorenzo Valla began to question Cicero's authorship of the *Ad Herennium*.[7]

Though there are some differences between the books — for example the *Ad Herennium* offers two methods of Arrangement while Cicero proposes only one — the basic doctrines are substantially similar. These rhetorical precepts remain standard for antiquity, the middle ages and the Renaissance, and have currency well into the eighteenth century. It is fair to say that there is such an entity as "Roman Rhetoric," characterized by the five-part division of the subject and by standard treatments of each of the parts.

This standardization was achieved by a resolute rejection of eclecticism after about 100 B.C. The *Ad Herennium* itself draws on a number of Greek sources ranging from pre-Aristotelian to contemporary Rhodean ideas. But this "synthesis of various teachings" (to use translator Caplan's term) petrifies the chosen ideas into a lasting framework. Cicero simply assumes that the five-part plan is standard, "as most authorities have stated" (I.6.9).

The basic theoretical proposal of this Roman rhetoric is that the speaking process involves four chronologically-arranged interior steps, followed by one exterior step. The speaker finds ("invents")

---

[7]For an account of the medieval reception of the book see Murphy, *Rhetoric in the Middle Ages: A History of Rhetorical Theory from Saint Augustine to the Renaissance* (University of California Press, 1974), 106-114. Interestingly, the book was virtually unknown until late antiquity.

ideas, then arranges them in an order, then puts words to them, then remembers all of this; finally, the exterior expression ("delivery") occurs through vocal sound, facial expression, and bodily gesture. By analogy the writing process is almost the same, with the physical hand-writing (*orthographia*) replacing oral delivery as the final step.

Invention was accomplished through two major processes. One was the use of "status" or "issue" questions which could be asked in any controversy. "Every subject which contains in itself a controversy to be resolved by speech and debate," Cicero says, "involves a question about a fact, or about a definition, or about the nature of an act, or about legal procedures" (I.8.10). The other method was to discover ideas through the use of "topics" or "commonplaces" such as Division, Consequence, Cause, Effect, or Definition; each of these is a "region of an argument," a mental pathway which can lead the mind to find a useful line of argument. So important was this method that Cicero wrote a separate book (*Topica*) on the subject.

Arrangement specified six parts of an oration: Exordium or introduction, Narration or statement of facts, Division or the outline to be followed, Confirmation or proof, Refutation or attack on the opposition's arguments, and Peroration or conclusion.

Style included both general discussion of desirable wording and a very specific treatment of "figures" like Synechdoche, Metaphor, Antithesis, and Isocolon. The fourth book of the *Rhetorica ad Herennium,* in fact, presents the first systematic treatment of Style in Latin, with the first discussion of 64 figures (*exornationes*) which give "distinction" (*dignitas*) to language. Declaring that there are three levels of style—Plain, Middle, and Grand—the author says that good style should have the three qualities of Taste, Artistic Composition, and Distinction. This Distinction is achieved by two kinds of figures:

> To confer distinction upon style is to render it ornate, embellish-
> ing it by variety. The divisions under Distinction are Figures of
> Diction and Figures of Thought. It is a figure of diction if the
> ornament is comprised in the fine polish of the language itself. A
> figure of thought derives a certain distinction from the idea, not
> from the words (IV.12.18).

Then follow definitions and examples for 45 figures of speech (diction) and 19 figures of thought; the treatment of the figures occupies more than a fourth of the total length of the book, primarily because of the extensive examples the author feels necessary to make his definitions clear. It is interesting to note that this particular set of figures—not particularly well organized and not always mutually exclusive—became a sort of canon for writers as late as the sixteenth century. The figures became an accepted part of Style for Roman rhetoricians from Cicero onwards, and Quintilian regards then as so important that he devotes two entire books (Eight and Nine) of his *Institutio oratoria* to their analysis.

Memory, "the storehouse of invention," was described as being either natural or artificial. The natural memory could be improved by exercise, just like a bodily muscle. The artificial or artistic memory employed a mnemonic system of "Images" and "Backgrounds," in which the mind could store symbols (Images) set in a visualized neutral space (Background). Here too the *Rhetorica ad Herennium* is the first to describe the image-background system, though the theory may well have been commonly known.

Delivery, the final exteriorization, involved detailed consideration of vocal tones, of facial expressions, and of body movements including the management of posture, arms, and fingers.

This five-part division of rhetoric had the virtue of being analytic, permitting further study of the individual parts without neglecting their relation to the whole. Cicero, as we have already seen, could write an entire book dealing only with Invention, and, within that area another treating only the topics. Quite naturally there were technical debates about sub-points—as, for instance, the question whether there were really four "issues" in Invention or as few as three or as many as five. Nevertheless the main framework held steady for centuries. Perhaps it was the logicality of the process description, the theory that idea-collection proceeds arrangement which precedes style and memory. As a working hypothesis for speech preparation it seems to have had a recognized value for a very long time.

At the same time the written treatises had the defect of being schematic at best, and mechanical at worst. The technical could, and did, become hypertechnical at times. When Cicero grew older he began to react against what he saw as an over-technical approach he had favored in his youthful *De inventione.* His dialogue *De oratore*,[8] written in 55 B.C., argues that a liberal education is more important for the orator than "rules"; while Cicero's spokesman Crassus does accept the familiar doctrines of Roman rhetoric, he also declares that "the prize must go to the orator who possesses learning" (III.35.141). The character Crassus in *De oratore* is the same historical personage Crassus who was one of the censors who had prohibited the Latin teachers of rhetoric from operating their schools in 92 B.C., and Cicero has him explain his motives for the act; Crassus replies that they had no sense of the humanities and "so far as I could see these new masters had no capacity to teach anything except audacity" (III.24.94). In a sense Cicero's *De oratore,* with its plea for a broad general education, is the last major objection against a well-organized, discourse-centered teaching program which was clearly already well rooted in Roman society.

Yet the treatises of *praecepta* were only a part of the picture. The *Rhetorica ad Herennium* concludes with an insistence on *exercitatio:* "All these faculties we shall attain if we follow up the rules of theory with the diligence of exercise (*diligentia... exercitationis*)" (IV.56.69).

What, then, does *exercitatio* mean in this context? What is the nature of the system in which rhetoric is embedded? The evidence indicates that the system was as standardized as its rhetorical precepts.

THE ROMAN EDUCATIONAL SYSTEM AS DESCRIBED BY QUINTILIAN

The most complete description of the Roman educational system appears in a work published in A.D. 95, a century and a half after the death of Cicero but reflecting a process already under way during Cicero's lifetime; it was destined to continue in substantially unchanged form throughout antiquity, to survive the barbarian invasions of late antiquity, and to become a major force in medieval and Renaissance education.

What makes Quintilian's *Institutio oratoria* so valuable as a

---

[8]Cicero, *De oratore,* trans. E.W. Sutton and H. Rackham. Two volumes. (Loeb Classical Library: Harvard University Press, 1967).

source of our understanding is that it was written by Rome's acknowledged master teacher, based both on twenty years of classroom experience and on years of courtroom practice.[9] Moreover it is Quintilian's method not only to discuss his own methods but to compare other approaches and to analyze the advantages and disadvantages of each; consequently the book offers a wide-ranging treatment of educational issues in addition to its specific descriptions of the Roman process.

Quintilian was born about A.D. 35 in Callaguris (modern Calahorra) in Spain.[10] When he was about sixteen he went to Rome, attaching himself, as was the custom, to a famous orator, Domitius Afer. At sixteen he would already have finished his formal education in Spain and taken on the toga of an adult. When Domitius Afer died in 59, Quintilian returned to Spain. He must have taken up a career as pleader and orator with some success, for he was among those who went to Rome in 68 with the governor of Spain, Galba, who became emperor in January, 69.

Quintilian was both teacher and pleader in Rome. He mentions (I.1.19) that he once pleaded a case before Queen Berenice, sister of the King Agrippa who questioned Saint Paul in Caesarea before the apostle was sent to Rome for trial. He also says (IV.2.86) that in many trials "the duty of setting forth the case was generally entrusted to me" — certainly a mark of his peers' respect for his oratorical abilities. He says (VII.2.24) that he published one of his courtroom speeches, but the text has been lost.

His reputation as a teacher, however, was even greater. He was among the rhetoricians provided an annual subsidy from the public treasury in 72 by the Emperor Vespasian. A famous epigram by Martial a few years later, in 84, is evidence of his continuing reputation:

---

[9]"The Empire's greatest professor of rhetoric," according to Brother E. Patrick Parks F.S.C. in *The Roman Rhetorical Schools as a Preparation for the Courts Under the Early Empire* (Johns Hopkins Press, 1945), 98.

[10]For biography see George A. Kennedy, *Quintilian* (New York: Twayne, 1969). There is of course a considerable bibliography. For a select bibliography see Murphy, *Quintilian On the Teaching of Speaking and Writing*, xlv-li. Keith V. Erickson has published a listing of about one thousand items in "Quintilian's *Institutio oratoria* and Pseudo-*Declamationes*," *Rhetoric Society Quarterly* 11 (1981): See also Kennedy, *The Art of Rhetoric in the Roman World* (Princeton University Press, 1972), 45-62.

Quintiliane, vagae moderator summe iuventae,
Gloriae Romanae, Quintiliane, togae.

O Quintilian, supreme guide of unsettled youth,
Glory of the Roman toga, O Quintilian.

Even the satirist Juvenal remarks on Quintilian's good influence on the young, while his pupils included such famous figures as Pliny the Younger and perhaps as well the historians Tacitus and Suetonius. The Emperor Domitian entrusted the education of his two grandnephews to Quintilian even after he had retired from teaching. His career was economically successful, as he himself notes (VI.Preface 4); on the other hand, as he laments in the same section, he suffered the loss of a beloved son, then his young wife, and finally a second son. Upon his retirement about the year 90, the Emperor Domitian granted him consular rank—a remarkable honor at that time for a rhetorician. There is no record of Quintilian after the murder of Domitian in 96, and Kennedy suggests that he may have died within a year or two of the publication of his *Institutio oratoria* in 95.

Quintilian says that he spent two years of his retirement preparing to write the *Institutio,* after refusing for a while the requests of his friends that he write a book on the "art of speaking." In his Preface addressed to Marcellus Victorius he charges that other books on the subject have failed to recognize that such an art depends on the educational foundation of the orator; a visible eloquence depends on an invisible preparation, "as the pinnacles of buildings are seen, while the foundations are hid." Hence his program is a comprehensive one:

> For myself, I consider that nothing is unnecessary to the art of oratory, without which it must be confessed that an orator cannot be formed, and that there is no possibility of arriving at the summit in any subject without previous initiatory efforts: therefore, I shall not shrink from stooping to those lesser matters, the neglect of which leaves no room for the greater, and shall proceed to regulate the studies of the orator from infancy, just as if he were entrusted to me to be brought up (Preface 5).

The result is a work, divided into twelve books, which proposes an educational process beginning in the cradle and lasting into retirement from public life. It starts with what we would call language acquisition, and ends with a discussion of honorable leisure in old age. Quintilian includes a detailed description of elementary and secondary education, with a book (Ten) on adult self-education, and a lengthy treatment of the five parts of rhetoric. The final book, Twelve, discusses the ideal orator as "a good man speaking well."

Charles E. Little describes the *Institutio* as four books blended into one: a treatise on education, a manual of rhetoric, a reader's guide to the best authors, and a handbook on the moral duties of the orator.[11] Quintilian's own description includes the moral flavor permeating the work:

> The first book, therefore, will contain those particulars which are antecedent to the duties of the teacher of rhetoric. In the second book we shall consider the first elements of instruction under the hands of the professor of rhetoric and the questions which are asked concerning the subject of rhetoric itself. The next five will be devoted to invention (for under this head will also be included arrangement); and the four following, to elocution, within the scope of which fall memory and pronunciation. One will be added, in which the orator himself will be completely formed by us, since we shall consider, as far as our weakness shall be able, what his morals ought to be, what should be his practice in undertaking, studying, and pleading causes, what should be his style of eloquence, what termination there should be to his pleading, and what may be his employments after its termination (I.Preface 21-22).

What then of the subject of rhetoric itself? Quintilian follows this passage with the statement that rhetoric will be taught throughout the whole program, where suitable:

> Among all these discussions shall be introduced, as occasion shall require, the art of speaking, which will not only instruct students in the knowledge of those things to which alone some have given the name of art, and interpret (so to express myself) the law of rhetoric, but may serve (also) to nourish the faculty of speech, and strengthen the power of eloquence; for in general, these bare treatises on art, through too much affectation of subtlety, break and cut down whatever is noble in eloquence, drink up, as it were, all the blood of thought, and lay bare the

---

[11]Charles E. Little, *Quintilian the Schoolmaster.* Two volumes. (Nashville, Tennessee: George Peabody College for Teachers, 1951), II, 41.

bones, which while they ought to exist and be united by their ligaments, ought still to be covered with flesh (I.Preface 23-24).

In other words, Quintilian provides an integrated approach in which a major subject—rhetoric—is shown in its proper setting. The author of the *Rhetorica ad Herennium* had specified that the three elements of Precept, Imitation, and Exercise were necessary to the art, but left unspecified what he meant by Imitation and Exercise. It is quite possible that he felt it unnecessary to do so for his contemporary readers, who would know from their own experience what went on in the schools. (As a matter of fact he does remind his readers [II.24.38] of the way "students in rhetorical schools" are taught to use Dilemma in argument.) As we have seen, Quintilian complains that previous books on rhetoric had ignored the fact that the subject was embedded in a total learning process; his great book fastens on the person who learns, not merely on the subject itself. The subject of rhetoric, important though it may be, is but one of the tools in that learning process. Quintilian's title is "The Education of the Orator" (*Institutio oratoria*), not "A Book of Rhetoric" (*De rhetorica*).

As Aldo Scaglione has observed, what we today call "composition" had no equivalent in ancient and medieval literary theory.[12] Instead, the movement from silent voice or empty page to fully-fashioned appropriate language was the province of rhetoric as assisted by its ancillary, grammar. The oral-ness or written-ness of the language was regarded as less important than its wholeness in fitting the situation at hand; that is why there is no separate "art of letter-writing" in Roman antiquity (as there is in the middle ages), no separate "art of historiography" or separate "art of poetry-writing."[13] The movement toward future language is the concern of an entire educational program built around rhetoric in its broadest

---

[12]Aldo Scaglione, *The Classical Theory of Composition from Its Origins to the Present: A Historical Survey*. University of North Carolina Studies in Comparative Literature, 53. (University of North Carolina Press, 1972), 3.

[13]For the close correspondence between Horace's *Ars poetica* and the standard rhetorical lore of the day, see George Converse Fiske and Mary A. Grant, *Cicero's De oratore and Horace's Ars poetica*. University of Wisconsin Studies in Language and Literature, Vol. 27. (University of Wisconsin Press, 1929). There was of course a separate art of verse-writing in the middle ages; see Murphy, *Rhetoric in the Middle Ages*, 135-193.

sense but including much more than rhetoric itself.

The objective of the program is the shaping of an adaptive man of discretion, capable of adjusting his language to suit any subject or occasion. This sort of schooling does not attempt to lay down "rules":

> But let no man require from me such a system of precepts as is laid down by most authors of books of rules, a system in which I should have to make certain laws, fixed by immutable necessity, for all students of eloquence...for rhetoric would be a very easy and small matter, if it could be included in a short body of rules; but rules must generally be altered to suit the nature of each individual case, the time, the occasion, and necessity itself. Consequently, one great quality in an orator is discretion, because he must turn his thoughts in various directions, according to the various bearings of his subject (II.13.1-2).

Nevertheless, even if Quintilian disdains reliance on "rules," his is a systematic, programmatic approach. However, it is possible that a modern reader, untrained in the technical processes of Roman education, may well overlook the architectonic framework lying behind Quintilian's readable style and sensible advice.

It has been noted that if there is an art which conceals art, Quintilian has an art which conceals method. His Latin style makes extensive use of periodic sentences, with frequent parallel structures which are sometimes quite complex by modern standards. (A good example may be found in the passage just quoted, or in the preceding quotation on the role of rhetoric in the teaching program.) Also, since he usually presents various viewpoints before declaring his own judgment on each point, only the most careful reader will be able to track his main threads of thought through such discussions. His highly personalized accounts of his own teaching methods may also mislead an unwary reader into believing that the *Institutio* is more of an autobiography than an exposition. All of this makes Quintilian extremely difficult to summarize.

For this reason it will be useful to present his educational plan in a prose summary of the teaching sections from Books One, Two, and Ten of the *Institutio*. With this survey of the book in mind, then, it will be possible in the subsequent section to discuss the specific teaching methods in more detail.

A Prose Summary from Books One, Two, and Ten
of Quintilian's *Institutio oratoria*[14]

BOOK ONE

Preface

Having been asked by friends to clarify previous writers on
the art of speaking and to reconcile contradictory opinions, I
was moved to comply. I hold that the art of oratory includes all
that is essential for the training of an orator and that it is
impossible to reach the summit of any subject unless we have
first passed through the elemental stages. My aim is the
education of the perfect orator. The first essential for such a
person is that he be a good man. Let our ideal orator have
genuine title to the name "philosopher."

1. Conceive the highest hopes for your children, for most
are quick to reason and ready to learn. There are degrees of
talent. Be particular concerning your child's earliest training. His
nurses must be of good character and speak correctly. Both
parents should be as highly educated as possible, mothers
included. The child's companions ought to be carefully chosen.

2. Public instruction has won wide favor as opposed to
private education. Public instruction is accused of corrupting
morals, but morals may be corrupted anywhere, even at home.

3. Concerning teaching methods, ascertain first the student's
ability and character. The surest indication is his power of
memory, which should be quick and retentive. The next
indication is his power of imitation. Finally, he who is really
gifted will above all else be good.

4. The art of writing is combined with the art of speaking.
The ability to read precedes the ability to engage in oral
interpretation. The teacher should assist students in becoming
critics of writing and speaking.

5. All areas of language could be studied. Style has three
positive attributes: correctness, clarity, and elegance. A student
should be taught to select the right word and the one that
sounds best for his desired effect. Proper style results when one
chooses the more euphonious word when confronted with exact
synonyms, when barbarisms (offenses of single words) are
eliminated, when solecisms (errors of more than one word) are

---

[14]The three following summaries are from "Quintilian and the *Institutio oratoria*"
by Prentice A. Meador in Murphy (ed.) *A Synoptic History of Classical Rhetoric* (Davis,
California: Hermagoras Press, 1983), 151-176.

eliminated, and when current words are chosen.

6. Proper spoken language is based upon reason, antiquity, authority, and usage. Reason provides proper language through analogy and etymology. As for antiquity, attractive archaic words should be used sparingly. Language from orators and historians is applicable if not out of date. I define usage as the agreed practice of educated men.

7. Concerning suggestions for proper writing, orthography is the servant of usage and changes constantly. Actually, words should be spelled as they are pronounced.

8. Regarding effective oral reading, the student must understand what he reads. Oral reading should be manly and dignified. Oral reading differs from acting in that characterizations are not created.

9. The student should engage in composition exercises preliminary to rhetorical study. These include paraphrasing of Aesop's fables and other miscellaneous exercises such as character sketches and moral essays.

10. Other preliminaries to rhetorical study include the study of music, which aids voice and body control, and the study of geometry, which is allied to logic. Both oratory and geometry require proof.

11. The final preliminary is the study of acting, which aids gesture, movement, and expression. Even the study of gymnastics would be helpful.

12. On the capacity of students, early age is the best time for such a curriculum of preliminaries. Variety serves to refresh and restore the mind. It is easier to do many things continuously than to do one thing continuously.

BOOK TWO

1. The rhetoricians and the teachers of literature must each be assigned to their proper sphere. A student should be sent to the rhetorician when he is fit. While grammar has stretched so as to include much more subject matter than it should, rhetoric should not shrink from its duties.

2. The rhetorician must be of good character for he leads the student by example and strict discipline. His instruction must be free from affectation, his industry great, his demands on his class continual, but not extravagant.

3. The student should be taught by the best teachers available. The task of unteaching is harder than that of teaching.

4. There are three forms of narratives: the fictitious narratives

of tragedies and poems; the realistic narratives of comedies; and lastly, the historical narratives, which are expositions of actual fact. Since poetic literature is the province of the teacher of literature, the rhetorician should begin with historical narrative, which has force in proportion to its truth.

5. The teacher of rhetoric should point to the strengths and weaknesses of the older orators that are serving as examples. At times, it will be of value to read speeches that are corrupt and faulty in style. The teacher should test the critical abilities of his students by studying the orations of the older orators.

6. The rhetorician should attempt to assist the student in his declamations through oral criticisms.

7. There is one practice at present in vogue that should be changed. Boys should not be forced to commit all their own compositions to memory. If one is to memorize, he should memorize the broadly acceptable work of a skilled orator and not that of a novice.

8. The good teacher should be able to differentiate between the abilities of his pupils. While the student should be strong in all phases of oratory, style should be especially encouraged.

9. The student should love his master not less than his studies and should regard his master as he does his parents. As it is the responsibility of the teacher to instruct, it is the responsibility of the student to learn.

10. The subjects chosen for declamations should be as true to life as possible. Unrealistic declamations will seem foolish to the intelligent observer. It is ludicrous to work oneself into a passion for the unrealistic.

11. The sound rhetorical student cannot discard all rules. Eloquent speeches are not the result of momentary inspirations but the products of research, analysis, practice, and application.

12. True art results from discrimination of what should be said. Carefully nurtured achievement of a student is the cause of such discrimination.

Book Ten

1. Eloquence is best attained by careful attention to writing, reading, and speaking.

2. Although invention came first and is all-important, it is expedient to imitate whatever has been invented with success. Simple imitation is not enough; one should build on the model.

3. Among the things that the orator cannot obtain from external sources, the pen is the one that brings at once the most

labor and the most profit. The roots and foundations of
eloquence are in writing.

4. Erasure is quite as important a function of the pen as
actual writing. Correction takes the form of addition, excision,
and alteration.

5. The point that concerns me now is to show from what
sources copiousness and facility may most easily be derived.
Translations from Greek to Latin are helpful for there is much
matter and art in the Greek writings worthy of imitation. The
paraphrase of Latin authors is helpful for it is one of the best
ways of learning the ideas of the best authors. Theses and
commonplaces are valuable, since one who has mastered these
simple forms will be more fluent in more complex subjects and
will be able to cope with any case, for all cases are built upon
these kinds of general questions.

6. Premeditation derives force from the practice of writing
and forms an intermediate stage between the labors of the pen
and the more precarious fortunes of improvisation; indeed I am
not sure that it is not more frequently of use than either.

7. But the crown of all our study and the highest reward of
our long labors is the power of improvisation. The man who
fails to acquire this had better, in my opinion, abandon the task
of advocacy and devote his powers of writing to other branches
of literature.

ROMAN TEACHING METHODS

Virtually every individual element found in the program
described by Quintilian was inherited from the Greeks. What was
not inherited, however, was the deftly-designed correlation of these
elements into a "system."[15] As a system the process could be — and
was — replicated over time and space. As a system it could be
promoted world-wide as a tool of public policy equal in geopolitical
value to the legions and the tax collectors in making the world
Roman; as the television commentator Alastair Cooke once
remarked, "Language is a dialect with an army and a navy," and
history does in fact tell us that for more than half a millenium the
Latin language and its schools served as a kind of social cement

---

[15]For a schematic overview of the five elements of the Roman teaching methods, see
the Appendix at the end of this chapter.

throughout the Western world.[16]

Quintilian is not the inventor of this system — he is merely describing a process already familiar to Romans for almost two centuries — but he is one of our best sources for both its philosophy and its details. Donald A. Russell in fact suggests that Quintilian could even be used as a guide to understanding earlier Greek developments:

> The conservatism of rhetorical teaching over such a long period makes it possible to give an account of it as a system, based on the late textbooks which survive, without feeling that one's conclusions are likely to be fundamentally wrong for the earlier period. Quintilian is undoubtedly the best guide.[17]

Some modern critics have argued that Quintilian is presenting an idealized or even wistfully utopian view of education. They point to his insistence on morality as a reaction to the decadence he saw around him, noting that many of his examples hearken back to the presumably more virtuous days of the pre-Imperial Republic. Yet he says that he bases the *Institutio oratoria* on his own teaching experience in a career that won the approbation of at least two Emperors, Vespasian and Domitian, and attracted the plaudits of writers like Juvenal and Martial.

What is more important, though, is that what Quintilian describes is consistent with other evidence about Roman education from the time of Cicero up to the fall of Rome to the barbarians in the fifth Christian century. It is also generally consistent with the evidence we have about the early middle ages, up to the late twelfth century at least. Obviously not every student went all the way through the course, just as today there are many "dropouts" in even the best of schools. The poor sent their children for only

---

[16]Robert Pattison offers a useful analysis of the power of the Latin language "in the service of authority" in his book *On Literacy: The Politics of the Word from Homer to the Age of Rock* (Oxford University Press, 1982): "As it began its expansion, Rome also began to develop formal, written Latin for the business of Empire. The soldier and the grammarian proceeded in lockstep to spread the Roman way, one by conquering the world, the other by providing it with correct Latin as a medium of organization" (67).

[17]Donald A. Russell, *Criticism in Antiquity* (University of California Press, 1981), 25. S.F. Bonner also stresses the systematic, devoting 162 pages of his *Education in Ancient Rome from the Elder Cato to the Younger Pliny* (University of California Press, 1977), to a section titled "The Standard Teaching Programme."

the most elementary education with the *ludi magister* for grammar or the *calculator* for basic numbers.[18] No doubt many students had to content themselves with the instruction in grammar without ever proceeding to more advanced studies with a rhetorician. Nor can we expect that every teacher had the mastery of a Quintilian; Seneca tells the story of the Spanish schoolmaster Porcius Latro who could declaim brilliantly before his pupils but was paralyzed with fright when called upon to speak in public.[19]

If nothing else, the homogeneous longevity of the system proves its efficiency. Pierre Riché remarks that even in the sixth century teachers of grammar, rhetoric, and law were still listed in the public budget under "barbarians" like Theodoric and his successor Athalaric. "When we look inside the schools of the grammarian and the rhetor," he adds, "we can observe that the program and methods of instruction had not changed."[20] The ever-practical Romans surely did not continue the system out of any philosophical regard for "liberal arts" — Cicero's *De oratore* in 44 B.C. was apparently the last major stand on that issue — but rather for the quite pragmatic reason that it worked. It provided literacy for many, competence for some, excellence for a few; the dividing line between these three levels of accomplishment was based simply on the length of time the student could spend in the program.

What one sees in Quintilian, then, is the complete system. Whether this or that student benefited fully from it depended more on socio-economic factors than on the integrity of the system itself.

Consequently it would seem useful to examine in a bit more detail the actual methods designed to produce what Quintilian calls *facilitas,* the ability to produce appropriate language on any subject in any situation. This examination covers Precept (Rhetoric and Grammar), Imitation, Progymnasmata, Declamation, and Sequencing.

---

[18]The most comprehensive account of ancient education is that of Henri I. Marrou, *A History of Education in Antiquity,* trans. George Lamb (New York: Sheed and Ward, 1956). He discusses Roman education in Chapters IV through VII (265-313). For a discussion of terms like *calculator* see E.W. Bower, "Some Technical Terms in Roman Education," *Hermes* 89 (1961): 462-77.

[19]Cited in Gwynn, *Roman Education,* 67.

[20]Pierre Riché, *Education and Culture in the Barbarian West Sixth Through Eighth Centuries,* trans, John J. Contreni. (University of South Carolina Press, 1976), 40.

Precept. Both grammar and rhetoric are included here. The *Rhetorica ad Herennium,* as we have seen, defines *praecepta* as "a set of rules that provide a definite method and system of speaking." Cicero's *De inventione* defines Eloquence as speaking based on "rules of art." Quintilian, as we have seen from his Preface, denies that such "rules" should be followed slavishly, and he adds in another place that "these rules have not the formal authority of laws or decrees of plebs, but are, with all they contain, the children of expediency *(utilitas)*" (II.13.6). For him they serve as guides rather than commandments. No doubt this attitude was that of the best rhetors, though we can imagine the worse masters—just as today—driven to a helpless reliance on the rules because they do not know their subject well enough to be flexible.

The exact Roman method of teaching rhetoric as precept is not clear. Quintilian suggests that the precepts operate throughout the program; this could mean either that the master introduced precepts at each stage, or that separate times were set aside for them. The *Institutio oratoria* does not describe any separate segment for teaching precepts, though it would seem logical that the older students preparing for Declamation would have to know the principles of at least deliberative and forensic rhetoric—the major fields covered in the imaginary cases students were asked to plead.

The Roman boy's educational progress was divided into three main steps: the acquisition of the most basic language skills, especially reading and writing; then a period of exercises with the *grammaticus;* then, when he was ready, training under the teacher of rhetoric (the *rhetor*). Book Two of the *Institutio* covers the teaching done by the rhetorician. One might expect a discussion of *praecepta* at this point. Yet what Quintilian describes is not a systematic instruction in rhetorical precepts, but instead a more advanced version of the same types of classroom exercises already handled under the *grammaticus*. In fact, Quintilian declares that the exercises are more important than the precepts: "I will venture to say that this sort of diligent exercise will contribute more to the improvement of students than all the precepts of all the rhetoricians that ever wrote." (II.5.14). When he does come to a treatment of rhetoric in Book Three he adds another caution about the relation of precept to exercise:

For the present I will only say that I do not want young men to

> think their education complete when they have mastered one of
> the small text-books of which so many are in circulation, or to
> ascribe a talismanic value to the arbitrary decrees of theorists. The
> art of speaking can only be attained by hard work and assiduity
> of study, by a variety of exercises and repeated trial, the highest
> prudence and unfailing quickness of judgment (III.13.15).

Since his discussion of rhetoric occupies eight of the twelve books
of the *Institutio,* however, it is clear that he regards the subject as
important. Yet Quintilian's whole approach is to teach students,
not subjects.

The most likely explanation is that rhetorical precept was not
taught in a block, all at once or even on assigned days; rather,
individual concepts must have been introduced whenever they
suited the exercise at hand. When Quintilian discusses Narration of
histories under the teacher of rhetoric (II.4.3-19), for example, he
outlines the qualities of good narration and then refers to his later
treatment of the subject under Judicial Oratory in his rhetoric
section. Quintilian's recurrent principle for the assignment of individual exercises to the student is "When he is ready." He criticizes
grammarians (II.1.2) for taking upon themselves some aspects of
rhetorical instruction for which the boys will not yet be ready.

One thing is certain. The rhetoric treatise was not a student
"textbook" in the modern sense of the word, with each student
having a copy to study. The 'textbook' in this sense is a product of
the printing age, when books became cheap enough to distribute in
a classroom. In any case Roman rhetoric was so homogeneous that
any reasonably well-educated teacher could master and transmit
the principles orally without much difficulty. There were rhetoric
texts available for study (they apparently sold well), even if public
libraries were comparatively rare.

No doubt students were asked to memorize some materials.
For example the "commonplaces" (topics) would be useful for
students to have ready to hand. Certainly we know that they were
obliged to memorize poetry and prose for the process of Imitation,
and in fact Quintilian prefers this over having them memorize their
own writing (even if doting parents preferred to hear their sons
recite their own compositions from memory for public presenta-
tions). His argument is that they might as well memorize the best
authors rather than perpetuating their own errors. But he says
nothing about memorizing precepts.

Grammar was another matter. Although Quintilian does refer to "those rules which are published in the little manuals of professors" (I.5.7), the subject of grammar was not nearly as well developed in his day as rhetoric had already been for more than two centuries. There was no standard treatise on the subject. As a consequence he feels obliged to devote a significant portion of Book One (Chapters 4 through 7) to such matters as "word," analogy, usage, spellings, barbarisms, solecisms, vocal tones, and the differences between Greek and Latin. Chapter 7 deals with Orthography, the art of writing words correctly on the page. He justifies this attention to apparently minor matters by arguing that correct language is the basis for every good use of language. "These studies," he says, "are injurious, not to those who pass through them, but only to those who dwell immoderately on them" (I.7.35).

Grammar is so foundational that students must be taught its precepts directly, especially in the earliest stages. In the exercise of Imitation the fine points of grammar are noted carefully in meticulous critiques of the models being studied. These two stages of instructions are pointed out in his definition of the subject. Quintilian defines grammar in what was already a traditional way: "the art of speaking correctly, and the interpretation of the poets" (I.4.2). Thus it includes what we would today call the "rules" of correctness, and also the study of what we would call "literature."

By the fourth Christian century there was available a widely-accepted manual of basic Latin grammar, the brief *Ars minor* of Aelius Donatus (fl. A.D. 350).[21] This book petrified for later centuries the concept of "eight parts of speech"; another work, his larger *Ars grammatica (Ars maior),* not only treats the eight parts of speech in greater detail but adds a section dealing with "schemes" (figures of speech) and "tropes" which would ordinarily have been treated by the rhetor rather than the grammarian. It was to be another two centuries before the appearance of what was to become the standard advanced Latin grammar text for more than a thousand years—the *Ars grammatica* of Priscian (fl. A.D. 500)

---

[21]It has been translated by W.J. Chase in *The Ars Minor of Donatus.* University of Wisconsin Studies in the Social Sciences and History, No. 36. (University of Wisconsin Press, 1926). The Latin text is in Henry Keil (ed.) in *Grammatici Latini.* Seven volumes. (Leipzig, 1864), IV, 355-66.

who was a teacher of Latin grammar in the Greek-speaking city of Constantinople. This work contains eighteen books, the last two dealing with "construction," or the elements of composition.[22]

Even without such books in the earlier periods of Roman history, however, all the evidence indicates a consistency of grammatical instruction in the schools. The *grammaticus,* after all, received a young boy who had only the rudiments of reading and writing skills; the exigencies of standard-setting through all the complex classroom exercises provided ample opportunity for the grammarian not only to teach the rules themselves but to insist on their proper application in both writing and speaking.

What is to be remembered above all about the role of Precept in the Roman schools is that it was only a part of an integrated system designed to produce not merely knowledge but ability. Quintilian reminds his readers of this fact in Book 10: "But these precepts of being eloquent, though necessary to be known, are not sufficient to produce the full power of eloquence unless there be united to them a certain Facility, which among the Greeks is called *Hexis,* 'habit'" (X.1.1). This "facility" is resident in the educated person, not in his knowledge.

To comprehend how the Romans produced this 'habit' in young men, it is necessary to understand the precise role played in the schools by Imitation and by the graded composition exercises known as Progymnasmata.

Imitation. The concept of *Imitatio (Mimesis)* is much misunderstood today. On one hand it could mean the artistic re-creation of reality by a poet or artist; on the other it could mean the deliberate modelling of an existing artifact or text.[23] Actually it was for the Romans the second of these, a carefully-plotted sequence of interpretive and re-creational activities using pre-existing texts to teach students how to create their own original texts. Each phase in the sequence has its own purpose, but takes its value from its place in the sequence. It would be a mistake therefore for a modern reader to assume that each of the parts is

---

[22]Text in Keil, *Grammatici Latini,* IV, 367-402.
[23]There is a good brief survey of ancient views in Russell, *Criticism in Antiquity,* 99-113.

independent of the others, or to think that the set of compositional activities is a kind of smorgasbord to be picked up and used at random. It is not mere eclecticism.

The concept is certainly an ancient one. Plato has Protagoras say that when schoolboys memorize the great poets they imbibe not only the poetry but the moral qualities of the great men described in the poems (*Protagoras* 325-326). Isocrates makes it a key teaching tool (*Antidosis* 276-277). Aristotle begins his discussion of drama with a statement of principle: "Imitation is natural to man" (*Poetics*). The *Rhetorica ad Herennium,* as we have seen, begins and ends with the injunction to use Imitation as well as Exercise to learn the art of speaking. Cicero—himself to be the object of fervid imitation during the Renaissance[24]—opens the second book of his *De inventione* with the statement that he has taken the best from many sources, just as the painter Zeuxis of Heraclea chose the five most beautiful girls from Croton as models for a painting of Helen the city had commissioned for its Temple of Juno. The continuity of Imitation is so strong throughout the Roman period that the first Christian rhetorician, Saint Augustine, writing in A.D. 426, declares in his *De doctrina Christiana* (IV.3) that Imitation is more important than Precept for the adult newcomer to rhetoric.

The Roman school system perfected a seven-step process of Imitation, with writing or the analysis of written texts being coupled to oral performance by the students before master and peers in the classroom. What we would call peer criticism is an integral part of the scheme; in the Roman interactive classroom the student-critic shapes his own critical judgment by assessing publicly what he hears and reads. The teacher is not merely to tell the students what to think, Quintilian says, "but frequently to ask questions upon them, and try the judgment of his pupils" (II.5.13).

[24]See Izora Scott, *Controversies Over the Imitation of Cicero as a Model for Style and Some Phases of Their Influence on the Schools of the Renaissance* (Columbia University Teachers College, 1910).

A brief explanation of the seven steps may show how Imitation works.[25]

A. Reading Aloud *(lectio)*. Either the master or one of the students could read a text aloud. Models are to be carefully chosen, though occasional faulty ones may be used. In the later stages when speeches become the texts for study, the master may declaim a speech or even declaim one of his own (though Quintilian prefers that the master use an acknowledged orator like Cicero rather than his own work). Quintilian introduces implicitly a major educational principle at this point—namely, that no exercise should be conducted for a single purpose only. The students hear not only the form of a text, including its rhythmical or other sonic patterns, but also take in unconsciously its subject matter. Hence the insistence on histories as well as poems, as offering salutary models of conduct.

B. Analysis of the Text *(praelectio)*. This is the beginning of the application of judgment. The master literally dissects the text. The immediate intent is to show the students how the author made good or bad choices in wording, in organization, in the use of figures, and the like; the long-range objective is to accustom the student to what today we could call a "close reading" of texts. Since it is a written text done orally, the exercise also trains the "ear" of the student for later exercises in analyzing the oral arguments used in orations. Both good models and bad models are to be presented. Quintilian's brief summary in Book Two of the *Institutio* seems straightforward enough; in the following passage he is explaining the method in respect to analyzing an oration, though the method is exactly the same for a poem or a history (as he points out in I.8.13-21):

> The master, after calling for silence, should appoint some one pupil to read (and it will be best that this duty should be imposed on them by turns), so that they may thus accustom themselves to clear pronunciation. Then, after explaining the

---

[25]A useful account of Imitation may be found in Donald Lemen Clark, *Rhetoric in Greco-Roman Education* (Columbia University Press, 1957), 144-176. Clark's account may be particularly interesting to readers concerned with teaching method, since he consistently analyzes the rationale for the exercises more clearly than other historians like Marrou or Bonner.

cause for which the oration was composed (so that what is said will be better understood), he should leave nothing unnoticed which is important to be remarked, either in the thought or the language: he should observe what method is adopted in the exordium for conciliating the judge; what clearness, brevity, and apparent sincerity is displayed in the statement of facts; what design there is in certain passages, and what well-concealed artifice (for that is the only true art in pleading which cannot be perceived except by a skilful pleader); what judgment appears in the division of the matter; how subtle and urgent is the argumentation; with what force the speaker excites, with what amenity he soothes; what severity is shown in his invectives, what urbanity in his jests; how he commands the feelings, forces a way into the understanding, and makes the opinions of the judges coincide with what he asserts. In regard to the style, too, he should notice any expression that is peculiarly appropriate, elegant, or sublime; when the amplification deserves praise, what quality is opposed to it; what phrases are happily metaphorical, what figures of speech are used; what part of the composition is smooth and polished, and yet manly and vigorous.

Nor is it without advantage, indeed, that inelegant and faulty speeches—yet such as many, from depravity of taste, would admire—should be read before boys, and that it should be shown how many expressions in them are inappropriate, obscure, timid, low, mean, affected, or effeminate (II.5.6-10).

When Quintilian and his colleagues say that they would "leave nothing unnoticed," they mean exactly that. The dissection of the text is intended to be microscopic. While a reader may cover whole sections with a sweep of the eye, the composing writer/speaker must commit himself to one word or even one syllable at a time. Hence the truly analytic reader needs to reach back through the wholeness of paragraph or argument to identify the microcosmic decisions made by the composer.

An excellent example of this micro-analysis may be found in a later work written by the grammarian Priscian about A.D. 500. Priscian's *Analyses of the First Twelve Lines of Virgil's Aeneid* is an extremely meticulous work, occupying 108 columns of type over 54 pages in the folio-size standard edition of Henry Keil. The beginning section provides a good example of the method:

Scan the line *Arma virumque cano Troiae qui primus ab oris.*
How many caesura are there? Two. What are they?

The penthemimera and the hephthemimera [*semiquinaria, semi-septenaria,* Priscian says in his barbarous Latin].
Which is which?
The penthemimera is *Arma virumque cano,* and the hephthemimera *Arma virumque cano Troiae.*
How many "figures" has it?
Ten.
Why has it got ten?
Because it is made up of three dactyls and two spondees.
[Priscianus takes no notice of the final spondee.]
How many words ["parts of speech"] are there?
Nine.
How many nouns?
Six — *Arma, Virum, Troiae, qui* [sic], *primus, oris.*
How many verbs?
One — *cano.*
How many prepositions?
One — *ab.*
How many conjunctions?
One — *que.*
Study each word in turn. Let us begin with *arma.* What part of speech is it?
A noun.
What is its quality?
Appellative.
What kind is it?
General.
What gender?
Neuter.
How do you know?
All nouns ending in -*a* in the plural are neuter.
Why is *arma* not used in the singular?
Because it means many different things.[26]

This kind of methodical treatment, carried on over all kinds of texts for ten or a dozen years, must surely have promoted a high degree of linguistic sensitivity in the students. It must be remembered, too, that the same treatment was given to the students' own compositions.

On the other hand the mere analysis of others' texts could

---

[26]Quoted in Marrou, *History of Education in Antiquity,* 279-280.

produce a sort of compositional paralysis, with the writer fearing his inability to do as well as the models. Quintilian is quite aware of what we would call "writer's block." He tells the story of a young man named Secundus, whose uncle, Julius Florus, found him in a dejected state one day; Secundus told his uncle that he had been trying for three days to write an introduction to a subject he had to write upon for school. Florus responded smilingly, "Do you wish to write better than you can?" (X.3.14). For improvement, Quintilian adds, there is need of application, but not of vexation with ourselves.

The close analysis of texts was of course not the only method used. It took its value from its place in the system. The next steps called upon the student to apply his own energies.

C. Memorization of Models. Quintilian is convinced that memorization of models not only strengthens the memory in the way that physical exercise strengthens a muscle but also provides the student with "an abundance of the best words, phrases, and figures" for possible use later on (II.7.4). Memorization is especially useful for the very young, who do not yet have the capacity for intellectual analysis of their texts. "The chief symptom of ability in children," he says, "is memory" (I.3.1). (He says the same thing about teaching a foreign language to the very young.) He is quite adamant about the virtue of memorizing good models rather than one's own writing, and in fact says that such memorization will equip the student better to recall his own compositions when necessary. As usual, though, he has a keen eye for the pedagogical opportunity—a student may be allowed to recite his own work from memory only as a reward, when he has produced "something more polished than ordinary" (II.7.5). The problem he sees is that otherwise the student may end up perpetuating his faults if he memorizes his own work.

D. Paraphrase of Models. The re-telling of something in the students' own words begins at the earliest stages of the program— for example, with first an oral and then a written paraphrase of a fable of Aesop (I.9.2)—but continues throughout the instruction of both the *grammaticus* and the *rhetor*. The more advanced students deal with more complex types of narrations such as plots of comedies or the accounts found in histories (11.4.2); here

Quintilian refers to the concepts of narration to be found in rhetorical doctrine, though he expressly reminds the reader that the exercise is a continuation of that begun earlier under the *grammaticus*.
(Here too is another example of the way in which formal
rhetorical precepts are fed into the system as the need arises.)

The ultimate purposes of paraphrase are two: to accustom
students to fastening on the structure of the model rather than its
words, and to begin the development of a personal style in
narration. "It is a service to boys at an early age," he says, "when
their speech is but just commenced, to repeat what they have
heard in order to improve their faculty of speaking. Let them
accordingly be made, and with good reason, to go over their
stories again, and to pursue them from the middle, either
backward or forward" (II.4.15).

It is in this section, dealing with the first efforts of the students
to compose in their own terms, that Quintilian lays down his
principles of classroom correction. The students should be shown
the faults in their writing and speaking, but should also be praised
for whatever they have accomplished. If the performance is so bad
that the student is asked to write again on the same subject, he
should be told that he can indeed do better, "since study is cheered
by nothing more than hope" (II.4.13). Quintilian applauds exuberance in compositions by the young, if it is made clear that later on
a more sophisticated standard will be demanded. He comments
that "the remedy for exuberance is easy, but barrenness is
incurable by any labor" (II.4.6). Elsewhere he refers to an ancient
aphorism that "it is easier to prune a tree than to grow one"
(II.8.9). Accordingly he urges the master to promote freedom of
invention in the early stages of the student's development, tolerating
(though noting) some stylistic faults which can be corrected as the
student becomes more adept in language.

E. Transliteration of Models. There is no precise English term
for the Roman exercises in text re-casting. The process could take
several forms: direct translation of the text from Greek to Latin or
Latin to Greek; re-casting of Latin prose to Latin verse; re-casting
of Latin prose to Greek verse, or vice versa; making the model
shorter, or longer, whether in verse or prose; altering the style
from plain to grand or vice versa. Transliteration could be an
extremely sophisticated assignment, demanding precise knowledge

of verse forms and prose rhythms as well as an extensive vocabulary. Indeed, Quintilian notes, the difficulty of the exercise is most serviceable. A sure knowledge of the model is a prerequisite. As for critics of this method, he points out agreement on the principle: "About the utility of turning poetry into prose, I suppose no one has any doubt" (X.5.4). Once the principle of usefulness for re-casting is established, he implies, there is no reason to shy away from other modes of accomplishing the same end.

A monolingual culture like the American, in which knowledge of foreign languages is severely limited, might be hard put to use some translative forms of the method, but other forms (e.g. verse-prose or prose-verse, or plain style-grand style) might well be considered as classroom tools.

F. Recitation of Paraphrase or Transliteration. The oral-written relationship is so strong in Roman educational practice that even Quintilian does not always make explicit what he clearly expects everyone to take for granted. This relationship is spelled out at the very beginning of his discussion of teaching methods: "Not only is the art of writing combined with that of speaking, but correct reading also precedes illustration" (I.4.3). The student, having "read" his text analytically, writes his own paraphrase or transliteration of it and then brings his own work into the public classroom for oral presentation. Sometimes it will be recited from memory, sometimes read aloud.

G. Correction of Paraphrase or Transliteration. The admonitions of the master concerning this performance are shared with all who hear, thus raising the standards of everyone. Quintilian argues that this is the prime advantage of public over private tutorial education:

> At home he can learn only what is taught himself; at school, even what is taught others. He will daily hear many things commended, many things corrected; the idleness of a fellow student, when reproved, will be a warning to him; the industry of anyone, when commended, will be a stimulus; emulation will be excited by praise; and he will think it a disgrace to yield to his equals in age, and an honor to surpass his seniors. All these matters excite the mind; and though ambition itself be a vice, yet it is often the parent of virtues (I.2.21-22).

This "exercise of judgment" as Quintilian calls it could also enroll the students themselves as critics. Not only was the Roman schoolroom interactive between master and students, but between students and students as well. Quintilian is quite explicit about this for the older boys doing formal declamations or practice orations: "Shall a pupil, if he commits faults in declaiming, be corrected before the rest, and will it not be more serviceable to him to correct the speech of another? Indubitably" (II.5.16). Even though he does not make the same kind of statement about the earlier stages of the program, the whole tone of the book—and especially Chapter Two of Book One on the virtues of the public classroom— argues for what he continually refers to as "activity of the mind" among the students. There is no reason to believe that this would exclude what we call "peer criticism." Perhaps Quintilian intends only the older boys to comment on each others' work, but everything else he says throughout the book is at least consistent with the possibility that he encourages student criticisms at every stage.

Two principles govern his use of correction. The first is that oral correction should be tailored to the capacities of the student involved; however, since correction is public the master must keep in mind the other hearers in the classroom, "who will think that whatever the master has not amended is right" (II.6.4). The second is that some early faults can be tolerated, as part of the student's natural development of a particular skill.

For the adult practitioner he discusses in Book Ten there is another kind of self-correction involved in the practice of writing. This involves personal decisions about what to add, to take away, or to alter (X.5.1), rather than the public pronouncements in a classroom about something just recited. Even so, it is logical to assume that Quintilian would ask the adult writer to analyze his own written text with the same methods used earlier in the classroom process of Imitation. He proposes lifetime use of methods learned in school.

The process of Imitation, then, is for Quintilian and other Romans a specific sequence of learning activities for students from the youngest to the oldest. The method remains the same over time, the only change being in the models imitated. The young lad who begins with a simple fable of Aesop ends up years later as a young adult doing the same thing with a complex speech of Demosthenes or Cicero. The student learns political science, history, morals, and literature by a kind of intelligent osmosis. His attention is focused on the style and structure of the particular text, but he cannot escape an awareness of historical circumstances or ethical problems as he moves through the various steps.

The objective, of course, is to enable the student eventually to compose his own texts: "For what object have we in teaching them, but that they may not always require to be taught?" (II.5.13). Free composition must be based on knowledge of the options available to the writer—and this knowledge comes only from Imitation. Imitation is thus a life-long pursuit. Quintilian remarks early in the *Institutio* that a child learns spoken language easily through natural imitation, so that even a two-year-old can speak and understand what is said to him. Writing, however, must be taught to him. The boy follows the forms of the letters of the alphabet before he is allowed to write them for himself, tracing indented patterns with his stylus to accustom his hand to the form of a letter before he writes it freely. "By following these sure traces rapidly and frequently, he will form his hand, and not require the assistance of a person to guide his hand with his own hand placed over it" (I.1.27). This kind of tactile Imitation is based on exactly the same principles as the school exercises and the self-learning activity recommended in Book Ten for adults to continue even into retirement. To put it into abstract terms, form precedes freedom. The writer who knows only one mode of writing is not free, but is bound to that one mode.

As valuable as Imitation is, however, it too is but one part of the total educational system. The Roman student also underwent a parallel program of specific writing/speaking exercises *(progymnasmata)*.

Progymnasmata (Graded Composition Exercises). This is one area of methodology in which Quintilian is less than thorough, perhaps because of what he calls "this haste of mine" (II.1.12). In the opening chapter of Book Two he discusses the proper spheres of *grammaticus* and *rhetor,* arguing that the teacher of rhetoric (as well as the teacher of grammar) "should not shrink from the earliest duties of his profession" (II.1.8). What he means is that both should teach the "little exercises" that ultimately prepare the boy to be an adept user of language. Then he rapidly lists nine exercises: narration, praise, blame, thesis, commonplaces, statement of facts, eulogy, invective, and refutation; then in Chapter Four he discusses some of these exercises and adds three more: comparison, cause and effect, which he calls a *chreia,* and praise or censure of laws. Earlier (I.8.3) he had named *prosopopeiae* in connection with proper oral reading. This makes thirteen altogether. He concludes Chapter Four with this observation: "On such subjects did the ancients, for the most part, exercise the faculty of eloquence" (II.4.41). In other words, he is simply listing rapidly a number of exercises long known and undoubtedly familiar to his readers — hence his brevity.[27]

What he writes about here is a set of graded composition exercises which had long since come to be called *progymnasmata* (though he himself does not use that term). The name comes from the function of the exercises: if the highest forms of school training are the Declamations or fictitious speeches (*gymnasmata* in Greek), then that which prepares for them is Pre-Declamation *(progymnasmata).* Even though the term itself is Greek, and the major ancient writers of textbooks on the progymnasmata were Greek, it is clear from Quintilian's account that the use of the exercises is already solidly entrenched in Latin schools.

The earliest surviving textbook defining and illustrating the exercises is that by Aelius Theon of Alexandria, writing probably in the latter half of the first Christian century — a contemporary of Quintilian though probably unknown to him. Two of the most popular Greek textbooks come long after Quintilian, written by Hermogenes of Tarsus[28] (second century) and Aphthonius of Antioch[29] (fourth century). Both these books had impact well beyond antiquity. Hermogenes' treatise was translated into Latin as *Praeexercitamenta* by the Latin Grammarian Priscian around A.D. 500, and had use during the middle ages and Renaissance. Aphthonius, however, eclipsed Hermogenes in antiquity by far, mainly because he included useful examples, and his work became a standard Byzantine textbook as well; when introduced to the

---

[27]A brief survey of the tradition may be found in Ronald F. Hock and Edward N. O'Neil, *The Chreia in Ancient Rhetoric: Volume I. The Progymnasmata* (Atlanta, Georgia: Scholars Press, 1986), 10-22. A good account with examples is in Clark, *Rhetoric in Greco-Roman Education,* 177-212.

[28]Translated by Charles S. Baldwin, *Medieval Rhetoric and Poetic* (New York: Macmillan, 1928), 23-38.

[29]Translated by Ray Nadeau, *Speech Monographs* 19 (1952), 264-285.

Latin West during the fifteenth century it achieved a new popularity extending even to colonial America.

Quintilian's concern with the proper role of the grammarian proved to be a prophetic one. It was not a question of whether the *progymnasmata* should be taught, but rather a question of who should teach them. Quintilian urges the rhetorician to keep some control, even if it means taking up "the earliest duties of his profession" by working with very young students just beginning narrations of fables. History tells us that the grammarians eventually won out in Roman schools, taking over the *progymnasmata* for themselves. As a practical matter this development may have meant little to the boys who came through the system, since they received the instruction in any case.

We see in Quintilian, then, a comparatively early stage in which these exercises still fall under the purview of both masters. It is true nevertheless that his brief account can show us the relation of the *progymnasmata* to the schools' objectives. Specifically he argues that the exercises train students in the exact functions needed in the real world:

> But what is there among those exercises, of which I have just now spoken, that does not relate both to other matters peculiar to rhetoricians, and, indisputably, to the sort of causes pleaded in courts of justice? Have we not to make statements of facts in the forum? I know not whether that department of rhetoric is not most of all in demand there. Are not eulogy and invective often introduced in those disputations? Do not commonplaces, both those which are leveled against vice (such as were composed, we read, by Cicero), and those in which questions are discussed generally (such as were published by Quintus Hortensius, as, "Ought we to trust to light proofs?" and "For witnesses and against witnesses"), mix themselves with the inmost substance of causes? These weapons are in some degree to be prepared, so that we may use them whenever circumstances require. He who shall suppose that these matters do not concern the orator, will think that a statue is not begun when its limbs are cast (II.1.10-12).

This argument is coupled with the proposal that the *grammaticus* continue to teach the students part of the time even after they join the *rhetor*. This, he says, will show the students the continuity of their instruction while providing them with variety in their masters.

"Nor need there be any fear," he adds, "that the boy will be overburdened with the lessons of two masters. His labor will not be increased, but that which was mixed together under one master will be divided. Each tutor will thus be more efficient in his own province" (II.1.13). Perhaps the futility of his argument lay in the fact that both masters used the same methods anyway, with the exception of Declamation belonging clearly to the *rhetor.*

In any case Quintilian does not define or illustrate most of the terms he uses for the exercises, so we must look elsewhere. The *Progymnasmata* of Hermogenes of Tarsus is as good a source as any, since it transmitted the well-accepted definitions which even the more popular Aphthonius used later as the basis for his own book. Even though Hermogenes is writing in the second Christian century he reflects a tradition going well back before the time of Cicero.

Donald Lemen Clark has an incisive statement about the educational value of the *progymnasmata* as found in Hermogenes and his successors:

> They all give patterns for the boys to follow. They present a graded series of exercises in writing and speaking themes which proceed from the easy to the more difficult; they build each exercise on what the boys have learned from previous exercises, yet each exercise adds something new.[30]

The key term here is "graded." Like other elements of the Roman system the *progymnasmata* are taught not for themselves but for habit-building in the mind of the student. With each accomplishment of the student there comes a new and more difficult challenge, just as Imitation moves by steps from the oral reading through model-based writing to the final free composition of the student. The "how" is carefully spelled out at each stage.

Hermogenes presents twelve *progymnasmata:* fable, tale, *chreia,* proverb, refutation and confirmation, commonplace, encomium, comparison, impersonation *(prosopopeia),* description, thesis, and laws. (Aphthonius makes these into fourteen by separating refutation and confirmation, and by making censure the opposite of encomium; Quintilian, as we have seen, adds cause and effect.)

---

[30]Clark, *Rhetoric in Greco-Roman Education,* 181. For a modern adaptation of this idea, see John Hagaman, "Modern Use of the Progymnasmata in Teaching Rhetorical Invention" *Rhetoric Review* 5 (1986): 22-29.

The twelve can be divided according to the three types of rhetoric:

Deliberative rhetoric: fable, tale, chreia, proverb, thesis, laws.
Judicial rhetoric: confirmation and refutation, commonplace.
Epideictic rhetoric: encomium, impersonation, comparison,
     description.

However apt this kind of division might be in terms of future usefulness to the student, though, it does not represent the order in which the *progymnasmata* were taught. (Indeed the concept of "three genera of speeches," introduced by Aristotle and followed by the Romans, was always more theoretical than practical in terms of speeches made in the real world; any one oration might require elements of all three genera, as Cicero's performances have shown.) The exercises were taught in a certain order, for the good reason that they naturally succeeded each other.

The following abstract of the twelve *progymnasmata* of Hermogenes is necessarily brief, since the inclusion of over-numerous examples would produce an account as long as the book itself; examples are provided only in those cases (e.g. the *chreia*) which might otherwise be difficult for a modern reader to understand.[31]

1. Fable. The first exercise is the re-telling of fables from Aesop. The re-telling may be either more concise than the original, or expanded beyond it with invented dialogue or additional actions to enhance the tale.

2. Tales. This is the recounting of something that happened (a history) or of something as if it had happened (an epic, a tragedy, a comedy, a poem). Hermogenes names five modes: direct declarative, indirect declarative, interrogative, enumerative, comparative.

3. *Chreia.* This is an exercise in amplification, dealing with what a person said or did. Hermogenes says there are three types of *chreia* to be used in this way:

Of words only: "Isocrates said that education's root is bitter, its
     fruit is sweet" (*Chreia* 43).
Of actions only: "Crates, having met with an ignorant boy, beat
     the boy's tutor" (Quintilian I.9.5).

---

[31]The following account is based largely on Clark.

Mixed, with both words and actions: "Diogenes, on seeing a youth misbehaving, beat his tutor and said, 'Why are you teaching such things?'" (*Chreia* 26).

Hermogenes notes that a *chreia* differs from a maxim in three ways: a maxim has no character speaking, does not involve actions, and does not have an implicit question and answer.

The main point, of course is the amplification asked of the student. Hermogenes suggests a sequence of eight means to write about a *chreia:* praise of the speaker quoted, an expanded restatement of the *chreia,* its rationale, a statement of the opposite view, a statement from analogy, a statement from example, a statement from authority, and an exhortation to follow the advice of the speaker.

Ronald F. Hock and Edward N. O'Neill have recently published translations of the *chreia* of seven ancient authors including Quintilian; an appendix listing 68 *chreia* shows a remarkable similarity among the various collections, whether the speaker named is Demosthenes, Diogenes, or Plato.[32] This is not surprising, since the books are written for teachers rather than students; utility not variety is the standard.

4. Proverb. This is an exercise in amplification of an aphorism *(sententia).* It is not radically different from the preceding exercise, but is intended as incremental repetition. Hermogenes suggests methods similar to those for the *chreia,* though of course without praise for a speaker or an action. The *Rhetorica ad Herennium* (IV.56-58) cites the Proverb as an element of a figure of speech called Dwelling On One Point *(expolitio);* seven means of amplification are offered for the proverb "Often one who does not wish to perish for the republic must perish with the republic."

5. Refutation and Confirmation. This involves disproving or proving a narrative; Quintilian (II.4. 18-19) makes credibility the main heading to be considered. Hermogenes, however, says that the elements of Destructive Analysis are obscurity, incredibility, impossibility, inconsistency, unfittingness, inexpediency, or obscurity. Constructive analysis takes the opposite of these.

6. Commonplace. This exercise asks the student to "color"— that is, to cast a favorable or unfavorable light upon—an established fact, a thing admitted. Hermogenes says the Commonplace is

---

[32]See note 27 above.

practice in arousing the emotions of an audience in the face of an established fact—for example, the discovery of a temple robber:

> Begin with the contrary, analyzing it, not to inform, for the facts are assumed, but to incite and exasperate the auditors. Then introduce a comparison to heighten as much as possible the point you are making. After that introduce a proverb, upbraiding and calumniating the doer of the deed. Then a digression, introducing a defamatory conjecture as to the past life of the accused; then a repudiation of pity. Conclude the exercise with the final considerations of legality, justice, expediency, possibility, decency, and the consequences of the action.[33]

This treatment is called a Commonplace, he says, because it can be applied to any temple robber or other miscreant.

7. Encomium. This is an exercise in praise of virtue and dispraise of vice, either in a thing or in a person. (Apthonius makes the positive [Encomium] and negative sides [Vituperation] of this exercise into two separate items, but most others keep them as one.) Since praise and blame are the function of Epideictic oratory, the exercise of Encomium could draw upon all the lore of that section of rhetorical theory. Theon is reported to have developed the topics of Encomium in 36 divisions and subdivisions. Hermogenes contents himself with ten ways to praise a person: marvelous events at his birth, his nurture, his education, the nature of his soul, the nature of his body, his deeds, his external resources, how long he lived, the manner of his end, and the events after his death. Quintilian praises this exercise because "the mind is thus employed about a multiplicity and variety of matters" (I.2.20), and because it furnishes the students with many examples for later use.

8. Comparison. This exercise builds on the preceding one of Encomium by doubling the subjects to be treated in one composition. The same methods are to be used.

9. Impersonation. Here the student is asked to compose an imaginary monologue that would fit an assigned person in certain circumstances. The task is to make the language appropriate not only to the person (his age, background, and emotional state) but to the circumstances in which he speaks. For example, what might Achilles say to the dead Patroclus, or what might Niobe say over

---

[33]Clark, *Rhetoric in Greco-Roman Education,* 194.

the bodies of her dead children? There were three standard divisions: *Ethopoeia* is the imaginary statement of a known person; *Prosopopoeia* is the imaginary statement of an imaginary person; and *Eidolopoeia* are lines written for the dead to speak. Despite these theoretical divisions of the textbooks, the term *Prosopopeia* (as in Quintilian) is often used to denote the whole range of impersonative exercises.

10. Description. The exercise in vivid description *(ecphrasis)* asks the student to write and speak so that he is "bringing before the eyes what is to be shown"—a phrase used by Theon, Hermogenes, and Aphthonius as well as Quintilian. Quintilian discusses this kind of imaging in Book Eight under Ornateness; the figure *enargeia* (Vivid Illustration), he says, portrays persons, things, and actions in lively colors, so that they seem to be seen as well as heard (VIII.3.61). Clark (p. 203) uses the term "epideictic word-painting" for *ecphrasis,* and quotes Hermogenes as saying that "The virtues of the ecphrasis are clearness and visibility." It requires a careful attention to detail—and here the *ecphrasis* builds on the earlier exercises of Commonplace and Encomium. The student does not simply say a wall is large, but describes its stones, its height, its thickness, its circumference, its battlements— dilation of detail until the reader/hearer can "see" it in his mind.

11. Thesis. This advanced exercise asks the student to write an answer to a "general question" *(questio infinita)*—that is, a question not involving individuals. Cicero states in his *De inventione* (I.6.8) that rhetoric does not deal with such General Questions, but only with those involving individuals. Quintilian too notes that a general question can be made into a persuasive subject if names are added (II.4.25). That is, a Thesis would pose a general question such as "Should a man marry?" or "Should one fortify a city?" (A Special Question on the other hand would be "Should Marcus marry Livia?" or "Should Athens spend money to build a defensive wall?") Hermogenes distinguishes the Thesis from the Commonplace by declaring that the Commonplace amplifies a subject already admitted, while the Thesis is an inquiry into a matter still in doubt. Since both negative and positive answers may be supported, the exercise calls on the students to marshall arguments—i.e. use his rhetorical skills—on the chosen side; as a consequence both Hermogenes and Aphthonius recommend the same structure that is used in orations.

12. Laws (Legislation). This final exercise asks the pupil to compose arguments for or against a law. Quintilian regards this as the most advanced of the set of exercises: "The praise or censure of laws requires more mature powers, such as may almost suffice for the very highest efforts" (II.4.33). That is, it requires almost as much skill as the most advanced student activity, the Declamation. He says that the chief topics to be considered are whether the law is proper or expedient; under "proper" he includes consistency with justice, piety, religion or similar virtues; the "expedient" is determined by the nature of the law, by its circumstances, or by its enforcability. Quintilian also complains that some teachers make too many divisions of the two topics he discusses; as a matter of act Hermogenes lists the six topics of evident, just, legal, possible, expedient, and proper.

The *progymnasmata,* then, offered Roman teachers a systematic yet flexible tool for incremental development of student abilities. The young writer/speaker is led step-by-step into increasingly complex compositional tasks, his freedom of expression depending, almost paradoxically, on his ability to follow the form or pattern set by his master. At the same time he absorbs ideas of morality and virtuous public service from the subjects discussed, and from their recommended amplifications on themes of justice, expediency, and the like. By the time he reaches the exercise of Laws he has long since learned to see both sides of a question. He has also amassed a store of examples, aphorisms, narratives, and historical incidents which he can use later outside the school.

The student is, in short, ready to take on the most complex of all the Roman school's learning experiences—the Declamation *(declamatio),* or fictitious speech. Declamation is the cap, the culmination of the whole process.

Declamation. The Declamation is a rhetorical exercise designed to develop skill in deliberative (political) and forensic (judicial) oratory.[34] The two main types, in fact, are the *suasoria* in which

---

[34]See S.F. Bonner, *Roman Declamation in the Late Republic and the Early Empire* (University Press of Liverpool, 1949). For pre-Roman declamation see D.A. Russell, *Greek Declamation* (Oxford University Press, 1983). Clark has an account in *Rhetoric in Greco-Roman Education,* 213-261. There are shorter descriptions in Gwynn, Marrou, Parks, and Kennedy.

the speaker urges an assembly or person either to act or not to act, and the *controversia,* in which the speaker prosecutes or defends a person in a given legal case. Here again the Romans adapt for the schools a Greek practice apparently in use well before the time of Aristotle. The earliest Latin rhetorical treatises take it for granted. The author of the *Rhetorica ad Herennium* describes several deliberative exercises he finds useful; for example, one finds Hannibal debating with himself whether to return to Carthage or stay in Italy (III.2.2). Cicero says in his *De oratore* that every day he made up fictitious cases and made practice orations on them.

Besides such private practice sessions there was a public form of declamation, first among friends for mutual edification and entertainment (as in the time of Cicero), then under the Empire as a regular type of public display or even competition—the Emperor Nero himself "won" such a competition on one occasion. Later, under the period of oratorical virtuosity known as "The Second Sophistic," the public declaimers attracted crowds and wealth which today only a rock star could command.[35]

Declamation thus has a curious history. Obviously any would-be orator would want to practice, and there is the famous story of Demosthenes delivering a practice oration on shore against the sound of the breakers to improve his speaking voice. No doubt speakers since the very earliest days have practiced their skills in made-up controversies, and it would not be surprising to find Greek teachers like Gorgias or Isocrates putting their students through such drills.

The great virtue of Declamation for the Roman schoolmaster, though, was that the whole technical apparatus of rhetorical theory was available as resource for the classroom activity of the oration. All that was needed was a set of subjects on which to deliver speeches. It is significant that Quintilian, after devoting most of the

---

[35]See, for instance Eunapius's account of the declamation which Prohaeresius delivered in Athens in the third century as part of his candidacy for the highly-paid position of *rhetor* in that city; the crowds were so great that soldiers had to be used to control the situation. Prohaeresius started his extempore speech on one side of a difficult theme, then switched to the opposite side—then challenged the shorthand reporters to check his accuracy as he repeated both impromptu speeches word for word! The story is in Eunapius, *Lives of the Philosophers,* in Philostratus and Eunapius, *Lives of the Sophists,* trans. Wilmer C. Wright. (Loeb Classical Library: Harvard University Press, 1922), 495-497.

first two books of the *Institutio* to the early education of the
student, turns briefly to Declamation (II.10.1-15)—and then begins
the detailed exposition of rhetoric which occupies eight of the ten
remaining books. Once Declamation is reached, in other words,
rhetoric becomes the master's concern. The complete oration, even
in the classroom, demands a full appreciation of the five parts of
rhetoric: Invention, Arrangement, Style, Memory, and Delivery.
Heretofore rhetoric has been used piecemeal in the preliminary
exercises, the precepts being introduced wherever useful.

The student facing an audience of colleagues and master, and
often facing a student opponent as well, had rhetorical problems
similar to those in the outside world. Quintilian has high
expectations for Declamation, rather sarcastically answering critics
who see no value in it:

> For, if it is no preparation for the forum, it is merely like
> theatrical ostentation, or insane raving. To what purpose is it to
> instruct a judge who has no existence? To state a case that all
> know to be fictitious? To bring proofs on a point on which no
> man will pronounce sentence? This is nothing more than trifling;
> but how ridiculous is it to excite our feelings, and to work upon
> an audience with eagerness and sorrow, unless we are indeed
> preparing ourselves, by imitations of battle, for serious contests
> and a regular field? (II.10.8).

These "imitations of battle" take a standard format in the
Roman schools. The master assigns a problem ("theme") to one or
more students; they prepare and deliver an oration before the class
in reply to the problem posed in the theme; the master delivers an
oral comment on the orations, perhaps adding to it a declamation
of his own to show how it might be done better. Quintilian in fact
proposes that the master ask the students to evaluate his own
declamation as a means of sharpening their critical skills (II.2.13).
An easy variation involves matching two students against each
other, especially in the forensic declamations *(controversiae).*

Typically the declamation is divided into the four parts of
proem, narration, proofs, and peroration (i.e. conclusion). A *divisio*
after the narration could lay out the overall plan the speaker
intends to follow; for example he might divide his remarks into
Letter of the Law *(ius)* versus Spirit of the Law *(aequitas).*
Classroom practice encouraged amplification as a means of testing
the students' powers, particularly in the use of weighty statements

(sententiae) or in the devising of novel approaches *(colores)*. To go into greater detail here about the methodology of the Declamation would be to rehearse the entirety of rhetorical theory. This is of course not our main concern.

What part did writing play in the exercise of Declamation? The answer is not clear. Quintilian does not specifically mention writing, though he does say of Declamation that "it comprehends within itself all those exercises of which I have been treating, and presents us with a very close resemblance to reality" (II.10.2). Certainly writing plays a major part in Imitation and in the *progymnasmata* which go before. Quintilian mentions the practice of providing outlines for students to follow in their declamations (II.6.2). Given Quintilian's whole orientation toward the relation of speaking and writing, it would not be surprising to find various written forms behind the oral performance. For one thing his constant admonitions about storing examples for future use imply written record as well as strong memory. And what he says in Book Ten about the writing orator (e.g. X.3.10) seems to imply that at least some of the oral was first the written. The Declamation itself was of course purely oral, but we are not yet sure how much writing lies behind it.

Certainly Quintilian urges the adult speaker to use writing both as a general preparation and as a tool for shaping certain parts of a speech in advance of its delivery: "By writing we speak with greater accuracy and by speaking we write with greater ease" (X.7.29). He makes this remark—one of his most famous aphorisms—in discussing the value of meditation as compared to the value of writing:

> As to writing, we must certainly never write more than when we have to speak much extempore; for by the use of the pen a weightiness will be preserved in our matter, and that light facility of language, which swims as it were on the surface, will be compressed into a body as husbandmen cut off the upper roots of the vine (which elevate it to the surface of the soil) in order that the lower roots may be strengthened by striking deeper. And I know not whether both exercises, when we perform them with care and assiduity, are not reciprocally beneficial, as it appears that by writing we speak with greater accuracy, and by speaking we write with greater ease. We must write, therefore, as often as we have opportunity; if opportunity

is not allowed us, we must meditate; if we are precluded from
both, we must nevertheless endeavor that the orator may not
seem to be caught at fault, nor the client left destitute of aid. But
it is the general practice among pleaders who have much
occupation, to write only the most essential parts, and especially
the commencements, of their speeches; to fix the other portions
that they bring from home in their memory by meditation: and
to meet any unforeseen attacks with extemporaneous replies.
(X.7.28-30).

Quintilian adds (X.7.30-31) that Cicero and many other orators
used written memoranda as aids in preparing their speeches.[36] His
personal recommendation is to use short notes and small memoran-
dum-books which may be held in the hand while speaking. In his
discussion of Memory in Book Eleven there are constant references
to written texts of orations for which the memory must be used
(esp. XI.2.25-49). If the adult speaker is urged to use writing, it
certainly seems likely that the young student preparing to be an
orator would be given the same instructions.

There have been many critics of the Declamation, both ancient
and modern. Tacitus complains in his *Dialogue on Oratory* (A.D.
85) about "the training merely of tongue and voice in imaginary
debates which have no point of contact with real life."[37] Quintilian
himself says that "The practice however has so degenerated
through the fault of the teachers, that the license and ignorance of
the declaimers have been among the chief causes that have
corrupted eloquence" (II.10.3). To this, however, he immediately
has a positive reply: "But of that which is good by nature we may
surely make a good use."

Many of the criticisms concern the subjects chosen for

---

[36]For a discussion of the role played by writing in Cicero's oratory, see Richard Leo
Enos, *The Literate Mode of Cicero's Legal Rhetoric* (Southern Illinois University Press,
1988). Orthography—the physical task of writing—is important to Quintilian; he urges
writers to use wax tablets for drafts to speed up composition without breaking the pattern
by having to dip a pen in ink (X.3.31-33). For a brief history of the wax tablet, see
Richard and Mary Rouse, "Wax Tablets" *Language and Communication* 9 (1989): 175-
191. See also Albertine Gaur, *A History of Writing* (London: The British Library, 1984);
the illustration of pens and a stylus on p. 52 may help illuminate Quintilian's remarks
noted above.

[37]Tacitus, *Dialogue,* 31 (p. 95).

classroom use.[38] Manifestly such subjects must be difficult enough to challenge the capacities of the students, yet generalizable enough to permit the students to work on them without vast research. As a consequence a large array of fantastic or even incredible topics come to be associated with Declamation, and especially with the forensic type. They feature pirates, seducers, wronged heirs, poison cups, cruel husbands, contradictory laws, cures for the blind, shipwrecks, and a host of other calamities and dilemmas calculated to present the student orator with difficulty. The deliberative type was generally more staid—"Cato deliberates whether to take a wife"—but the Romans always considered the forensic the more difficult and therefore exercised more ingenuity in posing its problems. One example from the collection of Seneca may suffice to show the level of complexity which was employed:

The Daughter of the Pirate Chief

"A young man captured by pirates writes his father for ransom. He is not ransomed. The daughter of the pirate chief urges him to swear that he will marry her if he escapes. He swears. Leaving her father, she follows the young man, who, upon his return to home, takes her to wife. A well-to-do orphan appears on the scene. The father orders his son to divorce the daughter of the pirate chief and marry the orphan. When the son refuses to obey, the father disowns him" (*Controversiae* I.6.6).[39]

S.F. Bonner, one of the most perceptive modern students of the Declamation, defends such classroom subjects on the very grounds that critics use to attack them. The subjects are deliberately more complex than real life, he says, as a test of the student's powers: "they were deliberately designed to provide an almost, but not quite, impossible hurdle."[40]

The publication of declamatory texts also shows a public interest in the topics and their treatment. While the published *progymnasmata* of Hermogenes and Aphthonius were for the use

---

[38]"The world of the declamation was a fantastic and melodramatic one," writes Martin Lowther Clarke, "and for that reason perhaps popular in a humdrum age." He makes the remark in *Rhetoric at Rome: A Historical Survey* (London: Cohen and West, 1953), 91.

[39]Quoted in Clark, *Rhetoric in Greco-Roman Education,* 231.

[40]Bonner, *Roman Declamation,* 83.

of teachers, the sets of declamations published by the elder Seneca and by the Pseudo-Quintilian[41] were intended for a general reader. Such works were successful enough that someone wrote two collections to which Quintilian's name became attached. The reason, of course, is that there were popular public declamations put on by adult orators to demonstrate their rhetorical virtuosity; the throngs attending such displays of extempore eloquence might well treasure a written form of what they had heard, just as sports fans today read eagerly the newspaper account of a game seen the day before.

In any case history shows that the Declamation served the Roman schools for many centuries—again, a case in which the very longevity of the practice demonstrates its perceived value. The Declamation is the remote ancestor of the *disputatio* of the medieval university, and of scholastic debate beginning in colonial American colleges and lasting into the present time. Like the *progymnasmata* and Imitation, Declamation may well have had far-reaching influences in Western culture not yet completely recognized by modern scholars.

Sequencing. The systematic ordering of classroom activities in Roman schools was to accomplish two goals: Movement, from the simple to the more complex; and Reinforcement, by reiterating each element of preceding exercises as each new one appears. To these can be added another principle: no exercise should be done for just a single purpose.

It is these principles which lead to the constant interrelating of writing, speaking, reading, and listening. Writing is a solitary activity, Quintilian notes, but recitation of the written is a public one. What is written by one student is heard by another when recited. What is read—and we must remember that reading in ancient times is generally vocalized, and therefore "heard" by the reader—becomes the model for the written. Writing makes

---

[41]See Seneca the Elder, *Controversiae. Suasoriae.* Ed. and trans. Michael Winterbottom. Two volumes. (Loeb Classical Library: Harvard University Press, 1974). Seneca says he wrote the declamations for his sons, but the work had a more general circulation anyway. Michael Winterbottom has edited the *Minor Declamations Attributed to Quintilian* (New York and Berlin: Walter de Gruyter, 1984), with a commentary which includes treatment of the subject of possible authorship of the collection.

speaking precise, Quintilian says, just as speaking makes writing easy. Listening prepares the student for analysis of the oral arguments he will later hear his opponent raise against him in forum or courtroom. Everything fits; there are no random activities in the Roman schoolroom.

Habituation is the key to success in the Roman school. For example a dozen years of re-tellings, from simple Aesop to complex Demosthenes, makes narrative skill second nature by adulthood. Likewise the analytic phases of Imitation make critical reading the norm. The step-by-step progression through the *progymnasmata* equips the student with powerful tools of amplification, just as the Declamation prepares him to see instinctively the two sides to any controversy. Quintilian declares Habit *(hexis)* to be the ultimate goal of the program. What he means is something a bit different from the modern idea of habit as something fixed and somewhat out of our control; his "habit" means a deep-rooted capacity (his word is *facilitas*) to employ language wherever needed, on whatever subject, in whatever circumstances. His meaning is close to Aristotle's, who defines rhetoric as a "faculty" of observing the available means of persuasion in a given case; this 'faculty' for Aristotle is seen as virtually a part of the personality *(ethos)* of the rhetor. In a sense, for both men, the person *becomes* rhetorical.

It is for this reason that Quintilian and other Roman masters are willing to set up this gruelling sequence of sometimes petty and dull exercises. The goal is no less than the perfect orator, whose molding is worth every effort. Quintilian would probably say that the way to train an architect is to start him as a boy on building bricks; the child need not know what a wall is, when he begins to make bricks, but later he can be taught how to make small brick piles, then walls, then houses, then palaces, and then even cities. This is just the way Roman schools approach language use. The master envisages word-cities even from the time the child begins to trace letters with his stylus, and then leads him incrementally through a nicely coordinated sequence of learning experiences which make efficient language use virtually a part of his personality. The letter of the alphabet becomes years later a stirring oration in the Roman Senate.

Many of the individual exercises can be used profitably today, of course, since each is largely self-explanatory. Nevertheless a modern reader should understand that the full power of their use resides in their interrelation to each other, and in their place in a proven sequence.[42]

THE CONTINUITY OF ROMAN TEACHING METHODS:
THE FIRST THIRTEEN HUNDRED YEARS

Almost exactly one thousand years after Quintilian finished his *Institutio oratoria* in A.D. 95, describing a system already two centuries old, a writer named William Fitzstephen visited a courtyard in medieval London. He was there for the occasion of a joint public ceremony involving young students from three schools: St. Paul's, St. Mary Arches, and St. Martin-le-Grand. The boys were twelve to fourteen years old. The year was 1170. Here is his description of what he saw:

> The scholars dispute, some in demonstrative rhetoric, others in dialectic. Some 'hurtle enthymemes,' others with greater skill employ perfect syllogisms. Boys of different schools strive against one another in verse, or contend concerning the principles of grammar, or the rules concerning past and future. There are others who employ the old art of the crossroads in epigrams, rhymes, and metre.[43]

The language was Latin. We may wonder, how did London schoolmasters get boys coming from Norman French, or perhaps even West Saxon or Irish at age six or seven, up to the point of using Latin well enough to improvise verse and dispute about grammar? During the middle ages Latin was always a foreign language, learned on top of some vernacular ("hearth language"). Just as Roman boys had to learn Greek on top of their family Latin, so did medieval boys have to learn Latin on top of their native tongues.

An answer to this question may be found in a passage written just a few years earlier by John of Salisbury in his *Metalogicon* (1159); the passage is lengthy, but John's attention to detail may give a better picture of the situation than any summary could:

---

[42]For a comment on modern use of the system see Murphy, "The Modern Value of Roman Methods of Teaching Writing, with Answers to Twelve Current Fallacies" *Writing On the Edge* 1 (1989): 28-37.

[43]Quoted in Murphy, "The Teaching of Latin as a Foreign Language in the Twelfth Century" *Historiographia Linguistica* 7 (1980): 160.

This method was followed by Bernard of Chartres, *exundissimus modernis temporibus fons litterarum in Gallia.* By citations from the authors he showed what was simple and regular; he brought into relief the grammatical figures, the rhetorical colours, the artifices of sophistry, and pointed out how the text in hand bore upon other studies: not that he sought to teach everything in a single session, for he kept in mind the capacity of his audience. He inculcated correctness and propriety of diction, and a fitting use of congruous figures. Realizing that practise strengthens memory and sharpens faculty, he urged his pupils to imitate what they had heard, inciting some by admonitions, others by whipping and penalties. Each pupil recited the next day something from what he had heard on the preceding. The evening exercise, called the *declinatio,* was filled with such an abundance of grammar that any one, of fair intelligence, by attending it for a year, would have at his fingers' ends the art of writing and speaking, and would know the meaning of all words in common use. But since no day and no school ought to be vacant of religion, Bernard would select for study a subject edifying to faith and morals. The closing part of this *declinatio,* or rather philosophical recitation, was stamped with piety: the souls of the dead were commended, a penitential Psalm was recited, and the Lord's Prayer.

For those boys who had to write exercises in prose or verse, he selected the poets and orators, and showed how they should be imitated in the linking of words and the elegant ending of passages. If any one sewed another's cloth into his garment, he was reproved for the theft, but usually was not punished. Yet Bernard gently pointed out to awkward borrowers that whoever imitated the ancients *(majores)* should himself become worthy of imitation by posterity. He impressed upon his pupil the virtue of economy, and the values of things and words: he explained where a meagreness and tenuity of diction was fitting, and where copiousness or even excess should be allowed, and the advantage of due measure everywhere. He admonished them to go through the histories and poems with diligence, and daily to fix passages in their memory. He advised them, in reading, to avoid the superflous, and confine themselves to the works of distinguished authors. For, he said (quoting from Quintilian) that to follow out what every contemptible person has said, is irksome and vainglorious, and destructive of the capacity which should remain free for better things. To the same effect he cited Augustine, and remarked that the ancients thought it a virtue in a grammarian to be ignorant of something. But since in school exercises nothing is more useful than to practise what should be accomplished by the art, his scholars wrote daily in prose and verse, and proved themselves in discussions.

John also cites Quintilian more directly in laying out the ideal learning program:

> One who aspires to become a philosopher should therefore apply himself to reading, learning, and meditation, as well as the performance of good works, lest the Lord become angry and take away what he seems to possess. The word "reading" is equivocal. It may refer either to the activity of teaching and being taught, or to the occupation of studying written things by oneself. Consequently the former, the intercommunication between teacher and learner, may be termed (to use Quintilian's term) the "lecture" *(prelectio);* the latter, or the scrutiny by the student, the "reading" *(lectio),* simply so called. On the authority of the same Quintilian, "the teacher of grammar should, in lecturing, take care of such details as to have his students analyze verses into their parts of speech, and point out the nature of the metrical feet which are to be noted in poems. He should, moreover, indicate and condemn whatever is barbarous, incongruous, or otherwise against the rules of composition."[44]

As a matter of fact the influence of Quintilian as an individual had had a major revival in French schools like Chartres and Bec in John's lifetime. Although there was no complete text of the *Institutio oratoria* available during the middle ages, the so-called *textus mutilatus* which was available retained almost all of the first two books concerning the *grammaticus* and *rhetor,* together with a fragment of Book Ten.[45]

The influence of the Roman teaching methods themselves was far greater. Basically the history is that the Roman school system remained intact even after the onset of barbarian invasions and the fall of Rome itself in 410 and the removal of the last Emperor in 467. The advent of Christianity did not materially change the picture, due in part to the influence of Saint Augustine. There was a sharp decline in the sixth to ninth centuries—the so-called "Dark Ages"—followed by localized revivals in various places

---

[44]Ibid., 171-172.
[45]Murphy, *Rhetoric in the Middle Ages,* 123-130.

throughout the West. (In Byzantium Greek rhetoric, with strong
reliance on the *progymnasmata,* never suffered the decline that
befell the Roman system).[46] Then, in twelfth century Europe, the
rapid dispersion of schools made possible the widespread increases
in literacy that have earned that period the title of "The
Renaissance of the Twelfth Century." The rise of universities—a
truly medieval invention—is a feature of this same period, causing
a radical re-structuring of education; the re-introduction of Aristotelian dialectic in new Latin translations tilted European education
in a new direction. What John of Salisbury and William
Fitzstephen show us is that the entire *trivium* of grammar, rhetoric,
and dialectic was being taught in twelfth century schools. But by
1215 Paris, the "Mother of Universities," made dialectic the core
subject for language study, relegating grammar to lower schools
and excluding rhetoric altogether. The result was that medieval
students learned grammar in local schools following an essentially
Roman teaching program—then went on to universities using
Aristotelian dialectic as their basic methodology; the formal
disputatio became the chief tool in every university subject for
both teaching and examinations for the next six centuries. The fate
of Roman rhetorical theory and its medieval offshoots is a subject
for another inquiry.

Evidence for continuity is pervasive, too massive to recount
here in detail. It should not be surprising that the Roman
geopolitics which made the Latin language a world-ordering device
should have cemented its teaching methods into the very warp and
woof of Western culture. The schools continued to pump out new
Ciceros long after the oratorical scene had changed beyond
recognition: the law courts under Emperors turned increasingly to
statutory law and written documentations, thus lessening opportunities for forensic oratory in the traditional sense, while autocratic
rule made public debate literally dangerous for speakers.[47] Only
epideictic oratory was left for public display.

At the same time the demand for schools continued, though

---

[46]The best account is George A. Kennedy, *Greek Rhetoric Under Christian
Emperors* (Princeton University Press, 1983).

[47]The suppression of free speech under the Empire is described vividly by Chester
G. Starr, *Civilization and the Caesars: The Intellectual Revolution in the Roman Empire*
(Cornell University Press, 1954).

more for reasons of upward mobility than for the ideals of a Cicero or a Quintilian. Robert A. Kaster has recently published a book, *Guardians of Language,* which provides splendid detail concerning the role of grammarians and rhetoricians in the Empire.[48] Imperial and municipal salaries were commonplace. As Marrou has observed, "The whole of the Empire was covered with a fairly dense network of academic institutions: elementary school teachers were to be found more or less everywhere, grammarians and rhetors in places of any importance."[49] Teachers often had valuable immunities from taxes or from military service, though their social status was not always high, and a certain Athenanaeus cites an old Greek proverb that "If there were no doctors there would be no greater fool than a schoolmaster."[50]

Pierre Riché, perhaps the greatest modern scholar of education in late antiquity and the early middle ages, makes two important observations about the period up to the eighth century. One is about the continuity of teaching methods: "When we look inside the schools of the grammarian and the rhetoric, we can observe that the programs and methods of instruction also had not changed."[51] The other is about historiography itself: is it that schools disappeared during the great barbarian invasions, or is it that our sources have disappeared? Noting that historians have been "astonished" at what they see as a "renaissance" later, he suggests the alternate possibility that the schools continued to exist without leaving the kind of written traces needed to prove their existence.

The period after the end of the twelfth century has its own history in respect to the history of writing instruction, and that is the subject of the next chapter by Marjorie Woods. Nevertheless it seems clear that the developments she describes are rooted in the teaching situations in schools of the twelfth century, which in turn depend on methods refined over twelve Christian centuries but

---

[48]Robert A. Kaster, *The Guardians of Language: The Grammarian and Society in Late Antiquity* (University of California Press, 1988). In addition to a wealth of detail about salaries, social status, reputation and the like, he provides (pp. 231-440) a "prosopography" or demographic records of hundreds of teachers from the period A.D. 250 to 565.

[49]Marrou, *History of Education,* 296.

[50]Ibid., 137.

[51]Riché, *Education and Culture in the Barbarian West,* 40.

originally laid down in ancient Rome during the first century before Christ.

CONCLUSION

This has been a story of system and continuity. It seems inconceivable that any human enterprise of such longevity could be valueless.

This is not to say that the enterprise was perfect or without fault. Its very longevity has provided ample opportunity for criticism, from Cicero and Tacitus to modern detractors like Martin Lowther Clarke who notes that "The Romans had administrative capacity in their bones, and it could survive even the follies of the lesser rhetoricians."[52] He complains that the schools fostered a cult of ornateness; that the system of Imitation and Invention by Topics prevented students from thinking for themselves; that truth was made less important than imagination; that directness in speech was discouraged; and that the same educational labor could well have been spent on something better. He concludes with the observation that Pliny is narrower than Cicero, and Fronto is narrower than Pliny. Others complain that the education was purely literary—that is, word-centered—thus training declaimers rather than orators. Still others maintain that the student was given no real sense of history, no training in philosophy except for a scattering of ethical commonplaces, no unifying picture of society or government; another criticism is that as an elitist mechanism the schools merely perpetuated the order of a ruling class.[53]

At the same time its pedagogical values surely seem worth studying. It might be well to conclude this chapter with an observation from Louis G. Kelly:

> Nobody really knows what is new or old in present-day language teaching procedures. There has been a vague feeling that modern experts have spent their time in discovering what other men have forgotten; but as most of the key documents are

---

[52]Clarke, *Rhetoric at Rome,* 162.
[53]Kaster (*Guardians of the Language,* 12-13) offers a succinct array of such charges.

in Latin, moderns find it difficult to go to original sources. In any case, much that is being claimed as revolutionary in this century is merely a rethinking and renaming of earlier ideas and procedures.[54]

APPENDIX

OVERVIEW OF ROMAN TEACHING METHODS
DESCRIBED IN THE *INSTITUTIO ORATORIA*

They fall into five categories: (1) Precept; (2) Imitation; (3) Composition exercises (*progymnasmata*); (4) Declamation; and (5) Sequencing.

1. Precept: "a set of rules that provide a definite method and system of speaking." Grammar as precept deals with "the art of speaking correctly, and the interpretation of the poets." Rhetoric as precept occupies eight of the twelve books of the *Institutio oratoria:*
   a. Invention
   b. Arrangement
   c. Style
   d. Memory
   e. Delivery
2. Imitation: the use of models to learn how others have used language. Specific exercises include:

[54]Louis G. Kelly, *25 Centuries of Language Teaching: An inquiry into the science, art, and development of language teaching methodology, 500 B.C.-1969.* (Rowley, Massachusetts: Newbury House Publishers, 1969), ix.

    a. Reading aloud (*lectio*)
    b. Master's detailed analysis of a text (*praelectio*)
    c. Memorization of models
    d. Paraphrase of models
    e. Transliteration (prose/verse and/or Latin/Greek)
    f. Recitation of paraphrase or transliteration
    g. Correction of paraphrase or transliteration
3. Composition exercises (*progymnasmata or praeexercitamenta*): a graded series of exercises in writing and speaking themes. Each succeeding exercise is more difficult and incorporates what has been learned in preceding ones. The following twelve were common by Cicero's time:
    a. Retelling a fable
    b. Retelling an episode from a poet or a historian
    c. *Chreia,* or amplification of a moral theme
    d. Amplification of an aphorism (*sententia*) or proverb
    e. Refutation or confirmation of an allegation
    f. Commonplace, or confirmation of a thing admitted
    g. Encomium, or eulogy (or dispraise) of a person or thing.
    h. Comparison of things or persons
    i. Impersonation (*prosopopeia*), or speaking or writing in the character of a given person
    j. Description (ecphrasis), or vivid presentation of details
    k. Thesis, or argument for/against an answer to a general question (*quaestio infinita*) not involving individuals
    l. Laws, or arguments for or against a law
4. Declamation (*declamatio*), or fictitious speeches, in two types:
    a. *Sausoria,* or deliberative (political) speech arguing that an action be taken or not taken
    b. *Controversia,* or forensic (legal) speech prosecuting or defending a fictitious or historical person in a law case
5. Sequencing, or the systematic ordering of classroom activities to accomplish two goals.:
    a. Movement, from the simple to the more complex
    b. Reinforcement, by reiterating each element of preceding exercises as each new one appears

Perhaps the most important aspect of these methods is their coordination into a single instructional program. Each is important for itself, but takes greater importance from its place within the whole.

CHAPTER THREE

THE TEACHING OF WRITING
IN MEDIEVAL EUROPE

MARJORIE CURRY WOODS

The Middle Ages constitute the longest definable period in the western tradition, more than two to ten times as long as that covered by any other essay in this collection.[1] It is also the period that in standard histories of rhetoric receives the shortest and often the least satisfactory treatment.[2] This situation has not been caused by deliberate neglect. Rather, the Middle Ages appear so problematic

---

[1]There has always been debate about when the Middle Ages actually begin and end. For some modern scholars the period begins with the fall of Rome, for others with the crowning of Charlemagne or the twelfth-century "renaissance" (in which case the earlier centuries become the "Dark Ages"). Its end is dated by some with the career of one or another of the more prominent humanists, such as Petrarch, by others at the invention of printing. James J. Murphy's *Rhetoric in the Middle Ages: A History of Rhetorical Theory from St. Augustine to the Renaissance* (Berkeley and Los Angeles: University of California Press, 1974) covers the period from A.D. 426 to 1416.

[2]E.g., Edward P.J. Corbett, *Classical Rhetoric for the Modern Student,* 2nd ed. (New York: Oxford University Press, 1971), 2 of 35 pages; George Kennedy, *Classical Rhetoric and Its Christian and Secular Tradition from Ancient to Modern Times* (Chapel Hill: The University of North Carolina Press, 1980), 29 pages out of 246; Brian Vickers, *In Defense of Rhetoric* (Oxford: At The Clarendon Press, 1988), 40 of 479 pages. Revisionist historians of rhetoric can be even more drastic: William A. Covino, *The Art of Wondering: A Revisionist Return to the History of Rhetoric* (Portsmouth, N.H.: Boynton/Cook, 1988), one sentence; C.H. Knoblauch and Lil Brannon, *Rhetorical Traditions and the Teaching of Writing* (Upper Montclair, N.J.: Boynton/Cook, 1984), no mention. A welcome exception is Bruce A. Kimball, who devotes two chapters in *Orators and Philosophers: A History of the Idea of Liberal Education* (New York: Teachers College Press, 1986) to the "Foundation of the *Artes Liberales*" and the "Rise of the Philosophical Tradition in the High Middle Ages" (62 of 241 pages).

Richard McKeon's classic essay, "Rhetoric in the Middle Ages," *Speculum* 17 (1942): 1-32, is not particularly helpful for those interested in the teaching of writing in

(continued on next page)

because of our approaches to the period itself and the assumptions about rhetoric with which we begin our investigations.

It has been difficult to see the Middle Ages whole because the study of this period is divided among so many modern disciplines, in each of which the study of medieval rhetoric, which means the study of medieval Latin, is a marginal field. With such a fragmented subject, it is not surprising that those who are trying to understand medieval rhetoric receive fragmentary and contradictory answers to the vexed question of "What do medieval rhetoricans want?"

Not only has finding out about medieval rhetoric been difficult for modern scholars; we have also failed to see what was there when we found it. Certain basic value judgments about rhetoric in general become less secure after a good, hard look at the Middle Ages; and rather than give up such value judgments, we have preferred to give up the Middle Ages. A summary of the kind of assumptions about rhetoric that are most problematic are conve-niently available at the beginning of George Kennedy's *Classical Rhetoric and Its Christian and Secular Tradition from Ancient to Modern Times.*[3] In the following paragraphs I have quoted and then paraphrased Kennedy's key statements so as to indicate some of the problematic results of encoding such value judgments in our tradition:

1. "Primary rhetoric is the conception of rhetoric as held by the Greeks when the art was, as they put it, 'invented' in the fifth century B.C." In other words, rhetoric is defined by one group of persons who say that they invented it, no matter what was accomplished before or after.

2. "Rhetoric was 'primarily' an act of persuasion; it was primarily used in civic life. ..." That is, only rhetoric associated with civic life is "primary." Those who are at any given time

---

[2](continued from previous page)
the Middle Ages. A more useful single essay is Martin Camargo, "Rhetoric," in *The Seven Liberal Arts in the Middle Ages,* ed. David L. Wagner (Bloomington: Indiana University Press, 1983), pp. 96-124; and see also Susan Miller's chapter on "Textual Literacy: Writing in the Middle Ages" in *Rescuing the Subject: A Critical Introduction to Rhetoric and the Writer* (Carbondale, Ill.: Southern Illinois University Press, 1989), pp. 71-802. An up-to-date, annotated, and inexpensive bibliography of scholarship in the field is the second edition of James J. Murphy, *Medieval Rhetoric: A Select Bibliography* (Toronto: University of Toronto Press, 1989).
[3]The quotations that follow are found on pages 4 and 5 of Kennedy's book.

excluded from participation in civic life are also, *ipso facto,* excluded from "primary" rhetoric and are, thus, rhetorically "second"-rate.

3. "[Rhetoric] was primarily oral. Primary rhetoric involves an act of enunciation on a specific occasion; in itself it has *no text,* though subsequently an enunciation can be treated as a text" (emphasis mine). Yet the only oratorical examples that we have inherited from the past are those that were written down, and those groups who traditionally have been forced to confine themselves "primarily" to oral rhetoric, that is, those with "secondary" status as citizens and those from "third"-world countries, are the most suppressed in modern rhetorical-political discourse.

4. "The primacy of primary rhetoric is a fundamental fact in the classical tradition: throughout the Roman Empire, whatever was the *real* situation of their students, teachers of rhetoric took as their *nominal* goal the training of persuasive public speakers..." (emphasis mine). That is, Kennedy's primary rhetoric is "primary" whether it is delusory or not.

5. "'Secondary' rhetoric... is the apparatus of rhetorical techniques clustering around discourse or art forms when those techniques are not being used for their primary oral purpose." That is, all rhetoric except that described above is secondary.

6. "The most frequent manifestations of secondary rhetoric are commonplaces, figures of speech and thought, and tropes in elaborate writing. Much literature, art, and informal discourse is decorated by secondary rhetoric, which may be a mannerism of the historical period in which it is composed. ..." That is, literature is "secondary" rhetoric because it is rhetorical.

7. "It has been a persistent characteristic of classical rhetoric... to move from primary into secondary forms. For this phenomenon the Italian term *letteraturizzazione* is convenient shorthand. *Letteraturizzazione* is a tendency of rhetoric to shift its focus from persuasion to narration, from civic to personal contexts, and from discourse to literature, including poetry." That is, literature is "secondary" rhetoric because it is literary.

8. "The primary reason for the *letteraturizzazione* of rhetoric is probably the place given rhetoric in education and the recurring tendency to teach it by rote to young children rather than to make it a more intellectually demanding advanced discipline." That is, teaching rhetoric, and more specifically teaching it to the young,

has degraded the art. Yet throughout the western tradition the rhetorical focus of pedagogical practices for the young has been much stronger and more continuous than that of adult discourse about rhetoric.

Because the Middle Ages, although the longest period in the western tradition, is nevertheless the one most marginalized by this system of interrelated values, I shall offer in my conclusion an alternate set of assumptions by means of which to approach the history of rhetoric, one that takes the Middle Ages as the norm. Heretical as such an argument sounds, it is in a number of important respects more accurate for other periods as well.

First, however, it is necessary to address the question of whether it is possible to consider the Middle Ages as a unit from any rhetorical perspective. After all, Brian Vickers argues in his new book, *In Defence of Rhetoric,* that the Middle Ages is responsible for the disintegration of rhetoric. (Fortunately for us, Vickers argues, the Renaissance reintegrated it.)[4] And there is no question that a period as long as the Middle Ages and one that embraced or spawned so many different cultures can appear to us confusing and self-contradictory. But fragmentation can be in the eye of the beholder, and recent historians of medieval rhetoric have remarked on the continuity of the medieval rhetorical tradition, especially from the perspective of "secondary" rhetoric, the rhetoric of the schools.[5]

My own research affirms the continuity of rhetorical teaching throughout the High Middle Ages. For example, the techniques of teaching grammar and rhetoric that John of Salisbury, writing in about 1150, describes in his eulogy of his master, Bernard of

---

[4]The relevant chapters are entitled "Medieval Fragmentation" and "Renaissance Reintegration."

[5]Several of the papers given in 1988 at the International Conference on Education in the Language Arts, sponsored by the National Endowment for the Humanities and held at The Medieval Institute, Western Michigan University, presented evidence for this continuity of the pedagogical tradition from the late antique to the medieval period and throughout the High Middle Ages. Plans are underway to publish these papers and additional essays.

For an description of changes in rhetorical pedagogy during the Middle Ages, however, a topic that I ignore in this paper, see Camargo, "Rhetoric," cited above, and Ronald Witt, "The Teaching of the *Ars dictaminis* in Fourteenth-Century Italy," forthcoming in this volume.

Chartres,[6] were used consistently throughout the thirteenth, four-teenth, and fifteenth centuries.[7] Bernard's methods included daily memorization of passages as well as short compositions in prose and verse based on these passages. In addition, Bernard also carefully and clearly explained to his students the rhetorical choices involved in different kinds of composition projects.

There is also an extraordinary coherence in the school texts on which literacy was based during the Middle Ages. The books that formed the basis of rhetorical education in composition at the beginning of the Middle Ages continued to be taught more than a thousand years later. The new works that were included as the period developed were seen not as replacing but as supplementing the earlier ones. For example, the introductory reader called the *Liber Catonianus* is a collection of late antique and early medieval short texts that continued in popularity throughout the Middle Ages and, in a slightly different form, well into the Renaissance. It was comprised of the following list of books:[8]

---

[6]John's famous discussion is found in *The Metalogicon of John of Salisbury: A Twelfth-Century Defense of the Verbal and Logical Arts of the Trivium,* trans. Daniel D. McGarry (Berkeley, 1955; reprinted Gloucester, Mass.: Peter Smith, 1971), 67-70. This section of John's text is also found in Lynn Thorndike, *University Life and Records of the Late Middle Ages* (New York: Columbia University Press, 1944), 7-9.

[7]I have edited and translated several versions of one teacher's commentary on a medieval text used to teach composition (*An Early Commentary on the "Poetria nova" of Geoffrey of Vinsauf,* Garland Medieval Texts, vol. 12 [New York: Garland Publishing, Inc., 1985]), and I am working on a book on all of the commentaries on this text. Examples of Bernard's techniques found in the commentaries on the *Poetria nova* will be discussed in a forthcoming article, "Some Techniques of Teaching Rhetorical Poetics in the Schools of Medieval Europe."

[8]The contents of this collection varied somewhat during the millenium under discussion here; see George L. Hamilton's still-useful treatment in "Theodulus: A Medieval Textbook," *Modern Philology* 7 (1909): 1-17 (169-185); the classic study by Marc Boas, "De librorum Catonianorum historia atque compositione," *Mnemosyne* 42 (1914), 17-46; and the short overview of "Curriculum Authors" in Ernst Robert Curtius, *European Literature and the Latin Middle Ages,* trans. Willard R. Trask (New York: Harper & Row, 1953), 48-54. The specific grouping that I take as exemplary here is from Paul Clogan, ed., *The Medieval Achilleid of Statius, Edited with Introduction, Variant Readings, and Glosses* (Leiden: E.J. Brill, 1968), 3.

1. *Distichs* of Cato (3rd century).[9]
2. *Eclogue* of Theodulus (10th century).[10]
3. *Fables* of Avianus (4th century).[11]
4. *Elegies* of Maximianus (early 6th century).[12]
5. *Achilleid* of Statius (1st century).[13]
6. *Rape of Proserpine* of Claudian (fl. ca. 400).[14]

This is the reader that students used after mastering the basics of Latin grammar from Donatus. All of the texts in it are in verse, and, except for the *Achilleid* and *Rape of Proserpine,* they are composed of short, interconnected stanzaic units. Such short units were easy to memorize, discuss, and imitate.

A different kind of reading list is outlined by Gervais of Melkley in the preface to his early thirteenth-century treatise on

---

[9]The standard edition is by Boas, *Disticha Catonis* (Amsterdam: North-Holland Publishing Co., 1952). A convenient text and translation are in J. Wight Duff and Arnold M. Duff, eds. and trans., *Minor Latin Poets,* Loeb Classical Library, vol. 434 (Cambridge, Mass.: Harvard University Press, 1934), II: 585-639. See also two articles by Richard Hazelton: "The Christianization of 'Cato': The *Disticha Catonis* in the Light of Late Mediaeval Commentaries," *Medieval Studies* 19 (1957): 157-173, and "Chaucer and Cato," *Speculum* 35 (1960): 357-380.

[10]The standard edition is J. Osternacher, *Ecloga Theoduli*...(Linz, 1902). A more convenient text is in R.B.C. Huygens, ed., *Bernard D'Utrecht, Commentum in Theodulum* (Spoleto: Centro Italiano di Studi sull'alto Medioevo, 1977), 9-18. I quote below from the translation in preparation by Harry Butler and Sandra Bernhard. See also Hamilton, cited above, and R.P.H. Green, "The Genesis of a Medieval Textbook: The Models and Sources of the *Ecloga Theoduli,*" *Viator* 13 (1982): 49-106.

[11]Avianus, *Fabulae,* ed. A. Guaglianone (Padua: In aedibus Io. Bapt. Paraviae, 1958); another text and translation are in Duff and Duff, *Minor Latin Poets,* II: 680-749.

[12]This work was edited most recently by T. di. Agozzino, *Elegie* (Bologna: Silva, 1970). The text has been translated by L.R. Lind in *Gabriele Zerbi, "Gerontocomia": On the Care of the Aged, and Maximianus, Elegies on Old Age and Love* (Philadelphia: American Philosophical Society, 1988), 309-336.

[13]The standard edition is by A. Marastoni, *P. Papini Stati Achilleis* (Leipzig: Teubner, 1974). Another Latin text and an English translation are found in Statius, *Works,* trans. J.H. Mozley, Loeb Classical Library, vol. 207 (Cambridge, Mass.: Harvard University Press, 1969), II: 508-595. A medieval version of the text, complete with medieval commentary, is available in Clogan, *Medieval Achilleid.*

[14]*De Raptu Proserpinae,* ed. J.B. Hall (Cambridge: Cambridge University Press, 1969). A translation is available in Harold Isbell, *The Last Poets of Imperial Rome* (New York: Penguin, 1971; reprinted 1982), 75-106. See also R.A. Pratt, "Chaucer's Claudian," *Speculum* 22 (1947): 419-429.

poetic composition, the *Art of Versifying*.[15] As Gervais tells us, his work was written for young boys, "the 'rough' ones" (*rudium*).[16] His numerous citations from the *Cosmographia* of Bernardus Silvestris show that such complex and, one would have thought, adult works as this one (more below) could be introduced to beginning students in small units illustrating particular rhetorical techniques. Although Gervais's work was not widely read, it is important to our understanding of the teaching of writing in the Middle Ages because of his statements about how different kinds of texts affect students differently. In the dedication at the beginning of his work, he places himself in the tradition of other teachers: Bernardus Silvestris; Matthew of Vendôme, who was Bernardus' student and Gervais' teacher; and Geoffrey of Vinsauf, whose *Poetria nova* has survived in more manuscripts than any other medieval art of poetry.[17] Gervais also recommends that older students consult the *Barbarismus* of Donatus, Horace's *Ars poetica,* and the *"Rhetorics"* (Rethoricas) of Cicero.[18] Gervais also distinguishes between authors like Priscian and Cicero who instruct "directly," that is, through example, and, authors like Donatus who instruct "indirectly by naming unfitting things," or faults of language.[19]

Gervais then praises a group of classical and medieval Latin literary works which were used widely in the schools. They exerted a powerful effect on students such as Gervais:

> Master John of Hanville, the breasts of whose teaching nourished my rough infancy, has indeed invented many elegancies, has handed several on to his hearers. In fact in his little book

[15]Jürgen Gräbener, ed., *Gervais von Melkley Ars poetica,* Forschungen zur romanischen Philologie, vol. 17 (Münster Westfalen: Aschendorffsche Verlagsbuchhandlung, 1965); unpublished translation by Catherine Yodice Giles, "Gervais of Melkley's Treatise on the Art of Versifying and the Method of Composing in Prose," Ph.D. diss. Rutgers University, 1973.

[16]Giles, 2; Gräbner, 2.2.

[17]Giles, 1; Gräbner, 1.9-11.

[18]Giles, 2; Gräbner, 2.2-5. The last title refers to Cicero's *De inventione,* also called the "rhetorica vetus," and the Pseudo-Ciceronian *Rhetorica ad Herennium,* called the "rhetorica nova."

[19]Giles, 3-4, translating "Directe nos instruunt Priscianus et Cicero, indirecte vero Donatus indecentias assignando" (Gräbner, 2.17-18).

concerning philosophical pilgrimage, which he calls *Architrenius,*[20]
he attended to a great many. Indeed, only looking into [his] little
book is sufficient to give form to a rough spirit.

The same may be said of Claudian, Dares the Phrygian,[21]
Bernardus Silvester. The same [may be said] of the ancients—
namely Lucan, Statius, and Vergil. You may also learn very much
from the little books of Ovid. The *Anticlaudianus*[22] teaches us
more fully indirectly than directly.[23]

These works belong, according to Douglas Kelly, to the genre of
"masterpiece," which provided examples of style and content for
students to use in their own writing.[24]

Medieval student compositions that have come down to us
illustrate how students reworked material from the literary texts that
they read. Most of those that have survived are based on the works
of Ovid, especially the *Metamorphoses,* whose interwoven narratives
provided medieval teachers with perfect topics for short composition assignments. For example, a pair of poems on Niobe,
probably written by the same student, show contrasting methods of
describing Niobe and the disastrous results of her display of pride

[20]Johannes de Hanvilla, *Architrenius,* ed. Paul Gerhard Schmidt (Munich: Wilhelm
Fink, 1974). This important text has not been translated into English.

[21]The narrator of a Latin work purporting to be an eye-witness account of the fall
of Troy, written by a Trojan; see *De excidio Troiae historia,* ed. F. Meister (1873),
translated by Richard M. Frazer, Jr., in *The Trojan War: The Chronicles of Dictys of
Crete and Dares the Phrygian* (Bloomington, 1966).

[22]Alan of Lille, *Anticlaudianus or The Good and Perfect Man,* trans. James J.
Sheridan (Toronto: Pontifical Institute of Mediaeval Studies, 1973); Latin text in Alain de
Lille, *Anticlaudianus,* ed. R. Bossuat (Paris, 1955).

[23]Giles, 4 (italics Giles); Gräbener, 3.20-4.3:

"Magister Iohannes de Hanvilla, cuius ubera discipline rudem adhuc mihi
lactaverunt infantiam, multas quidem elegantias adinvenit, plures auditoribus suis tradidit.
In libello vero suo de peregrino philosopho, quem Architrenium vocat, plurimas
observavit. Cuius quidem libelli sola sufficit inspectio studiosa rudem animum informare.

Idem de Claudiano, de Frigio Darete, de Bernardo Silvestri. Idem de antiquioribus,
scilicet Lucano, Stacio et Virgilio. Maxime etiam de libellis Ovidii sentiatis. Sed
Anticlaudianus indirecte nos instruit plenius quam directe."

[24]See Kelly, "The Scope of Medieval Instruction in the Art of Poetry and Prose:
Problems of Documentation and Interpretation," to be published (see note 5).

in her reproductive capacities.[25] The first poem of the pair is an exercise in composing rhetorical figures; there are three figures of words in the first six lines:

> How stupid, how insane, how wicked it is to vex the gods,
> 　　you teach by your cry, oh daughter of Tantalus.
> Swollen in heart, swollen in speech, you are swollen in deed
> 　　as you prepare to surpass Latona's progeny with your own.
> Why do you do this? Why do you affect this? Why do you
> 　　believe that in this
> 　　you can profit? You make no gains, but inflict losses.[26]

In all, twenty-one figures in forty-six lines.[27] The companion piece to this poem, only six lines long, emphasizes in epigrammatic form the emotional and dramatic aspects of Niobe's self-absorption:

> Distinguished Niobe, fertile, powerful, noble,
> 　　she boasts of riches, she rejoices in offspring, she recounts
> 　　her ancestors.

---

[25]The poems discussed in this paragraph are found in Glasgow MS Hunterian V. 8. 14, an important thirteenth-century collection of texts that also contains most of the treatises on verse composition produced during the late twelfth and early thirteenth centuries. The collection is analyzed and some of the student poems are described by Edmond Faral in "Le manuscrit 511 du 'Hunterian Museum' de Glasgow," *Studi medievali* n.s. 9 (1936): 18-119. Bruce Harbert edits all of the poems in the manuscript except the composition treatises in *A Thirteenth-Century Anthology of Rhetorical Poems: Glasgow MS Hunterian V. 8. 14* (Toronto: Centre for Medieval Studies, 1975). Harbert, following Faral, argues that one and possibly two groups of poems in the manuscript are student compositions. The pair discussed below come from the first of Harbert's groups. A translation of this first group, numbers 15-25 in Harbert (14-24 in Faral), is in preparation by Cheryl Eve Salisbury and Wilma Wierenga, who have provided the excerpts quoted below.

[26]Quam stultum, quam uesanum, quam sit sceleratum
　　irritare deos, Tantale, uoce doces.
Corde tumes, sermone tumes, actuque tumes, dum
　　Latone prolem uincere prole paras.
Quid facis hoc? quid proficis hoc? quid credis in hoc te
　　posse lucrificere? non lucra — dampna facis. (Harbert, 24.1-6)

[27]Faral gives the Latin names of the figures in the margins of his text ("Le manuscrit 511," pp. 34-35). The *Poetria nova,* found in this same manuscript and praised by Gervaise of Melkley, contains similar virtuoso displays of figures; see Nims, pp. 56-60 and 62-70. Faral notes (p. 36) that most of the figures in the first Niobe poem are identified in the margin by a fourteenth-century hand, and most of the manuscripts of the *Poetria nova* that I have looked at contain identifications of the rhetorical figures in the margins.

A king for a husband, beauty for a dowry, of divine lineage,
she shows herself greater in offspring to the people, and she
swells.
Even her husband Amphion puffs up as author of a royal
family—she a grandaughter, he a son of Jove.[28]

Although both poems are short, Edmond Faral notes their complementarity in length as well as focus and treatment.[29]

Another group of student poems, including some by Gervais of Melkley himself when he was a student, are based on another story from the *Metamorphoses,* that of Pyramis and Thisbe, a theme that

occupied a privileged place in the curriculum of a number of important schools in France, Germany, and probably England in the decades before and after 1200. ... Although other pairs of lovers were certainly well known and often treated in medieval literature, I can find no other theme so often attested as a basis for the learning of grammar and rhetoric.[30]

Matthew of Vendôme, Gervais's teacher, had also written a school poem on this same topic and, like Gervais, quoted it in his own treatise on poetic composition.[31]

After working on short exercises for some time, students learned to analyse the larger structure of works. For example, a teacher's commentary on the *Poetria nova* emphasizes the double structure of the text and the effective transitions from part to part, "like Ovid's from story to story."[32] When studying narratives

---

[28]Insignis Niobe, fecunda, potens, generosa,
   iactat opes, gaudet prole, recenset auos.
Rege viro, dote faciei, stirpe deorum,
   se populo prolis plus probat, atque tumet.
Vir suus Amphion turgescit ut auctor auorum
   stemate—neptis ea, filius ille Iovis. (Harbert, 25.1-6)

[29]Faral, 36.

[30]Robert Glendenning, "Pyramus and Thisbe in the Medieval Classroom," *Speculum* 61 (1986): 71.

[31]Glendenning, 62. According to Glendenning (73), these poems are part of the tradition of lyrics, many of which were produced in medieval schools, that helped to convert the topos of "one mind in two bodies" from one describing intense male friendship to one evoking heterosexual love.

[32]Woods, *Early Commentary,* 67 ("sicut Ouidius de fabula ad fabulam"), from the gloss on line 737.

medieval students were taught to look at arrangement in terms of both natural and artificial order. Thus the *Aeneid* displays artificial order by beginning *in medias res,* but it also demonstrates natural order when the first six books are interpreted as an illustration of the six stages of a man's life.[33] Such double orders were particularly prized and emphasized during the Middle Ages.[34]

During the fourteenth and fifteenth centuries, the *Poetria nova* was taught in a number of universities in central Europe while it still remained an important text in the schools as well. The emphasis in the university commentaries is on the theory of rhetoric, rather than on the specific rhetorical texts and specific applications for imitation and composition that are the focus for younger students.[35]

Thus, one can say that medieval training in rhetoric began for young students with tropes and figures, or *elocutio,* accompanied by exercises in memory and delivery, *memoria* and *pronunciatio;* then students proceeded to the study of larger structures, or *dispositio,* and only at the end to *inventio* or theoretical content.[36] Such a sequence is unexpected. We have interpreted the progression of invention, disposition, style, memory, and delivery as chronological rather than programmatic. But the medieval approach is pedagogically sound. Recent work in teaching children how to write poetry demonstrates the importance of specific words, word-

---

[33]See the preface and the summaries of each book in *The Commentary on the First Six Books of Virgil's "Aeneid" by Bernardus Silvestris,* trans. Earl G. Schreiber and Thomas E. Maresca (Lincoln: University of Nebraska Press, 1979), pp. 3-4, 6, 16, 17, 24, and 28. (The attribution to Bernardus Silvestris is doubtful.)

[34]See Woods, "*Verba* and *Sententia* and Matter and Form in Medieval Lectures on Poetic Composition," forthcoming in a Festschrift for Judson B. Allen.

[35]Woods, "The Commentaries on the *Poetria nova,*" to be published. For medieval university prose composition in letter writing, see Camargo and Witt, cited above; Camargo, "Toward a Comprehensive Art of Written Discourse: Geoffrey of Vinsauf and the *Ars Dictaminis,*" *Rhetorica* 6 (1988): 167-94; and Carol Dana Lanham, "Freshman Composition in the Early Middle Ages: the Theory and Practice of Letter Writing before the *Ars diotaminis,*" forthcoming (see note 5).

[36]See Douglas Kelly, "The Scope of the Treatment of Composition in the Twelfth- and Thirteenth-Century Arts of Poetry," *Speculum* 41 (1966): 261-78; and Camargo, "Rhetoric," 107.

play, repetition, and performance in their creative endeavors.[37]

One of the most distinctive—and to a modern reader unexpected—aspects of the word-play in the texts used to teach rhetoric and composition to young students during the Middle Ages is the intense figuration and suggestiveness of the language, even in the introductory reader, the *Liber Catonianus.* The last work in the collection, Claudian's *Rape of Proserpine,* was famous throughout the Middle Ages as an example of extended *descriptio* or ekphrasis, particularly for its evocation of the coupling, through Pluto's "rape" of Proserpine, of darkness with light, death with life. The conversion of the inhabitants of the underworld into happy wedding guests is an example of the oxymoronic quality of this marriage:

> The furies lost their wrath and made a bowl of wine
> from which they drank. The snakes that live on their foreheads
> lifted their mouths to the wine and became happy
> like all the monsters and fiends of Hell.[38]

The physical union between Pluto and Proserpine is not described, but it is anticipated by Pluto's violent rupturing of the earth in his passion to reach the surface, "When the island of Sicily felt Pluto's blow/and opened herself,"[39] and it is echoed later when Proserpine's mother dreams "that a spear pierced the body of her child."[40]

The *Achilleid* of Statius is more explicit. Achilles' mother, fearing the prediction of his death, dresses him in girl's clothing and hides him in what is virtually a harem, where he is able to rape with impunity the young girl whom he loves, an accepted form of seduction in many classical texts. The *Achilleid* encom-

---

[37]See, for example, Elizabeth McKim and Judith W. Steinbergh, *Beyond Words: Writing Poems with Children* (Green Harbor, Mass.: Wampeter Press, 1983).

[38]Isbell, *Last Poets of Imperial Rome,* p. 93. In Hall's edition the lines are as follows:
  Oblitae scelerum formidatique furoris
Eumenides cratera parant et vina feroci
crine bibunt flexisque minis iam lene canentes
extendunt socios ad pocula plena cerastas
et festas alio succendunt lumine taedas. (II, 326-27)

[39]Isbell, *Last Poets,* 89; "Postquam victa manu duros Trinacria nexus/solvit et inmenso late discessit hiatu..." (II. 186-87).

[40]Isbell, *Last Poets,* 96; "namque modo adversis invadi viscera telis" (III, 71). The plural "spears" (*telis*) in the Latin is less explicit.

passes cross-dressing, sexual exploration, the literal taking up of arms, and escape from an anxious and protective mother — a cornucopia of adolescent male fantasies. Although the text is unfinished, it ends with the hero's passing from puberty and his final movement away from his childhood's dominant attraction and power, his mother: "So much do I remember, friends, of the training of my earliest years, and sweet is their remembrance; the rest my mother knows."[41]

Just as startling, and in an earlier position in the reader, is the *Eclogue of Theodulus.* This poem is the story of a composition contest between Pseustis, a pagan shepherd "born in Athens" because, as one of the glosses says, "that's where there are clever shepherds,"[42] and a shepherdess named Alithea, a "virgin from the seed of David."[43] Each tries to top the other's quatrain by singing of a related story in his or her textual tradition, with such traditional pairings as Noah's flood with Deucalion's.

Yet the correspondences sometimes involve an almost lurid sensibility. In one pair of stanzas, for example, first Pseustis describes the metamorphosis of Phyllis into a cork tree, and the reaction of her beloved, Demophon, who, "returning there, moistens the trunk with upturned mouth."[44] Then Alithea answers with the story of Lot's "faithless wife," who is turned "Into an effigy of salt — animals lick the rock-crag."[45] These complementary images of licking are unforgettable, and the capping of the first one by the moralizing of the second only heightens the startling effect.

But such suggestive sensuality seems not to have bothered medieval teachers or their young students.[46] Ovid, for example, needed to be "moralized" not for children learning to read and

---

[41]Trans. Mosley, II, 166-67 ("hactenus annorum, comites, elementa meorum/et memini et meminisse iuvat: scit cetera mater").

[42]"'Ab Athenis natus' ibi siquidem callidiores fuere pastores 'cognomine Pseustis'" (lines 13-14), commentary of Bernard of Utrecht (cf. note 10).

[43]"Virgo decora nimia David de semine" (9).

[44]"Ille reversus eo truncum rigat ore supino" (113).

[45]"In salis effigiem, lambunt animalia cautem" (116).

[46]Glendenning remarks of the Pyramus and Thisbe theme, "The exposure of boys in early adolescence to this morally ambiguous theme, precisely in connection with the use of rhetoric, with its many antithetical devices for exploring irony and paradox, is a subject of considerable interest in itself..." ("Pyramus and Thisbe," 17).

write from his texts, but rather for adults.[47] And most other medieval school texts also contain explicit sexual imagery. The *Cosmographia* of Bernardus Silvestris, which Gervase of Melkley quotes constantly in his book on poetic composition for beginners, is famous for its celebration of natural sexuality. This work, which depicts the creation of man in the image of the cosmos, ends with a description of man's sexual organs:

> The phallus...carefully rejoins the vital threads severed by the hands of the Fates. Blood sent forth from the seat of the brain flows down to the loins, bearing the image of the shining sperm. Artful Nature molds and shapes the fluid, that in conceiving it may reproduce the forms of ancestors.
>
> The nature of the universe outlives itself, for it flows back into itself, and so survives and is nourished by its very flowing away. For whatever is lost only merges again with the sum of things, and that it may die perpetually, never dies wholly.[48]

The texts that were used as for instructing older students are sometimes more judgmental. Alan of Lille's *Plaint of Nature* is a sequel to the *Cosmographia;* in it Nature laments the condition of the created world, and especially the prevalence of male homosexuality. Alan describes the "unnaturalness" of homosexuality in images of incorrect grammar:

---

[47]Cf. Ralph Hexter, *Ovid and Medieval Schooling: Studies in Medieval School Commentaries on Ovid's "Ars Amatoria," "Epistulae ex Ponto," and "Epistulae Heroidum"* (Munich: Arbeo-Gesellschaft, 1986), 10-11.

[48]*The "Cosmographia" of Bernardus Silvestris,* trans. Winthrop Wetherbee (New York: Columbia University Press, 1973), "Microcosmus" 14, p. 126. The Latin text of this important medieval work is edited by Peter Dronke (Leiden: E.J. Brill, 1978); the lines translated here are the following:

Militat adversus Lachesim sollersque renodat
  Mentula Parcarum fila resecta manu.
Defluit ad renes, cerebri regione remissus,
  Sanguis, et albentis spermatis instar habet.
Format et effingit sollers Natura liquorem,
  Ut simili genesis ore reducat avos.
Influit ipsa sibi mundi natura, superstes,
  Permanet et fluxu pascitur usque suo:
Scilicet ad summam rerum iactura recurrit,
  Nec semel — ut possit sepe perire — perit. ("Mic." 165-174)

The active sex shudders in disgrace as it sees itself degenerate into the passive sex. A man turned woman blackens the fair name of his sex. The witchcraft of Venus turns him into a hermaphrodite. He is subject and predicate; one and the same term is given a double application. Man here extends too far the laws of grammar. Becoming a barbarian in grammar, he disclaims the manhood given him by nature. Grammar does not find favour with him; he prefers a trope. This transposition [*translatio* 'metaphor'], however, cannot be called a trope. The figure here more correctly falls into the category of defects.[49]

The twelfth century did see an outpouring of homo-erotic verse. Marbode of Rennes, for example, a famous rhetorician and teacher, wrote ironic and haunting lyrics about the arbitrariness of desire and the genders of the bodies that evoke it.[50] And grammatical jokes could also be made on behalf of homosexuality. In the "Debate between Ganymede and Helen," about the respective merits of homosexual and heterosexual sex, Ganymede argues that

...[T]he right way is like with like.
Man can be fitted to man by elegant conjunction.

---

[49] James J. Sheridan, trans., *Plaint of Nature* (Toronto: Pontifical Institute of Mediaeval Studies, 1980), I, meter 1. The standard edition is *De planctu naturae*, ed. Nikolaus M. Häring, *Studi Medievali*, 3rd. ser., 19.2 (1978): 797-879. The lines translated are as follows:

Actiui generis sexus se turpiter horret
Sic in passiuum degenerate genus.
Femina uir factus sexus denigrat honorem,
Ars magice Veneris hermafroditat eum.
Predicat et subicit, fit duplex terminus idem.
Gramatice leges ampliat ille nimis.
Se negat esse uirum Nature, factus in arte
Barbarus. Ars illi non placet, immo tropus.
Non tamen ista tropus poterit translatio dici.
In uicium melius ista figura cadit. (15-24)

[50] See, for example, the poems translated by John Boswell in *Christianity, Social Tolerance, and Homosexuality: Gay People in Western Europe from the Beginning of the Christian Era to the Fourteenth Century* (Chicago: University of Chicago Press, 1980), Appendix II, pp. 370-71, and by Thomas Stehling, *Medieval Latin Poems of Male Love and Friendship* (New York: Garland Publishing, Inc., 1984), pp. 30-39, especially numbers 46 and 47. Translations and analyses of important lyrics by Marbode, including "De Molesta Recreatione" ("Troubled Recreation"), are forthcoming in Gerald Bond, *Reforming Desire*.

If you don't know this, look at the gender of their articles:
Masculine should be coupled with masculine by the rules of
grammar.[51]

Adult medieval discourse about discourse, however, especially
the scholastic university training that emphasized logic and philosophy, was suspicious of particulars of all kinds, whether categories,
or books, or bodies. Sexuality, like textuality, was to be avoided.[52]

Such polarization of the techniques of teaching rhetoric to older
and younger students and the sensuousness of the language used to
teach children seem strange to us, nourished as we are on the
humanist tradition, which tries to find means whereby a certain
decorous control over language can be maintained. But the polarization of medieval teaching does make possible the fulfillment of the
most extreme aspects of the appropriation of codes of discourse.[53]

Taking seriously this highly successful medieval tradition of
pedagogical rhetoric allows us to rephrase, even turn around, key
issues, values, and judgments in the modern study and appropriation of the classical rhetorical tradition. What follows, for example,
is an inversion of the statements cited above from George
Kennedy's *Classical Rhetoric and Its Christian and Secular*

---

[51]Stehling, number 114, p. 113, ll. 141-44, translating
...recte par cum pari,
eleganti copula mas aptatur mari.
Si nescis: articulos decet observari,
hic et hic gramatice debent copulari.
The poem is also translated by Boswell in Appendix II, pp. 381-89. Boswell notes that
this poem "was recited aloud to students and known by heart by many educated persons"
(p. 256).

[52]Medieval allegorization of classical texts has been widely studied, as has the
debate about teaching classical texts in Christian schools. That such debate and
allegorization had little impact on the early training in the Latin classics received by all
young students is less widely recognized, but see Hexter, cited above.

[53]The medieval polarization of learning about discourse seems to me to be in some
ways analogous to Freud's primary and secondary processes; a discussion of Freud that is
useful in this context is Kaja Silverman, *Subject of Semiotics* (New York: Oxford, 1983),
especially 77-86. This analogy becomes especially important when we remember that,
after about the eighth century, all medieval students were learning to appropriate a new
language in their rhetorical training; see James J. Murphy, "The Teaching of Latin as a
Second Language in the Twelfth Century," *Historiographia Linguistica* 7 (1980): 159-75;
and Elaine Fantham, "The Teaching of Quintilian: The Approach to Composition in
Primary, Secondary, and Adult Education," forthcoming (see note 5).

Tradition. I offer these statements as a new basis on which to build a more accurate assessment of the whole of the western rhetorical tradition and one that reflects the centrality, in all meanings of the word, of the medieval part of that tradition. My statements are in inverse order and thus lead from the more secondary to the primary assertions:

8. The emphasis on adult civic discourse in our teaching and theory of rhetoric has limited our recognition of rhetorical accomplishment only to those with social, political, and financial power. But the basis of rhetoric has always been the pedagogical tradition, a realm of experience where expressive as well as persuasive communication is recognized.

7. Rhetoric moves from narration to persuasion, from personal to public contexts, and from literature, including poetry, to civic discourse. Our learning experience works best when it follows the same path.

6. Literary language, with its intense rhetorical decoration, is the genesis of communication, not its decadent offshoot.

5. Secondary rhetoric is the apparatus of rhetorical techniques clustering around public discourse, whose demands are imposed from without rather than generated from within.

4. Throughout the western tradition, whatever was the *nominal* goal of training persuasive public speakers, teachers took as their *real* goal the passing on of a textual heritage to serve as the basis of verbal communication and creativity.

3. Rhetoric combines whenever possible the elements of the permanent and the transitory, both the recorded — whether by memorization or written production — and the performed — whether in the presence of others or in the imagination.

2. Rhetoric is used in all shared aspects of life.

1. Primary rhetoric is our inheritance of written and spoken texts.

In conclusion, let us consider the primary rhetorical artifact of the western tradition, the *Iliad.* The part of the *Iliad* most likely to be analyzed in a modern class in rhetoric or composition is Book IX, the embassy to Achilles, which contains three successive pieces of unpersuasive rhetoric. These are found in the middle of the *Iliad,* that is, in its weakest part rhetorically speaking. But earlier rhetoricians like Plato knew that the beginning of the *Iliad,* as of any text, is far more important than the middle, which is why Plato chose the beginning of the *Iliad* to paraphrase in book III of the *Republic* (392e-394a) in a successful pedagogical exercise[54] to demonstrate how to deprive the text of its rhetorical power. It is the power of an old man, whose speech is unpersuasive to Agamemnon in its narrative context but moving to us, as to the earlier audiences of the work, that Plato wants to suppress.

Yet even the beginning of a work, though more important than the middle, is not the most rhetorically significant part. As that deft medieval manipulator of words, Chaucer's Pandarus, knew, "The end is every tale's strength." The *Iliad* ends not with the victorious Greeks but with the defeated Trojans, and those who speak for them are four women and a fallen, shattered old man. The final speakers have power only to praise their dead hero. One speaker is mad, another is going insane, and all are bereft and without hope. But they all can speak and move us.

Medieval rhetoric may, indeed, be a fragmentation of classical rhetoric as we have *nominally* defined it. But the rhetoric of the classical era was, *really,* something else, closer in many ways to the rhetoric of the Middle Ages: taught in the classroom, based on the memorization and imitation of texts, and expressed in giving voice as much to those who could not persuade as to those who did prevail.

---

[54]This is not Plato's only use of a pedagogical exercise. Duff and Duff point out that "In Plato's *Phaedo,* 60-61, Socrates says a dream led him to turn Aesopic fables into verse," as in *Phaedrus* 259, *Symposium* 203, and *Protagorus* 320-321 (*Minor Latin Poets* II, p. 681, n. c.). Note the importance of the dialogues containing fables to our assessment of Plato's discourse on language.

CHAPTER FOUR

RHETORIC AND WRITING IN RENAISSANCE EUROPE AND ENGLAND

DON PAUL ABBOTT

In *The English Grammar Schools* Foster Watson claims that "there is no evidence of the systematic school-teaching of Rhetoric in the Middle Ages—beyond the rules of verse-making and the very slight reading of the poets. It [rhetoric] is a Renaissance subject."[1] While historians of medieval rhetoric may dispute his claim, Watson is certainly correct in identifying it as a Renaissance subject, or, more accurately, *the* Renaissance subject. As he further explains: "Indeed, if there is one school subject which seems to have pre-eminently influenced the writers, statesmen and gentlemen of the 16th and 17th century, in their intellectual outfit in afterlife, probably the claim for this leading position may justly be made for Rhetoric and the Oration."[2] Rhetoric dominated the thoughts of Renaissance intellectuals and the curriculum of Renaissance schools to a degree that is extraordinary. So extensive was rhetorical inquiry that James J. Murphy calls Renaissance rhetoric the subject with "one thousand neglected authors."[3] Such an immense subject as this must be limited if a discussion of it is to be useful for present purposes.

---

[1] Foster Watson, *The English Grammar Schools to 1660* (Cambridge: Cambridge University Press, 1908; reprint, London: Frank Cass, 1968), 440.

[2] Ibid.

[3] James J. Murphy, "One Thousand Neglected Authors; The Scope and Importance of Renaissance Rhetoric," in *Renaissance Eloquence: Studies in the Theory and Practice of Renaissance Rhetoric* (Berkeley: University of California Press, 1983), 20-36.

I have, therefore, chosen to look primarily to one institution: the English grammar school. Scrutiny of this institution offers a number of advantages for an investigation of the teaching of writing in the Renaissance. First, and perhaps most importantly, an examination of the grammar school insures an emphasis on the pedagogical rather than the theoretical issues. The schoolmasters were intensely interested in how their young students should be taught to write and, fortunately, left considerable testimony as to their methods. Second, it was in these schools that rhetoric was most often taught. Although rhetoric was also a university subject, philosophy and theology, broadly defined, frequently overshadowed rhetoric in higher education. Third, a look at these schools maintains an emphasis on the development of the English language and the educational system ultimately inherited by the United States. At the same time, however, this orientation does not entirely neglect the developments on the Continent. The English grammar school was, after all, inspired by European rhetoricians — Erasmus and Vives in particular — and the dominance of Latin ensured the widespread use of Continental texts. Finally, an emphasis on the grammar schools permits this study to be limited to a discrete period of time — the "golden age" of these institutions from the middle of the sixteenth century to the middle of the seventeenth century.

Thus the curriculum of the English grammar school provides an extremely useful case study for considering the question of how writing was taught in the Renaissance. In particular, by contrasting grammar school practices with current methods we can perhaps draw some conclusions that are relevant to current needs. Before looking at the specific issues involved, however, let me first briefly outline the nature of the English grammar school.

THE ENGLISH GRAMMAR SCHOOL

The English grammar school is a sixteenth-century invention. Although the term "grammar school" was mentioned in England as early as 1387, Dean Colet's founding of St. Paul's School in 1510 marks the real beginning of a new educational movement. The grammar schools were inspired by the ideals of the European humanists and, in the case of St. Paul's, directly encouraged and assisted by Desiderius Erasmus. These schools, were, in a very real sense, an effort to put the educational theories of the Humanists into pedagogical practice. Thus the main aim of the schools was also a major goal of Renaissance Humanism: the creation of elegant and eloquent expression. The grammar schools sought to teach the kind of expression known to Cicero, but lost in the Middle Ages. Thus the art of expression was necessarily conceived in the language of classical rhetoric. In the minds of the humanists and in the grammar school classrooms rhetoric and humanism were intertwined.[4] The term grammar may be, therefore, slightly misleading to modern readers. In its narrowest sense, grammar meant Latin grammar. Knowledge of Latin gave students access both to the classical masters of expression and to the current scholarly and political communication in the international language. The educational goal, therefore, was to provide something far more than a rudimentary acquaintance with a foreign tongue. What grammar really meant to the masters of the grammar schools was what it meant to Quintilian. After a boy has learned to read and write, says Quintilian, he is then turned over to a *grammaticus,* a teacher of literature and language. The concern of this profession, says Quintilian, "may be most briefly considered under two heads, the art of speaking correctly and the interpretation of the poets; but there is more beneath the surface than meets the eye. For the art of writing is combined with that of speaking, and correct reading precedes interpretation, while in each of these cases criticism has its work to perform."[5] Grammar, then, may be best understood as signifying an integrated curriculum of oral and written composition combined with literary criticism.

　　This literary and Latinate curriculum was advocated by a wide variety of humanists, but it was Erasmus who most directly inspired the English grammar schools. In T.W. Baldwin's phrase,

---

[4]For an excellent survey of the relationship between rhetoric and humanism see John Monfasani, "Humanism and Rhetoric," in *Renaissance Humanism: Foundations, Forms, and Legacy,* ed. Albert Rabil, Jr., Vol. 3, *Humanism and the Disciplines* (Philadelphia: University of Pennsylvania Press, 1988) 171-235. For a discussion of the educational practices of the humanists see Anthony Grafton and Lisa Jardine, *From Humanism to the Humanities* (Cambridge: Harvard University Press, 1986).

[5]Quintilian, *Institutio oratoria,* trans. H.E. Butler (Cambridge: Harvard University Press, 1980), I. IV. 2-4.

Erasmus "laid the egg" of the grammar schools. Baldwin asserts that "anyone who wishes to understand the principles upon which the sixteenth-century grammar school was founded in England would be very unwise to begin anywhere else than with Erasmus."[6] In his small book *De ratione studii* Erasmus proposes a course of study which would become the basis of the grammar schools. Although not published until 1512, *De ratione studii* went through any number of earlier versions, including one which Erasmus sent to Colet for the latter's reaction. Colet responded that he read the "epistle about studies" and told Erasmus that "I not only approve it all, but I truly admire your genius, and art, and learning, and copiousness and eloquence. I have often wished too, that the boys at our school could be taught in the way you explain."[7] In due time the boys at St. Paul's and the other grammar schools would indeed come to be taught in the way Erasmus had explained. The method of study which Erasmus advances is very much dependent on Quintilian "who has left a very thorough treatment of these matters, so that it would seem the height of impertinence to write about a subject he has already dealt with."[8] So agreeable is Quintilian to humanists like Erasmus that it is reasonably accurate to say that the grammar school curriculum is a combination of Quintilian and Christianity. So strong is Quintilian's influence that the methods outlined by Professor Murphy in Chapter 2, could, with slight revision, serve to describe the education of sixteenth-century England.

Erasmus begins *De ratione studii* by concurring with the ancient position that knowledge is "of two kinds: of things and of words," that is, of ideas, truths, and of language.[9] The knowledge of words comes first, but knowledge of things is ultimately more important. Although Erasmus distinguishes two types of knowledge, the two are interdependent, and "a person who is not skilled in

---

[6]T.W. Baldwin, *William Shakspere's Small Latine and Less Greeke* (Urbana: University of Illinois Press, 1944), I:77.

[7]Cited in Baldwin, I:78.

[8]Erasmus, *Collected Works of Erasmus,* ed. Craig R. Thompson, Vol. 24, *Literary and Educational Writings: De copia / De ratione studii,* trans. Betty I. Knott (Toronto: University of Toronto Press, 1978), 672.

[9]Ibid., 666.

the force of language is, of necessity, short-sighted, deluded, and unbalanced in his judgment of things as well."[10] Knowledge of Latin and Greek is essential in the acquisition of knowledge because humankind's greatest ideas are to be found in these two languages. Thus grammar comes first, but only as a means to an end. Erasmus recommends only enough grammar as is necessary to allow the students to get on with the important tasks of reading, writing, and speaking. As students become increasingly familiar with the classical languages, more complex grammatical matters can be introduced. Erasmus is generally impatient with excessive attention to rules. He wishes Latin to be a truly living language to be used, rather than to be analyzed and systematized. As soon as the basics have been mastered, then, students should begin to read increasingly complex classical and Christian sources. These texts become the objects of imitation; students are expected to imitate both the eloquence of the "words" and the morality of the "things." Thus the educational program of Erasmus is at once both literary and moral. So confident is Erasmus of his approach that he makes this promise: "given youth who are not totally incompetent intellectually, I would with less trouble, and within fewer years, bring them to a credible degree of eloquence in each language than those notorious instructors who force their charges into their own stammering form, or rather lack, of expression."[11]

Precisely how the followers of Erasmus would bring students to "a credible degree of eloquence" can be seen from the records of what was taught in the grammar schools. That curriculum is particularly remarkable because the grammar school was intended to educate boys from about the ages of seven to fifteen. Before attending a grammar school, students would likely have gone to a "petty" or "elementarie" school. Richard Mulcaster, in *The Elementarie* (1582) says that such a school should consist of five activities: "reading, writing, drawing, singing, & plaing."[12] The first two of these activities were typically the most important. The primary accomplishment of most petty schools was probably the teaching of the alphabet and basic vernacular literacy. The

---

[10]Ibid.

[11]Ibid, 691.

[12]*Mulcaster's Elementarie,* ed. E.T. Campagnac (Oxford: Clarendon Press, 1925), 59.

grammar school thus served a kind of middle school between the "elementarie" and the university. Yet the grammar school was, in many ways, the heart and soul of English education: students attended it longer than any other stage of education and in the sixteenth-century, at least, the grammar school was at the forefront of educational innovation.

The humanistic curriculum of the grammar schools was predicated upon the recommendation of Erasmus that students be given a grammatical introduction followed by increasingly complex reading and writing accompanied by additional grammar when necessary. The schools were divided into five to eight classes or "forms." These forms were in turn divided into two broad groupings according to the instructor. The lower forms usually presented the rudiments of Latin grammar and were taught by an "usher." Beginning typically with the third form a more accomplished teacher, the "master," took over to teach advanced Latin grammar, Greek grammar, and, especially, rhetoric. The following specimen of a late sixteenth-century grammar school time table illustrates the thoroughness and complexity of the teaching methods. The numbers in parentheses indicate the days of the week.

USHER'S FORMS
First Form
7-11 a.m.

The Royal Grammar (2; 3; 4; 5).

Repetition of the work of the week (6).

Examination on the lecture of the previous afternoon (7).

1-5 p.m.

English Testament, or psalms of David in English (2; 3; 4).

Half Holiday (5).

Repetition of the work of the week continued (6).

Lecture on Aesop's Fables (6).

Writing out the catechism in English (7).

Second Form
7-11 a.m.

Lecture on the Colloquies of Erasmus, or on the Dialogues of Corderius (2; 3).

Lecture on the Cato senior, or Cato junior (4; 5).
Repetition of the week's lectures (6).
Examination of the lectures of the previous afternoon (7).

1-5 p.m.
Translation from English into Latin. Home lessons and exercises given out and prepared (2; 3; 4).
Half Holiday (5).
Repetition of the week's lectures continued. Lecturers on Aesop's Fables (6).
Writing out the catechism in English. Arithmetic (7).

MASTER'S FORMS

Third Form

7-11 a.m.
Lecture on the Letters of Ascham, or Sturm's Cicero's Letters, or Terence. Paraphrase of a sentence (2).
Lecture on Ascham, etc., as on Monday. Vulgaria in prose (3).
Lecture on Palingenius, or the Psalms of Hess. Paraphrase of a sentence (4).
Lecture on Palingenius, or the Psalms of Hess (5).
Vulgaria in prose, and repetition of the week's lectures (6).
Examination in lecture of the previous afternoon (7).

1-5 p.m.
Latin syntax, or Greek grammar, or the figures of Sysenbrote [Susenbrotus]. Home lessons given out and prepared (2; 3; 4).
Half Holiday (5).
Repetition of the week's work continued. Lectures on Erasmus' Apothegms (6).
Catechism and New Testament (7).

Fourth Form

7-11 a.m.
Lecture on Cicero *de Senectute,* or *de Amicitia,* or on Justin (2; 3).
Lecture on Ovid's *Tristia,* or *de Ponto,* or Seneca's Tragedies (4: 5).
Verse Theme, and repetition of the week's lectures (6).
Examination on the lecture of the previous afternoon (7).

1-5 p.m.

Prose Theme (2; 4).

Latin Syntax, or Greek Grammar, or Figures of Susenbrotus. Home lessons and exercises given out and prepared (2; 3; 4).

Half Holiday (5).

Repetition of the week's lectures continued, and lecture on Ovid's *Fausti* (7).

Catechism and New Testament (7).

Fifth Form

7-11 a.m.

Prose Theme (2; 4).

Lecture in Cicero or Sallust or Ceasar's Commentaries (2; 3). Verse Theme (3; 6).

Lecture in Virgil or Ovid's Metamorphosis, or Lucan (4; 5).

Repetition of the week's lectures (6).

Examination of the lecture of the previous afternoon (7).

1-5 p.m.

Latin Syntax, or Greek Grammar, or Figures of Susenbrotus. Home lessons and exercises given out and prepared (2; 3; 4).

Half Holiday (5).

Repetition of the week's lectures continued, and lecture on Horace on Horace, or Lucan, or Seneca's Tragedies (6).

Declamation on a given subject by several senior scholars. Catechism and New Testament (7). [13]

This timetable presents a reasonably complete view of what an English grammar school student would be expected to endure. While there was some variation in texts and assignments, the pattern of teaching was remarkably constant throughout England. Students at St. Paul's, Eton, Winchester, Rotherham, and the other grammar schools could expect to engage in much the same grammar, reading, lectures, examinations, themes, and declamations. What the timetable does not fully reveal are the exact methods used to teach the attainment of elegant expression in Latin. Teaching methods, however, were remarkably consistent from school to school.

---

[13]Appendix P, A. Monroe Stowe, *English Grammar Schools in the Reign of Queen Elizabeth* (New York: Teachers College, Columbia University, 1908), 185-188.

With this brief sketch of the English grammar school curriculum we are now in a position to look more closely at the nature of writing instruction in sixteenth-century England. The remainder of this chapter, then, will concentrate on the master's forms, that is, the "upper division," of the grammar school where composition, literature, and rhetoric were most fully taught. A closer look at the master's forms will make clear certain critical features of the grammar school approach to writing—features which, for better or for worse, separate so much of our current practice from our humanist tradition.

Perhaps the most fundamental aspect of the grammar school curriculum was that it was in its entirety a linguistic and literary curriculum. The original and fundamental purpose of the institution was to make the students eloquent in Latin. This intent is clearly revealed in the complete title of Roger Ascham's educational treatise of 1570: *The Scholemaster, Or plaine and perfit way of teachyng children, to understand, write, and speake, the Latin tong, but specially purposed for the private brynging up of youth in Jentlemen and Noble mens houses, and commodious also for all such, as have forgot the Latin tonge, and would, by themselves, without a scholemaster, in short tyme, and with small paines, recover a sufficient habilitie, to understand, write, and speake Latin.*[14] In order to ensure that children would indeed understand, write, and speak the Latin tongue, grammar school statutes commonly required both masters and scholars to speak Latin at all times while on school premises. The instruction in Latin was to be so complete and unremitting that the ancient language could not help but become as familiar as the vernacular. Thus Charles Hoole, in *A New Discovery of the Old Art of Teaching Schoole* (1660) would have his scholars in the fifth form translate an oration or a passage from Sallust, Livy, or Tacitus every day and then to recite these efforts in Latin and English each week. In the sixth form Hoole requires that the students "continue to make *themes* and *verses,* one week in Greek and another in Latine; and ever and

---

[14]Roger Ascham, *The Scholemaster,* ed. John E. B. Mayor (London; Bell and Daldy, 1863; reprinted, New York: AMS Press, 1967).

anon they may contend in making *Orations* and *Declamations.*"[15]

This intensive instruction in Latin was not designed to teach the vernacular, but of course a second language can only be taught by employing the native tongue of the students. Consequently, the grammar schools also taught composition in English. The process of translating from English to Latin and back into English began early and continued throughout the forms. Juan Luis Vives, who, like his mentor Erasmus, exercised considerable influence on English education, recommends that "as soon as they have learned syntax, let the pupils translate from the mother-tongue into Latin, and then back again into the mother-tongue."[16] Ascham enthusiastically endorses this "double translation" as far superior to a single translation from one language to another. Invoking the authority of Pliny the Younger Ascham claims that

> this exercise of double translating is learned easily, sensiblie, by litle and litle, not onlie all the hard congruities of Grammar, the choice of aptest wordes, the right framing of wordes and sentences, cumlines of figures and formes, fite for every matter and proper for everie tong, but that which is greater also, in marking dayly and folowing diligentlie thus the steppes of the best Authors, like invention of argumentes, like order in disposition, like utterance in Elocution is easelie gathered up: whereby your scholar shall be brought not only to like eloquence, but also to all trewe understanding and right judgement, both for writing and speaking.[17]

For these reasons, says Ascham, "I am moved to think this way of double translating, either onlie or chiefly, to be the fittest for the spedy and perfit atteyning of any tong."[18] The act of translating from English to Latin and back again, all the while attending to the principles of rhetoric, could not help but perfect the student's ability to compose in English. Moreover, the vernacular made steady inroads into the province of rhetoric in the late

---

[15]Charles Hoole, *A New Discovery of the Old Art of Teaching Schoole,* English Linguistics 1500-1800, ed. R. C. Alston, no. 133 (Menston, England: Scolar Press, 1969), 173, 200.

[16]Juan Luis Vives, *On Education [De tradendis disciplinis],* ed. and trans. Foster Watson (1913; reprinted, Totowa, N.J.: Rowman and Littlefield, 1971), 114.

[17]Roger Ascham, *The Scholemaster,* 103-104.

[18]Ibid., 104.

sixteenth and seventeenth centuries. Many vernacular textbook authors simply adapted, with little alteration, the methods of teaching Latin composition and applied them to English.[19] The program of the grammar school might best be thought of, then, as a kind of bilingual education. Latin was the primary language, but English was never far behind.

So complete was the domination of rhetoric and Latin in this curriculum that there was simply very little room for anything else. For example, what science was taught was often subservient to literary demands. In *De ratione studii* Erasmus recommends wide knowledge in order to facilitate the literary explication of ancient poets and other writers. Geography, says Erasmus, "which is useful in history, not to mention poetry, must also be mastered ... Here the main object is to have observed which of the vernacular words for mountains, rivers, regions, and cities correspond to the ancient."[20] Similarly, "astronomy must not be passed over, especially that of Hyginus, since the poets liberally sprinkle their creations with it. The nature and essence of everything must be grasped, especially since it is from this source that they are accustomed to draw there similies, epithets, comparisons, images, metaphors, and other rhetorical devices of that kind. Above all, however, history must be grasped. Its application is very widespread and not confined to the poets... In short, there is no branch of knowledge, whether military, agricultural, musical, or architectural which is not useful for those who have undertaken an exposition of the ancient poets or orators."[21] For Erasmus and his followers in the grammar schools, non-literary knowledge was useful primarily for its ability to assist in the development of eloquence.

Language occupied this preferred position in the grammar school curriculum because it is a defining characteristic of the human being. Vives says: "The first thing man has to learn is speech. It flows at once from the rational soul as water from a

---

[19]David Thomson demonstrates that late medieval grammar masters in England simply translated the Latin grammars of Priscian and Donatus into English. See *A Descriptive Catalogue of Middle English Grammatical Texts* (New York: Garland, 1979), esp. 1-49.

[20]Erasmus, *Collected Works,* 24:673.

[21]Ibid., 674-5.

fountain. As all beasts are bereft of intellect, so are they also lacking in speech. Discourse is also the instrument of human society, for not otherwise could the mind be revealed, so shut in is it by the grossness and density of the human body. Like as we have the mind by the gift of God, so we have this or that language, by the gift of art."[22] Vives continues by noting that "language is the shrine of erudition, and as it were a storeroom for what should be concealed, and what should be made public. Since it is the treasury of culture and the instrument of human society, it would therefore be to the benefit of the human race that there should be a single language, which all nations should use in common."[23] Latin was, of course, just such a "single language" and as such well-deserved its singular place in the schools. Latin made possible, for the Europeans and the English, at least, an international exchange of ideas, commerce and diplomacy. While suited to the needs of the present, Latin, without any native speakers, inevitably also kept its users cognizant of the past. Its users were especially cognizant of the literature of the Romans and were well aware that the oration was the literary form that dominated Rome. So it was in the grammar school classroom.

THE DOMINATION OF THE ORATION

The technological advances of the Renaissance made the teaching of writing more possible and practical than ever before. The printing press arrived in England in 1477 and paper production began in the first years of the sixteenth century. The use of books — textbooks for students to read and copybooks in which to write — made the act of writing far more central to the educational endeavor. Thus Richard Brinsley in *Ludus Literarius: or, The Grammar Schoole...* (1612) devotes an early chapter to a discussion of how the act of writing might be facilitated:

1. The schollar should be set to write, when he enters into his Accidence; so euery day to spend an hour in writing, or very neere.

---

[22]Vives, *On Education,* 90.
[23]Ibid., 91.

2. There must be special care, that every one who is to write, haue all the necessaries belonging thereunto; as penne, inke, paper, rular, plummet, ruling-pen, pen-knife, &c.

3. The like care must be, that their inke be thin, blacke, cleere; which wil not run abroad, nor blot: their paper good; that is, such as is white, smooth, and which will bear inke, and also that it be made in a book. Their writing books would be kept faire, strait ruled, and each to haue a blotting paper to keep their books from soyling, or marring under their hands.

4. Cause euery one of them to make his own pen; otherwise the making, and mending of pens, will be a very great hinderance, both to the Masters and to the Schollars. Besides that, when they are away from their Masters (if they have not a good pen made before) they wil write naught; because they know not how to make their pens themselves.[24]

Brinsley then presents an equally detailed account of how a pen is to be made, from the selection of the quill to the cutting of the nub. The remainder of the chapter involves instructions for holding the pen and for perfecting the techniques of writing. All of this detail is, in part, necessary because of the relative newness of writing with pen and ink in the classroom. Yet despite the obvious importance and practicality of writing in the grammar school, treatises treat writing primarily as a physical activity *(orthographia),* while the mental activities continue to be expressed in oral terms. That is, the conceptual and expressive functions of composition continue to be expressed in the terminology of classical oratory. Despite the rapid advances in printing, the oration remained fixed as the supreme form of discourse, just as it had been for the Romans. In the opinion of Walter Ong, the oration "tyrannized over ideas of what expression as such — literary or other — was."[25]

This oratorical "tyranny" is certainly apparent in the four principal composition exercises of the grammar school: letter-writing, verse-making, the theme, and the oration. The oration is invariably the final, and hence presumably the most difficult to

---

[24]John Brinsley, *Ludus Literarius,* English Linguistics 1500-1800, no. 62, (Menston, England: Scolar Press, 1968), 29.

[25]Walter Ong, "Tudor Writings on Rhetoric, Poetic, and Literary Theory," in *Rhetoric, Romance, and Technology; Studies in the Interaction of Expression and Culture* (Ithaca: Cornell University Press, 1971), 53.

accomplish, of these various assignments. Practically speaking, however, the three exercises which preceded the oration followed much the same rules of composition. Letter-writing, the most elementary exercise, provided a convenient introduction to the elements of rhetoric. In *The English Secretorie. Wherein is Contayned, a Perfect Method, for the inditing of all manner of Epistles and familiar letters...* (1586) Angel Day indicates that letter-writing may be divided into three parts: invention, disposition, and elocution. Of the five parts of classical rhetoric, Day omits only memory and delivery, the two most fully oral parts of the ancient division.[26] Likewise, Day also directs that the letter be organized precisely as a classical oration: *exordium, narratio, propositio, confirmation, confutatio,* and *peroratio.*[27] Indeed, any kind of discourse could be, and should be, organized in just this way. Citing Aphthonius, Brinsley says that he gives his students "a Theame to make, following the example in their booke, to prosecute the same parts of the Theame; as *Exordium, narratio, confirmatio, confutatio, conclusio.*"[28] It is no exaggeration to say that the rules of the classical oration were applied to every kind of discourse.

The oratorical domination of poetry is perhaps most surprising today, but it is simply another example of how completely ancient rhetoric governed all expression. There is no very clear demarcation between rhetoric and poetry in the Renaissance and the language of rhetoric is always deemed the appropriate idiom for the analysis of the poetry.[29] Thus Abraham Fraunce's *Arcadian Rhetorike* (1588), is, as the title suggests, a rhetoric which uses Sydney's epic, as well as the poetry of Boscan, Garcilaso, Tasso, and other vernacular poets as a source of rhetorical precepts. A few years later Sydney wrote his *Defense of Poesie* (1595) in the form of an oration.[30]

---

[26]Angel Day, *English Secretorie,* English Linguistics 1500-1800, no. 29 (Menston, England: Scolar Press, 1967), 19-20.

[27]Ibid., 22.

[28]*Ludus Literarius,* 172-3.

[29]For a complete treatment of this relationship see Brian Vickers, *Classical Rhetoric in English Poetry* (London: Macmillan, 1970; reprinted, Carbondale: Southern Illinois University Press, 1989).

[30]See K. O. Myrick, *Sir Philip Sydney as a Literary Craftsman* (Cambridge: Harvard University Press, 1935), especially 46-83.

This union of rhetoric and poetic and all other genres was possible, indeed even essential, because all discourse shared the same end: to speak well and to speak persuasively. The civic and forensic origins of rhetoric are never out of sight in Renaissance literature. That is, literature, like rhetoric itself, is always argumentative and persuasive, never neutral.[31] There is no conception of a use for language that is merely expository, or merely descriptive, or merely narrative. Such functions existed only insofar as each promoted the ultimate end of persuasion. Nowhere is this more apparent than in the work of John Milton. D.L. Clark has demonstrated that Milton, while a student at St. Paul's School in London had learned his lessons well. Milton's famous essay on freedom of the press was modeled after an Isocratean oration and is entitled "Areopagitica; A Speech of Mr. John Milton For The Liberty Of Unlicensed Printing. To The Parliament Of England."[32] Similarly, "Paradise Lost" is "An Oration to Justify The Ways of God to Men."

IMITATION AND LEARNING

The "Areopagitica" demonstrates the appeal of classical models to even a creative genius like Milton. "That Milton should aspire to such literary and oratorical ideals as moved the orators and poets of antiquity is natural enough," says Clark, "for he had an early education very like their own."[33] In basing his essay on a classical pattern Milton was simply doing what he had been taught to do. If there is one constant in Renaissance education it is a belief in the necessity, indeed, the inevitability of *imitatio* as the principle method of learning. Imitation is made necessary by the human condition. Says Vives: "Although it is natural to talk, yet all discourse whatsoever belongs to an 'art' which was not bestowed upon us at birth, since nature has fashioned man, for the

---

[31]See Ong, "Tudor Writings," 65.

[32]Donald Lemen Clark, *John Milton at St. Paul's School: A Study of Ancient Rhetoric in English Renaissance Education* (New York: Columbia University Press, 1948). See also Wilbur E. Gilman, "Milton's Rhetoric: Studies in His Defense of Liberty," *University of Missouri Studies* 14 (1939): 12-13.

[33]*John Milton at St. Paul's School,* 3.

most part, strangely hostile to 'art.' Since she lets us be born ignorant and absolutely skilless of all arts, we require imitation. Imitation, furthermore, is the fashioning of a certain thing in accordance with a proposed model."[34] Human expression, in particular, requires imitation to perfect. According to Ascham "all languages, both learned and mother tonges, be gotten onlie by *Imitation.* For as ye used to heare, so ye learne to speake... And therefore, if ye would speake as the best and the wisest do, ye must be conversant, where the best and the wisest are."[35] The best and the wisest are to be found, more often than not, in classical literature: "in the Greek and latin tong, the two onlie learned tonges, which be not kept in common taulke, but in private bookes, we finde alwayes wisdom and eloquence, good matter and good utterance, never or seldom a sonder."[36]

The belief in a literary education which favors imitation over rules naturally requires great authors to imitate. But which great authors? The answer, invariably, was the best writers from the best periods. That, in turn, almost always meant Cicero. There was considerable debate about whether or not Cicero was the only model for imitation, but there was little disagreement that he should be at the very least, one of the models.[37] Says Vives: "There are those who, out of all authors, select only Cicero, whom alone they imitate. Cicero is indeed the best, though he does not contain every merit. Nor is he the only author with good style. When he delights and teaches us he is admirable beyond the rest." The conclusion, says Vives, is that "if Cicero is the best and most eminent stylist, others are not, on that account, bad or contemptible."[38] In other words, Cicero is first among the ancients, but only one of a number of worthy models. Among many others, Vives himself suggests, "for an intellectual and learned circle, the

[34]Vives, *On Education,* 189.
[35]Ascham, *Scholemaster,* 134.
[36]Ibid., 136.
[37]In the *Ciceronianus* Erasmus rejects the imitation of Cicero to the exclusion of all other models. See *The Ciceronian: A Dialogue on the Ideal Latin Style,* trans. Betty Knott, Vol. 28, *Collected Works of Erasmus.* For a complete account of the debates about Ciceronianism, see Izora Scott, *Controversies over the Imitation of Cicero as a Model for Style and Some Phases of their Influence on the Schools of the Renaissance* (New York: Teachers College, 1910).
[38]Vives, *On Education,* 191-2.

speeches of Demosthenes are suited. So, too, are those to be found in Livy, in whose histories orations are interwoven. For sweetness and rhythym we have Isocrates. Plato has a still higher flight."[39] Each Renaissance educator has a favorite list of authors, but all agree on the need to imitate the greats of antiquity.

Vives suggests how this process of imitation should proceed: "the zealous imitator will study, with the greatest attention, the model he has set up for himself, and will consider by what art, by what method, such and such was achieved by the author, in order that he himself with a similar artifice may accomplish his own intention in his own work."[40] With the assistance of the master, then, the student should first analyze the appropriate model to determine the method of composition and then gradually attempt to apply these methods in their own writing. Naturally, a child needs considerable assistance in analyzing models and generating sophisticated prose and verse. The grammar school sought to facilitate this process by engaging the students in a series of increasingly complicated imitative exercises. Ascham discusses five such exercises. Although the fifth is explicitly called "imitation," all five are predicated on the emulation of models. The five are: 1) translation, especially double translation; 2) paraphrase, "not onlie to expresse at large with moe wordes, but to strive and contend (as *Quintilian* saith) to translate the best latin authors into other latin wordes"[41]; 3) metaphrase, the translation of prose into verse and verse into prose; 4) epitome, the distillation of classical works into their essences. This is an exercise Ascham much "mislikes" for it emphasizes only matter and disregards expression and it can cause students to lose sight of the original model. Finally, after much translation, paraphrase, metaphrase and perhaps epitome, the student is ready for 5) imitation proper: the careful scrutiny and creative emulation of an approved model.

This emphasis on imitation naturally meant that there must be sufficient material to imitate. While the models of imitation were to be found in the ancient masters, the Renaissance educators also devised various devices to make the words and ideas more readily

---

[39]Ibid., 194.
[40]Ibid., 195.
[41]Ascham, *Scholemaster,* 106.

accessible to young minds. Thus there are innumerable books of
lists which serve as guides for composition. These collections,
compendia, and anthologies of adages, apothegms, commonplaces,
and figures all provide handy sources of the wisdom of the
ancients. Thus Erasmus' *Adagia* began as a collection of 818
proverbs and ultimately grew to include 4151 adages. These
proverbs, which Erasmus culled from classical sources, contribute,
he says, four things to discourse: "philosophy, grace and charm in
speaking, and the understanding of the best authors."[42] Thus the
proverbs contained in this collection should be studied for their
merits and then applied where appropriate in a composition. A
similar work is Robert Cawdrey, *A treasvrie or Storehouse of
Similies: Both pleasaunt, delightfull, and profitable, for all estates
of men in general. Newly collected into Heades and Common
places* (1600). Cawdrey's 858 page book contains similes arranged
alphabetically from "Accusation" to "Zeale." Much like the
apothegms of Erasmus, these similes serve as a ready source of
philosophically sound illustrative material for composition. The
term "commonplace" in the title is indicative of Cawdrey's
purpose. As Joan Lechner explains, the commonplace, in this
sense, may be thought of "as a little oration or as a 'speech within
a speech.'"[43] These "little speeches which were regularly inserted
in longer orations for purposes of amplification, exposition,
persuasion, and description were thought of as 'commonplaces'
because they provided ready-made 'arguments' which in some way
magnified (or minimized) a subject."[44] These collections of commonplaces, figures, proverbs and all the rest served as a source of
approved material which could be inserted directly or altered to fit
individual needs.

   In addition to these collections of "little speeches" and other
relatively short devices, students could also make use of collections
of more complete discourses. Angel Day's *English Secretorie,* for
example, is comprised of "sundry examples of euery Epistle." Day

---

[42]Erasmus, *Adages,* trans. Margaret Mann Phillips, Vol. 31, *Collected Works of
Erasmus,* 14.
   [43]Sister Joan Marie Lechner, O.S.U., *Renaissance Concepts of the Commonplaces,*
(New York: Pageant Press, 1962, reprinted, Westport, CT: Greenwood Press, 1974), 3.
   [44]Ibid.

includes at least one example of deliberative, confirmatory, laudatory, hortatory, dehortatory, suasory, disuasory, and all the other genres of letters that he identifies. Another work which provides complete examples of discourse is Richard Rainolde's *A booke called the Foundacion of Rhetorike* (1563). *The Foundacion of Rhetorike* is an English adaptation of Reinhard Lorich's Latin version of Aphthonius' *Progymnasmata.*[45] The *Progymnasmata,* or a set of introductory exercises, is comprised of fourteen progressively more difficult compositional models from simple fables to complex questions of law. Rainolde readily acknowledges his debt to his ancient source:

> Aphthonivs a famous man, wrote in greke of soche declamacions, to enstructe the studentes thereof, with all facilitie to grounde in them, a most plentious and rich vein of eloquence. No man is able to inuente a more profitable waie and order, to instructe any one in the exquisite and absolute perfection, of wisedome and eloquence, then Aphthonius Quintilianus and Hermogenes.[46]

Thus Rainolde expresses both his conviction in the efficacy of imitation and his faith in the ancients whom he is himself imitating. In his enthusiasm for Aphthonius Rainolde is by no means alone; Aphthonius is one of the most widely accepted authorities for writing instruction. Brinsley, for example, bases his instructions for the teaching of themes on Aphthonius.[47]

In addition to the works of Rainolde and Day and all the various "storehouses" of epitomes, adages, and figures that were printed in the sixteenth and seventeenth centuries, students were also expected to collect their own commonplaces and enter them in their "copie" books. After recommending a number of authors which students might profitably read, Hoole next advises: "let every one take one of those books forementioned, and see what he

---

[45]Richard Rainolde, *The Foundation of Rhetoric,* English Linguistics, no. 347 (Menston, England: Scolar Press, 1972). Aphthonius's *Progymnasmata* was widely printed in the Renaissance and Lorich's version, with twenty-eight editions in the sixteenth and seventeenth centuries, was especially popular. See James J. Murphy, *Renaissance Rhetoric: A Short Title Catalogue* (New York: Garland Publishing, 1981), 22.

[46]Rainolde, "To the Reader."

[47]See *Ludus literarius,* 172-190.

can finde in it for his purpose, and write it down under one of those heads in his Commonplace book."[48] The students should then "all read what they have written, before the Master, and every one transcribe what others have collected, into his own book; and thus they may always have store of matter for invention ready at hand, which is far beyond what their own wit is able to conceive."[49] These student commonplace books functioned in concert with the various published collections to insure that the students would have a sufficient storehouse of material for the process of writing.

When grammar school students were finally faced with actually writing a theme they were at least theoretically well-stocked with material which would make the process relatively easy. In actual fact, of course, the process could be painful. In his dialogue *Ludus literarius* one of Brinsley's characters admits that the themes which "my children have done hereby for a long time, they have done it with exceeding paines and feare, in harsh phrase, without any inuention, iudgement; and ordinarily so rudely, as I have been ashamed that anyone should see their exercises. So as it hath driuen mee into exceeding passions, causing me to deale ouer rigorously with the poore boies."[50] Indeed, the grammar school curriculum appears extremely rigorous by any standard, and it is easy to imagine that many of those who experienced it were less than enthusiastic in their studies. Despite the frustrations of the Masters and the recalcitrance of the boys, the grammar schools certainly provided their charges with the opportunity to develop the ability to write comprehensively on virtually any subject.

Grammar school students were rather young, and they were never really expected to write discourse which would exceed the models they were constantly reading. Nevertheless, students in the later forms were expected ultimately to write themes that, while in the spirit of their models, were not simply slavish reproductions of them. Thus Hoole recommends that the master should not tie the students "to the words of any Authour, but giving them liberty to

[48]Hoole, *New Discovery,* 183.
[49]Ibid.
[50]Brinsley, *Ludus literarius,* 173.

contract, or enlarge, or alter them as they please; so that they still contend to go beyond them in purity of expression."[51] Ultimately, says Hoole, once the master determines that "they have gained a perfect way of making Themes of themselves, you may let them go on to attain the habit by their own constant practice."[52]

The "perfect way of making themes" was naturally dependent on the accumulation of material for imitation. The actual assembly of this previously gathered material was governed by the process of *amplificatio* — the achievement of copiousness or "copie." Amplification was, in effect, the active implementation of imitation. As such, the process combined the classical divisions of invention, style, and arrangement. Although the sixteenth-century educational reformer Peter Ramus had attempted to make invention the sole property of logic, this re-arrangement did little to banish invention from the grammar school where invention and style combined in the process of amplification.[53] Brinsley and Hoole could therefore, recommend Ramistic texts and still discuss invention without any sense of anomaly. Brinsley advises that students should "trie what reasons they can inuent of themselves according to the chiefe heads of Inuention" such as causes, effects, subjects, and adjuncts.[54] Later he admits that this approach may be too hard for children "who haue read no Logicke," but he nevertheless continues to advocate the use of these topics.

It is in the work of Erasmus, however, that the union of invention and elocution within the rubric of amplification is most apparent. Ascham calls Erasmus "the ornament of learning in our tyme"[55] and this veneration in large part is due to the Erasmus' *De duplici copia verborum et rerum. De copia* may be thought of as

---

[51]Hoole, *New Discovery,* 185.

[52]Ibid., 186.

[53]The standard account of "Ramism" is Walter Ong, S. J., *Ramus, Method, and the Decay of Dialogue* (Cambridge: Harvard University Press, 1958). For the first modern English translation of a work by Ramus see *Arguments in Rhetoric Against Quintilian: Translation and Text of Peter Ramus's Rhetoricae Distinctiones in Quintilianum (1549),* trans. Carole Newlands, with an introduction by James J. Murphy (DeKalb: Northern Illinois University Press, 1986).

[54]Brinsley, *Ludus literarius,* 180.

[55]Ascham, *Scholemaster,* 140.

the first grammar school textbook; in fact Erasmus wrote it for that purpose. In a letter to Dean Colet, the founder of St. Paul's school, he says:

> I thought it would be appropriate for me to make a small literary contribution to the equipment of your school. So I have chosen to dedicate to the new school these two new commentaries *De copia,* inasmuch as the work in question is suitable for boys to read and also, unless I am mistaken, not unlikely to prove helpful to them, though I leave it to others to judge how well-informed this work of mine is, or how serviceable it will be.[56]

De copia was judged very serviceable as a textbook upon its first publication in 1511. Indeed, "so widespread did its use become that it was worth pirating, summarizing, excerpting, turning into a question-and-answer manual, and making the subject of commentaries."[57] The frequency with which *De copia* was reprinted "testifies to the significance of the work and to its influence during the first three-quarters of the sixteenth century in both arousing and ministering to a particular stylistic ideal."[58]

That stylistic ideal is captured in the Latin word *copia* which is rendered "abundance" in the standard English translation of the work.[59] But as Donald B. King explains, there is no entirely suitable English word: "as used by Erasmus, copia encompasses within its meaning the meaning of four English words: *variation, abundance* or richness, *eloquence,* and the *ability* to vary and enrich language and thought."[60] Erasmus believes that the development of *copia* is necessary because "exercise in expressing oneself in different ways will be of considerable importance in general for the acquisition of style."[61] More particularly, "variety is so powerful in every sphere that there is absolutely nothing, however brilliant, which is not dimmed if not commended by variety. Nature above all delights in variety; in all this huge concourse of

---

[56]*Collected Works of Erasmus,* 24:285.

[57]Ibid., 283.

[58]Ibid.

[59]*Copia: Foundations of Abundant Style, Collected Works of Erasmus,* Vol. 24.

[60]Erasmus, *On Copia of Words and Ideas,* trans. Donald B. King and H. David Rix (Milwaukee: Marquette University Press, 1963), "Note to the Reader," 9.

[61]*Collected Works of Erasmus,* 24:302.

things, she has left nothing anywhere unpainted by her wonderful technique of variety."[62] Practically speaking, "this form of exercise will make no insignificant contribution to the ability to speak or write extempore, and will prevent us from standing there stammering and dumbfounded."[63] Ultimately, says Erasmus, "if we are not instructed in these techniques, we shall often be found unintelligible, harsh, or even totally unable to express ourselves."[64] *Copia,* then, is the very foundation of style.

After these introductory remarks Erasmus says that he will now "give some brief advice on the exercises by which this faculty may be developed."[65] The next three hundred or so pages are devoted to this "brief advice" on achieving copiousness in both words and ideas. For the most part, variety in words is achieved by the use of figures and tropes, variety in ideas by the rhetorical topics. There is, however, very little discussion of the theory of figurative or topical language in *De copia.* Rather, the emphasis in Erasmus' book, as in the grammar school classroom, is on practical application in discourse. This approach culminates in a "practical demonstration" of abundance in Chapter 33 of *De copia.* Erasmus promises to "take one or two sentences and see how far we can go in transforming the basic expression into a Protean variety of shapes."[66] As it turns out, Erasmus can go so far as to produce 195 variations on the sentence "your letter pleased me mightily."[67] This demonstration is followed by 200 variations on "always, as long as I live, I shall remember you."[68] In this virtuoso performance Erasmus is being intentionally extreme. He deliberately takes a "not particularly fertile" sentence and creates some 200 variants to show his readers the infinite fecundity of human language. Erasmus does not recommend going quite this far in the classroom; it is rather a dramatic testimony to the plasticity of language to those who might not believe it.

---

[62]Ibid.
[63]Ibid.
[64]Ibid.
[65]Ibid., 303.
[66]Ibid., 348.
[67]Ibid., 348-54.
[68]Ibid., 354-64.

There is nothing terribly original about Erasmus' *De copia.*
The work is based on broad reading in the classics, a knowledge of
rhetorical theory, and great practice in composition. In short,
Erasmus' work is the result of an education much like that he had
in mind for young boys. *De copia,* and the grammar school
curriculum, were together a celebration of the centrality of language in human affairs. When a student left the grammar school,
he might not be able to generate two hundred versions of the same
sentence, but he would certainly be prepared to write on any
subject with skill, dispatch, and perhaps even eloquence.

RENAISSANCE RHETORIC AND MODERN WRITING

It is appropriate that a discussion of the English grammar
school should begin with Erasmus. In many ways the grammar
school was the implementation of Erasmus' vision of what
education should be. But the vision did not belong to Erasmus
alone; rather, his works captured the spirit shared by an entire
culture. Humanism assumed that the end of education was to
endow human beings with eloquence. Furthermore, this eloquence
was to be a special kind: the classical eloquence of Cicero's
citizen-orator. The theory and practice of Cicero and the pedagogy
of Quintilian shaped a curriculum reverential toward the past and
yet attentive to the present. These Latin grammar schools could,
therefore, teach an ancient language and also prize eloquence in
the vernacular. The rhetorical tradition was so persistent that
despite the influence of printing, the spoken word of the classical
oration remained the dominant pattern for all discourse. Just as
the oration remained pre-eminent, so too did the educational
methods of antiquity. The inescapable necessity of imitation as the
only way to master expression was virtually unchallenged. In these
fundamental ways the teaching of writing in the Renaissance
differs from current practices.[69] Yet the differences may be neither
as great or as insurmountable as they appear.

From the writing teacher's standpoint, at least, the grammar
school masters had a clear advantage over their successors. The

---

[69]Dale L. Sullivan has recently detailed the "modern inability to appreciate
imitation as a serious pedagogical method" in "Attitudes toward Imitation: Classical
Culture and the Modern Temper," *Rhetoric Review* 8 (1989): 5-21.

curriculum of the grammar was entirely literary; the teaching of reading, writing, and speaking was the sole effort of the master, every day and every form. It is improbable that many would want to claim such an advantage and surrender the infinitely more diverse curriculum of our own time. Nor could a technological society ever accept an exclusively literary education. While we cannot return to the Renaissance we can perhaps approximate some of the best of the grammar school curriculum and find in the work of great educational theorists and practitioners inspiration for present efforts.

The real advantage of the grammar schools, and Renaissance education generally, was an approach to language instruction which was concentrated and unified, whereas ours has been, in contrast, diluted and diffuse. What Renaissance educators combined, we have fragmented and departmentalized. The Renaissance recognition of the primacy of language and the unity of all acts of expression is, however, beginning to reassert itself. "Writing across the curriculum" is the most obvious, but not the only manifestation of this attitude. While we have not approached the Renaissance pervasiveness of language in education, we increasingly recognize that the teaching of writing cannot be restricted to one hour three times a week. While we are unlikely to restore years of instruction in Latin grammar, we increasingly realize that Americans are not well-trained in foreign languages and this neglect disadvantages us in important ways. What the grammar school experience suggests is that the study of languages, native or foreign, should complement each other rather than be thought of as independent or even mutually irrelevant subjects.

Just as a reunion of languages, native and foreign, is endorsed by Renaissance practice, so too is a reintegration of the spoken and written word. The historically recent division of "English" and "Speech Communication" into separate departments would confound any grammar school master or, for that matter, virtually any rhetorician before, say, 1900.[70] The revival of rhetoric has already

---

[70]For discussions of the separation of the written and spoken word in American education see James A. Berlin, *Rhetoric and Reality: Writing Instruction in American Colleges, 1900-1985* (Carbondale: Southern Illinois University Press, 1987) and James J. Murphy, *The Rhetorical Tradition and Modern Writing* (New York: Modern Language Association, 1982).

begun to subvert this division, but the divisions between disciplines are still very potent.

This disunity of the discourse arts is apparent, too, in present approaches to reading and writing. Literary criticism as we know it cannot be said to exist in the grammar school. Classroom literary analysis was designed to provide the student with appropriate moral and philosophical ideas for discourse and to demonstrate the possibilities of style which could ultimately be emulated. In other words, reading served writing. To the grammar school master, the reflexive nature of most critical inquiry would be simply incomprehensible. Reading, writing, and reciting existed as closely correlated activities, but writing and speaking were always the end — reading and textual analysis were the means to that end.

The study of language is certainly a major preoccupation of the twentieth century. Yet that study is dispersed over a wide variety of fields, some of which are oblivious to the practical pursuit of any kind of eloquence. In the Renaissance that interest in language was concentrated in the study of "grammar," broadly defined, and rhetoric. It is this concentration that gives Renaissance rhetoric much of its effectiveness. Brian Vickers has recently suggested that the Renaissance "reintegrated" the study of rhetoric after the "fragmentation" of the art following the fall of Rome.[71] The twentieth century may very well be poised for yet another "reintegration" of rhetoric in contemporary education.

---

[71]Brian Vickers, *In Defence of Rhetoric* (Oxford: Clarendon Press, 1988), Chapter 5, "Renaissance Reintegration," 254-93.

CHAPTER FIVE

WRITING INSTRUCTION IN GREAT BRITAIN: EIGHTEENTH AND NINETEENTH CENTURIES

WINIFRED BRYAN HORNER

Writing instruction within any society is subject to social and political influences, and nowhere is this more true than in eighteenth- and nineteenth-century Britain, that territory that encompassed England, Scotland, Wales, and Ireland. In addition, strong religious movements and a special linguistic situation during this period shaped where and how writing was taught. In this essay, I shall look closely at some of the social, political, and religious influences and their effect on the schools and universities in the eighteenth and nineteenth centuries.[1]

The eighteenth century in Britain was a period of transition as the agricultural population migrated to the cities in large numbers. Industrialization was rapid. Between 1700 and 1800 England saw the rise of the industrial centers of Manchester and Liverpool, while Scotland changed from a poor agricultural society to a relatively industrialized one with an increase in population from 84,000 to 500,000 during the nineteenth century. Preparatory schools and universities were not available or adequate. At the beginning of the eighteenth century England had two universities, Oxford and Cambridge. Although Scotland had four well-established Universities,

[1]I should like to acknowledge the support of the National Endowment for the Humanities, the National Council of Teachers of English, the University of Edinburgh Institute for the Advancement of Studies in the Humanities, and Texas Christian University for support of my work in Scottish rhetoric.

Ireland had one, and Wales none.

The eighteenth century was also a period of upward mobility, and "good English" became a rung on the ladder. With economic stability established, the large and powerful merchant class and those aspiring to better themselves saw education in general and language in particular as one of the ways to move up. In response, the school teachers and grammarians, with a strong belief in rationality and rules, set out to standardize the language, firm in the beliefs that change was a sign of deterioration and that Latin was the standard by which all languages should be measured.

During the period there was also a rise in nationalism, which resulted in a new reverence for English language and literature. Although men and women of culture read their own vernacular literature, it was still considered folk literature improper for university instruction. Lectures, coffee houses, and journals proliferated, however, providing an active forum for such interests. The literary scene in London and Edinburgh was intellectually lively and out of this milieu came the popular literary journals like the *Spectator* and *Rambler* that helped to both standardize and valorize English. In the middle of the century the lectures of Adam Smith and Hugh Blair were first delivered in Edinburgh and were well attended by the local populace. When lectures in English literature were brought into the universities in the nineteenth century, the lectures were still marked by a strong sense of nationalism. John Nichol, professor of English literature at Glasgow University in 1861, like most of his colleagues, saw the teaching of English as a patriotic endeavor.

> The study of our literature encourages the best sort of patriotism—
> our pride in our great men. It enlarges our ideas by enabling us
> to penetrate into their minds, and stimulates us to emulate by
> setting forth the qualities that made them great.[2]

As the Nichol statement illustrates, nationalism in the teaching of English literature was coupled with a strong moral flavor. In 1828, Thomas Dale confirmed this idea in his "Introductory Lecture delivered in the University of London."

> But in all my Lectures, more particularly when treating upon that

---

[2]John Nichol, *An Inaugural Address* (Liverpool: F.S. Gibbons, 1851), n.p.

glorious and inexhaustible subject, the LITERATURE of our
country—I shall esteem it my duty—and I trust I shall find it
my delight—to inculcate lessons of virtue, through the medium
of the masters of our language.[3]

Instructors of the eighteenth and nineteenth centuries felt that in
teaching literature they were teaching a moral vision of the
world—an idea that lingered on in academia well into the
twentieth century. Since most of the teachers in the eighteenth
century were preachers and most university students were training
for the ministry, education was understandably closely connected
with religion. Religion was considered the rationale and basis of
education, and education the route to virtue. Religion and politics
both played important parts in the drama of education and writing
instruction in the eighteenth and nineteenth centuries, and the two
were never separate after the Jacobite defeat in 1746.

This fact had been emphasized in the act of Union in 1707,
which, while uniting the parliaments of Scotland and England,
allowed Scotland to retain its independence in education and
religion. Its universities were well-established and highly respected
on the continent and in England. When the 1662 Act of Uniformity
was passed, under which all teachers and students were required to
swear allegiance to the Church of England, Scottish Schools and
Universities were exempt. Consequently, students flocked to the
Scottish Universities or to the continent, where there were no
religious constraints. By the eighteenth century the Dissenting
Academies, which provided a university-equivalent education, were
numerous, while at the same time Oxford and Cambridge had
become decadent both morally and educationally. As a result the
Academies drew Anglican students as well as Dissenters.[4] It is in
these Academies and in the Scottish Universities that innovations
took place, that English as an academic subject flourished: instruction

---

[3]Cited in D.J. Palmer, *The Rise of English Studies: An Account of the Study of
English Language and Literature from Its Origins to the Making of the Oxford English
School* (London: Oxford University Press, 1965), 20.

[4]Thomas P. Miller, "Why Didn't College English Studies Originate in the English
Colleges?" Paper presented at the Conference of College Composition and Communication, March 1989. Tom Miller's excellent article gives a thorough picture of the
dissenting academies and credits them in large part with the origin of English studies.

in writing came to mean writing English instead of writing Latin.

The Catholic population did not fare as well as the Dissenters, and since most of the Catholic aristocracy in Ireland employed private tutors and then sent their children to continental universities, they did not, for the most part, participate in the British intellectual life of the period.[5]

THE LINGUISTIC SITUATION

In addition to the strong religious and political forces, there were three factors in the linguistic situation of the eighteenth and nineteenth centuries that altered the way writing was taught. The first was the gradual abandonment of Latin as the language of education and culture, the second was the shift from an oral culture to a basically literate culture—from emphasis on speaking to an emphasis on writing—and the third was the proliferation of books and periodicals.

Cultured persons in the eighteenth century read and wrote in Latin. In their grammar schools, they had learned grammar and had written extensively—in Latin. Their religious exercises were in Latin, and they sang psalms in the classical languages. At many schools, all discussion was in Latin except in family groups.[6] Literacy was defined as the ability to read and write Latin. It was during this period, however, that objections to such practices were heard as education began to have a more utilitarian end for merchants and men of business. Although the change from Latin to English was gradual, it was during the eighteenth and nineteenth centuries that the shift to English began in the schools, the Dissenting Academies, and the universities.

Another important pedagogical shift that began in the eighteenth century and continued through the nineteenth is the shift from the spoken to the written, the oral to the literate. Rhetoric had been the study of oratory, and university examinations had been

---

[5]Nicholas Hans, *New Trends in Education in the Eighteenth Century* (London: Routledge & Kegan Paul Ltd., 1951), 22.

[6]Herbert McLachlan, *English Education under the Test Acts: Being the History of the Non-Conformist Academies 1662-1820* (Manchester: Manchester University Press, 1931), 34.

oral until almost the middle of the eighteenth century. In the English Universities oral examinations were called "tripos" after the name of the three-legged stool on which the examiner sat. In Scotland, such examinations were called "Blackstone examinations" after "ye blak stane" on which the student sat while being quizzed orally and in Latin.[7] Oxford and Cambridge did not introduce written exams until the last part of the eighteenth century.[8] Until well into the nineteenth century most important exams still remained oral as the Ph.D. dissertation defense is today.

Writing instruction had been primarily confined to letter writing and sermons prior to the eighteenth century. As peoples' interests were increasingly served by government representatives and the legal profession during the eighteenth century, oratory became less important and writing increasingly became the medium of communication and record. Rhetoric traditionally associated with oratory lost favor as a school subject, leaving only elocution, a truncated rhetoric dealing only with stylized delivery, as its unsavory residue. Wilbur Samuel Howell, in his discussion of elocution, emphasizes its reductive nature during the two centuries by contrasting the opening line of an elocutionary manual, "Always breathe through the nostrils," to that of Aristotle's *Rhetoric*, "Rhetoric is the counterpart of dialectic."[9]

Another factor in the linguistic situation in this period is the great increase in the reading and writing public, which, in turn, produced a large class of writers who wrote specifically for that public. At the same time that English was making its way into the classroom at all levels, a spirited exchange in writing ensued in the numerous printed publications of the period—books, pamphlets, and periodicals. Public and private libraries increased in number and size. The new interest in the national language resulted in a reexamination of the older English texts already stored in libraries such as the British Museum, the Bodleian at Oxford, and the

---

[7]Alexander Morgan, *Scottish University Studies* (London: Oxford University Studies, 1933), 60.

[8]S. J. Curtis, *History of Education in Great Britain* (London: University Tutorial Press Ltd., 1957; 4th ed.), 137.

[9]Wilbur Samuel Howell, *Eighteenth-Century British Logic and Rhetoric* (Princeton: Princeton University Press, 1971), 145-256.

University Library at Cambridge. Jo McMurtry claims that "by the end of the nineteenth century they [Victorians] had found, edited, and published virtually the entire canon of English literature" in addition to many of the tools necessary for scholarship, such as concordances and dictionaries.[10]

Writing manuals and textbooks in the latter half of the nineteenth century became more and more numerous to serve this reading and writing public. In the last part of the seventeenth century and the first part of the eighteenth, textbooks were still largely in Latin. As the lectures changed to English, more and more textbooks in the native tongue were introduced. At first English and Latin texts were used side by side, since good English textbooks were not available. At some of the academies Latin textbooks "were abridged and translated by students before being used by them."[11] Often instructors wrote their own; more often, though, dictated lectures became the textbooks for the course in the Scottish Universities and in the Academies.

SCHOOLS AND UNIVERSITIES

The eighteenth-century English grammar schools developed out of a variety of cathedral, abbey, collegiate, parish and song schools from the fifteenth and sixteenth centuries. Their aim was to turn out students who could read and write Latin. They were called grammar schools for good reason — the students embarked on an intensive course of grammar — but it was Latin grammar. This endeavor occupied them in the early years. They then studied Greek and rhetoric while continuing to improve their proficiency in Latin by writing Latin verses. After attending a high school equivalent, they entered the university. In Scotland, where preparatory schools were scarce, allowance was always made for the "lad o'parts"—usually a gifted young man who was tutored by the local parson in a parish school—who then went early to the university—sometimes as young as fourteen or fifteen.[12] Thomas Carlyle, the

[10]Jo McMurtry, *English Language, English Literature: The Creation of an Academic Discipline* (Hamden, CT: Archon, 1985), 34.

[11]McLachlan, 22.

[12]Findlay, 9-10.

eldest of nine children, walked eighty miles from his home in Ecclefechan to the University of Edinburgh at the age of fourteen.[13]

By 1830 the central government began to intervene by imposing a standard on preparatory schools, but the standard was based on English models. The widespread assumption in the south was that elementary schools provided elementary instruction for the poor students who were not going on to higher education. The English upper classes provided tutors for their children or sent them to grammar schools to prepare for the university. On the other hand, the Scottish public schools, including both parish and burgh schools, drew from a wider social spectrum in preparing students for the university.[14]

Eighteenth- and nineteenth-century British students who sought out higher education in their own country might attend one of the older universities — Oxford or Cambridge — one of the Dissenting Academies, or one of the Scottish institutions. Toward the end of the nineteenth century their choice also included the University of London and the many newly established teaching colleges. Since Catholics and non-Anglicans were firmly excluded from Oxford and Cambridge during the eighteenth century, students' choices depended largely on religious affiliation, economic status, and the region in which they lived.

Oxford and Cambridge

By the eighteenth century Oxford and Cambridge had degenerated into a "preserve for the idle and the rich."[15] They were expensive: the annual cost for an undergraduate in the 1830's was between 200 and 300 pounds. They were also elitist: undergraduates of noble birth were carefully distinguished from the poorer students by their embroidered gowns of purple silk and a college cap with a gold tassel. In addition, such students were excused from all exams which led to a degree (even though the standards

---

[13]Ian Campbell, *Thomas Carlyle* (New York: Charles Scribner's Sons, 1974).

[14]Douglas Myers, "Scottish Schoolmasters in the Nineteenth Century: Professionalism and Politics," in *Scottish Culture and Scottish Education: 1800-1980*, eds. Walter M. Humes and Hamish M. Paterson (Edinburgh: John Donald Publishers Ltd., 1983), 81.

[15]H.C. Barnard, *A History of English Education From 1760*, 2nd ed. (London: University of London Press, 1961), 24.

of the tests were low), and were only required to be in residence for thirteen weeks out of the year.

Nicholas Hans in his statistical study of eighteenth-century education points out that "all the leading men of the eighteenth century—Bentham, Butler, Gibbon, Adam Smith, Vicesimus Knox and many lesser lights—condemned the two Universities from their personal experience as students."[16] Vicesimus Knox, headmaster of Tonbridge School from 1778 to 1812, called the requirements for the Oxford degree a "set of childish and useless exercises" which "raise no emulation, confer no honour and promote no improvement." He describes the Fellows as persons "who neither study themselves nor concern themselves in superintending the studies of others."[17] R.L. Archer, a twentieth-century scholar, describes eighteenth-century Oxford as "a university in which professors had ceased to lecture, and where work was the last thing expected." These students "entered the University not to feed on solid intellectual food, but to enjoy a costly luxury." Oxford at the time was marked by "extravagance, debt, drunkenness, gambling, and an absurd attention to dress."[18] Cambridge did not fare quite so badly as Oxford in the press, but during the eighteenth century the southern universities were the preserves of the traditional and an increasingly decadent culturally elite.

In the late eighteenth century, Oxford and Cambridge offered little that was new for students who came well prepared. Class attendance was low. At Oxford in 1850, "out of 1500 or 1600 undergraduates, the average annual attendance at the modern history course was 8; at botany 6 and at Arabic, Anglo-Saxon, Sanskrit and medicine, none."[19] Lectures were dubbed "wall lectures" because the lecturers had no other audience than the walls.[20] Reform came slowly to Oxford and Cambridge in the middle of the nineteenth century under the Oxford University Act

---

[16]Hans, 42. Hans sets out in his work, *New Trends in Education in the Eighteenth Century,* to refute the commonly held view of Oxford and Cambridge in the eighteenth century, especially the view that the poor students had deserted the Universities, but his arguments are not always convincing against the large evidence to the contrary.

[17]Cited in Barnard, 25-26.

[18]R.L. Archer, *Secondary Education in the Nineteenth Century* (Cambridge: At the University Press, 1921), 7.

[19]Barnard, 82.

[20]Archer, 9.

and the Cambridge Reforms of 1854-56. The Founder's Kin
scholarships were opened to competition, and for the first time
University business could be carried on in English instead of
Latin.[21] Life fellowships were abolished and celibacy was no longer
required for the college Fellows. In 1871 religious tests for the
degree were finally abolished. New professorships were established,
the curriculum was broadened, and examinations were made more
stringent. In spite of these nineteenth-century reforms, Oxford and
Cambridge continued to be aristocratic and extremely conservative
throughout the period. It is thus to the Scottish Universities and
the Dissenting Academies that we look for educational innovations
and the establishment of English as an academic study in the
eighteenth and nineteenth centuries.

The Dissenting Academies

The Dissenting Academies, in contrast to Oxford and Cambridge, were innovative and strong during the eighteenth century.
They are often credited with being the real originators of English
studies.[22] Thomas P. Miller states that as early as the last quarter of
the seventeenth century, English composition and literature were
being taught in the Dissenting Academies to college-age students in
"a systematic and concerted way" but adds that "contemporary
scholars may be hesitant to accept a group of Presbyterian divines
teaching in their homes as the first professors of English."[23] They
owed their existence to the 1662 renewal of the Act of Uniformity,
originally passed in 1559, by which all schoolmasters and students
were required to take the oath of conformity and to renounce the
Scottish covenant. As a result, on August 24 of that year, nearly
2,000 rectors and vicars resigned.[24] The early Academies were
illegal, but after the Act of Toleration in 1689, the English
grammar schools and high schools were opened to all comers,

---

[21]Barnard, 123.
[22]Miller and Alan Hollingsworth, "Beyond Literacy," in *Bulletin of the Association
of Departments of English* (May 1973).
[23]Miller, 11.
[24]McLachlin, 1.

though the universities still maintained their religious restrictions. The Academies filled the gap by offering an education equivalent to that of the English Universities. It was at these academies that English composition and literature were first taught in England. Founded by some of the finest scholars of the time, often educated on the continent and in Scotland, they brought a seriousness to these schools lacking at Cambridge and Oxford.[25] Originally, the Academies were designed for the sole purpose of educating ministers. In the eighteenth century, however, they broadened their scope and took on a practical and utilitarian purpose. They turned to "English study as a means of economic advancement and political reform."[26] Since these academies had been founded for training ministers, elocution was regularly stressed.

The nonconformist Academies were small and their staffs were limited, but there were many of them. Consequently, students were in the habit of moving from one school to another since "what could not profitably be learnt at one academy might be acquired at another." Herbert McLachlin cites the case of one student who attended five Academies and studied under five tutors.[27] The Academies were academically superior to Oxford and Cambridge and their curricula much stricter. Terms were longer and vacations were shorter. "Work often began before breakfast, for lectures at six or seven in the morning were by no means uncommon, and the evening studies were carefully prescribed."[28]

As in the Scottish Universities, the students were young, sometimes starting their studies as early as age 14 or 15 since their preparatory education was limited. Freed from religious restrictions, these institutions opened their doors to the brightest and best of eighteenth-century British youth, turning out a generation of brilliant men of letters as well as an avid reading public.

Irish and Welsh students were not so fortunate and had few options open to them. In the eighteenth and early nineteenth century, educational institutions including universities were primarily regional; Wales had few grammar schools and no Universities,

---

[25]Miller, 27.
[26]Ibid., 10.
[27]McLachlin, 23-24.
[28]Ibid., 25.

while Ireland with its largely Catholic population fared little better. Upper class Catholics could afford tutors and travel to continental universities, but the middle and lower classes often had no formal education. Irish protestants, such as Jonathan Swift, fared better gaining an education through the Academies.

The Scottish Universities

The Scottish philosophy of education was different from the English and Irish in that it was more democratic and contained few religious restrictions for admission or degrees. Michael Hans gives statistical evidence that the University of Dublin was as aristocratic as Oxford and Cambridge during the nineteenth century.[29] It is mainly in the Scottish universities that students from the families of merchants, farmers, and factory and land workers are found. In the north, education was considered a public and state responsibility in addition to an individual/voluntary one. The Scots felt strongly that basic education should be available to all and that the talented student should have access to higher education.[30] (These deeply held beliefs were very much like the ones held by leaders in the United States during the same period.) During the eighteenth century, their universities attracted students not only from the surrounding regions but also from England and the continent. Edinburgh University's well-known medical school attracted students from America as well.

Before the fifteenth century, Scottish students went to Oxford, but nearly four times as many went to the continent, especially to Paris and Bologna. Consequently when the Scottish Universities of Glasgow, St. Andrews, and Aberdeen were founded in the fifteenth century, they were modeled on the continental rather than the English pattern, a fundamental difference that became particularly important during the eighteenth century. While Oxford and Cambridge were notoriously aristocratic, the Scottish Universities retained their more broadly democratic flavor and their philosoph-

---

[29]Hans, 31.
[30]Myers, 80.

ically based education.[31]

The Scottish Universities offered a general education, characterized by the regent system where a single professor stayed with one
group of students during their entire program. He was expected to
teach all of the subjects in the arts curriculum: Latin, Greek,
Mathematics, Chemistry, Natural Philosophy, and, in the final year,
Logic, Moral Philosophy, and Rhetoric. Practice in composition —
Latin composition — came under the regent's purview. Regenting
was abolished at Edinburgh in 1708, at Glasgow in 1727, and at
St. Andrews in 1747. It persisted in King's College in Aberdeen
until 1798 because of the influence of Thomas Reid. Even after the
establishment of a number of professorships, the philosophy of
regenting persisted and the holders of these chairs moved quite
easily from one course to another, often presenting the same set of
lectures. After 1760 "good theologians and classical scholars were
appointed to scientific chairs as a means of reward," and often
professors "shifted from one chair to another on seniority rather
than qualifications."[32] The sinecure appointments were held for life
and housing was furnished. The students did not seem to suffer,
however, since ordinarily such professors had quite able assistant
lecturers who conducted their classes, lectured for them, and
customarily took over their chairs at their deaths.

During both the eighteenth and nineteenth centuries, the
Scottish Universities and the Dissenting Academies were distinguished by able professors who greatly influenced the direction of
English studies in both Britain and America in the nineteenth and
twentieth centuries. Such men wrote widely themselves in the
journals of the day and were innovators in other fields besides
philosophy and rhetoric. Adam Smith is better known today for
his *Wealth of Nations* (1776) than for his course in rhetoric, and
Joseph Priestley for his discovery of oxygen. Their textbooks, often
in the form of published lectures, were widely used on both sides
of the Atlantic. The importance of Campbell, Blair, and Whateley

---

[31]George Elder Davie, *The Democratic Intellect: Scotland and Her Universities in
the Nineteenth Century* (Edinburgh: Edinburgh University Press, 1961).

[32]Hans, 52.

in the eighteenth century has been well-documented.[33] The nine-teenth century included three less well-known but equally influential educators: Edward Edmonstone Aytoun at Edinburgh, Alexander Bain at Aberdeen, and George Jardine at Glasgow. These three men had a profound effect on the future of English studies and writing instruction.

Edward Edmonstone Aytoun held the chair of Rhetoric and Belles Lettres at Edinburgh from 1845 to 1865. He did not believe in instruction in formal rhetoric. "I believe the ancient systems to be unsuited to the circumstances of our time" (NLS MS 4913, fol. 29v).[34] During his tenure of the chair the title was altered and at his request he became the Professor of English Language and Literature. In his course, Aytoun covered the principles of vernacular composition with an examination of style as exhibited by eminent English authors. He also covered the rules of spoken discourse and included a critical review of British literature and occasional lectures on ancient and medieval literature. In writing to a friend about his teaching, he complained that he had enough themes to read to "roast an ox," eloquent testimony to the fact that students did write and receive instruction in composition in his course.[35] But his course came to include more and more of the native literature—a trend that was popular with his students who paid fees directly to Aytoun for the course. Largely due to its popularity, the study of English literature became an important part of the curriculum. In 1861, a Royal Commission recommended that English be added to the curriculum of all four of the Scottish Universities, and since none of the other universities (Aberdeen, Glasgow, and St. Andrews) had such a course at the time,

---

[33]See James L. Golden and Edward P. J. Corbett, *The Rhetoric of Blair, Campbell, and Whately* (New York: Holt, Rinehart and Winston, Inc., 1968) and Wilbur Samuel Howell.

[34]Edward Edmonstone Aytoun's lectures in his own hand are contained in manuscripts 4897-4911 in the collection of the National Library of Scotland. These manuscripts attest to the fact that Aytoun was constantly changing and updating his lectures, a factor that has made their editing and publication a formidable task. It is evident from these manuscripts that he was a lively and informative lecturer. Eric Frykman's book (cited below) contains excerpts from Aytoun's lectures.

[35]Erik Frykman, *W. E. Aytoun, Pioneer Professor of English at Edinburgh*, ed. Frank Behre (Gothenburg Studies in English, No. 17, 1963).

instruction was assigned to the professor of logic. At the outset, "English" might well include English history and geography. At the time the concept of literature was broad enough to include historical and scientific essays as well as "works of the imagination."

Alexander Bain, professor of Logic and Rhetoric from 1860 to 1880 at the University of Aberdeen, influenced writing instruction in a different way. The description of his course from the 1864 Calendar demonstrates his emphasis: The Professor of Logic "has two classes, one in the English Language and Literature, and the other in logic." The class of English includes "the higher Elements of English Grammar; the Principles of Rhetoric, applied to English Composition, and some portion of the history of English Literature."[36] Drawing students from the northern districts, Bain faced problems different from those of his colleague at Edinburgh. The students who went to Aberdeen were in general younger, less well-prepared, with dialects marked by what were called "rusticisms." It became the perceived duty of the universities to teach such students how to read, write, and speak a cultivated English which, at the time, was the London received standard. Alexander Bain, coming from just such a Scottish background, took as his own the responsibility of educating these students from the northern provinces. He comes down to us a double personality: first, an immensely popular teacher in psychology and now recognized as one of the early leaders in that discipline, and second, as an immensely unpopular teacher in composition and rhetoric, which was largely grammar and composition. Many of the characteristics of early twentieth-century rhetoric can be traced directly to his influence. He is generally credited with originating the "modes of discourse" which he delineated as narration, description, exposition, argument and poetry. He also stressed the topic sentence and the "organic" paragraph. His textbook, *English Composition and Rhetoric,* went through six editions in ten years. He felt strongly that the way to good English, written and spoken, was primarily through a knowledge of grammar, which he conscientiously drilled into his students. Bain was teaching a basic English course to

---

[36]Alexander Bain, *English Composition and Rhetoric: A Manual* (London: Longmans, 1866), n.p.

students from the northern districts. His mode of teaching was as unpopular for his nineteenth-century students as his methods are with twentieth-century composition theorists.

Like Bain, George Jardine recognized the Scottish students as ones "who are not qualified, either in respect to age or previous acquirements,"[37] but he approached this lack in a very different way. His enlightened teaching methods in many ways prefigure modern composition's pedagogical methods. During his long tenure as Professor of Logic and Rhetoric at the University of Glasgow from 1774 to 1827, Jardine was deeply involved in the educational issues of the day, a strong champion of the Scottish system. While formerly education was exclusively preparation for church and state, he recognized that the Scottish Universities were designed for "young men destined to fill various and very different situations in life."[38] He understood that knowledge was not enough, however, and admonished his students that "a man may be capable of great reflections but if he cannot communicate it to others, it can be of but little use" (GUL Ms. Gen. 737, vol.2, 157).[39] His remarkably enlightened teaching methods are described in his book *Outlines of Philosophical Education Illustrated by the Method of Teaching the Logic Class in the University of Glasgow.* He urged peer evaluation, promoted writing as a way of learning, and made frequent sequenced writing assignments.[40]

These three men—Aytoun at Edinburgh, Bain at Aberdeen, and Jardine at Glasgow—shaped future instruction in writing at both British and American Universities.

----

[37]George Jardine, *Outlines of Philosophical Education Illustrated By the Method of Teaching Logic, or First Class of Philosophy in the University of Glasgow* (Glasgow: Printed by Andrew & James Duncan, Printers to the University, 1818), 427.

[38]Ibid., 31.

[39]Much of the material on the Scottish Universities is based on lecture notes taken by students, which are housed in the manuscript sections of the Scottish libraries. These notes are "dictates" and represent, in most cases, word for word representations of a professor's lectures. I have included further manuscript references within the text and used the following abbreviations: University of Edinburgh Library, EUL; Glasgow University Library, GUL; and National Library of Scotland, NLS.

[40]Winifred Bryan Horner, "Rhetoric in the Liberal Arts: Nineteenth-Century Universities" in *The Rhetorical Tradition and Modern Writing,* ed. James J. Murphy (New York: The Modern Language Association, 1982).

Women in the Universities

Another shaping factor in the British Universities of the eighteenth and nineteenth centuries was the gradual influx of women, first to instruction in the universities, then to examinations, and finally at the end of the period to degrees. The rise of the middle class gradually brought political and economic recognition to women. Middle class women have traditionally been the guardians of culture, a fact recognized by scholars from Cicero to the modern linguist William Labov, so it is not surprising that women made up a significant portion of the audience in the popular city lectures of the nineteenth century. English literature was accessible to them, but their interest in it did nothing to champion its cause as a legitimate academic discipline. As Jo McMurtry points out, "any field of endeavor which is associated with a lower status group is itself going to be assigned lower status." Thus, although they filled the lecture halls and classes as soon as they were admitted, "they became an implicit liability when it came to demonstrating how hard the subject was."[41]

Not all persons were unsympathetic to women's ability to pursue a university education. As early as the seventeenth century, Daniel Defoe decried the "barbarous custom of denying the advantages of Learning to Women":

> We reproach the Sex everyday with Folly and Impertinence, while I am confident, had they the advantages of Education equal to us, they wou'd be guilty of less than ourselves.[42]

Charles Kingsley, in his introductory lecture at Queen's College, states:

> God intended woman to look instinctively at the world. Would to God that she would teach us men to look at it thus likewise. Would to God that she would in these days claim and fulfil to the uttermost her vocation as the priestess of charity.[43]

---

[41]McMurtry, 13,

[42]Cited in D.P. Leinster-Mackay, *The Educational World of Daniel Defoe* (University of Virginia, 1981), 37.

[43]D.J. Palmer, *The Rise of English Studies: An Account of the Study of English Language and Literature from Its Origins to the Making of the Oxford English School* (London: Oxford University Press, 1965), 39.

It was not uncommon for women to attend the grammar schools of the eighteenth century. Traditionally, however, the purpose of secondary and higher education was to train persons for service in the church and state, and women had never been included in that group. Higher education gradually opened its doors to women in the latter part of the nineteenth century. In 1848-49 Queen's College and Bedford College for Women were founded in London, although examinations and degrees were still closed to them. In 1865 Cambridge, Edinburgh, and Durham opened their local examinations to women and the University of London followed in 1868. It wasn't until 1871, however, that a house of residence was opened for women at Cambridge, and, although in 1874 the University of Edinburgh issued a certificate for women, it was not until 1887 that Victoria University, formed from the union of the colleges at Manchester, Liverpool, and Leeds, admitted women to degrees. The four Scottish Universities followed suit in 1892 and the Federated University of Wales in 1893, but it was not until 1920 that Oxford admitted women students to full university status.

The University of London

Another important development in the nineteenth century, was the founding of the University of London and, toward the end of the century, the development of the many so-called "red-brick" universities where the education offered was practical and without religious constraints. The beginning was slow. A meeting called by the Lord Mayor of London resulted in the opening of University College in 1828. It was run by shareholders as a joint stock company and was to be "undenominational." Its great advantage was that it was inexpensive compared to Oxford and Cambridge, with fees of only 25 to 30 pounds per year.[44]

There were no tests and no theology within a curriculum that tended toward science and medicine and other modern studies. It was here that the first professorship of English literature in England was established. University College was referred to as

---

[44]Barnard, 87.

"that Godless institution on Gower street" by Arnold.[45] It had an uphill battle against the prevailing opinion that religion was an essential part of all education and that the ultimate purpose of education was moral and religious improvement. As a consequence King's College was founded in 1831 with a curriculum based more on religion. Neither college was allowed to grant degrees, largely because of opposition from Oxford and Cambridge. In 1836, the University of London was chartered to grant degrees and students from King's College and University College could be admitted as candidates. After this date the University of London became an examining body admitting all students to examinations without inquiring about their preparation.

It was from this beginning that the non-sectarian and non-residential colleges were founded during the second half of the nineteenth century as teaching rather than degree-granting colleges. These institutions furnished instruction, but were not allowed to grant degrees. The University of Manchester was founded in 1871, Liverpool University in 1881, Leeds in 1877, and Newcastle in 1871. The College of Aberystwyth in Wales was founded in 1872. All of these institutions evolved from colleges of various types, originally supported by funds from private individuals and business and civic institutions. At the beginning all of these institutions sent their students to examinations for degrees at the University of London, until finally they were allowed to grant degrees themselves. In 1898, the University of London was still the primary degree-granting institution but provision was finally made for internal instruction. All of these institutions emphasized a departure from a purely classical education and counted proficiency in writing English as a necessary component of a student's education.

METHODS OF WRITING INSTRUCTION

It is difficult to document the way writing was actually taught during this period, since much instruction was oral and since instruction in writing was a part of every course and considered the responsibility of every instructor. Ian Michael, in his study of

---

[45]Ibid., 84.

textbooks of the period, maintains that there is "less textbook evidence for the teaching of composition than for any other aspect of English."[46] Other sources are not much more productive. In this essay, I have drawn from textbooks, lectures, student notes of lectures, books on education, and university calendars for the nineteenth century. Such sources are not always reliable, because in many cases, they deal with what individuals felt ought to be done either by themselves or others and not with what was actually done in the classroom. Because of the wide practice of dictating lectures, student notes are more reliable than they might appear.

During the eighteenth and nineteenth centuries, the teaching of writing proceeded in a number of different ways and in a number of different courses. Most important, all teachers in the Scottish Universities and the Academies from grammar school on felt that writing proficiency was their responsibility. The separate composition course as we know it today is a twentieth-century, largely American, idea and had no place in the eighteenth- and nineteenth-century British curriculum.

Medieval pedagogy lasted well into the eighteenth and nineteenth centuries. The trivium of grammar, logic, and rhetoric provided solid training in communication skills during the early part of the eighteenth century. Memorization and modeling were common methods of improving students' writing, and instructors believed that to learn to read one had first to learn to spell and that the study of grammar was basic to writing instruction. But the grammar was the grammar of Latin since writing instruction was writing Latin. Throughout the period and well into the twentieth century, grammar and writing instruction are closely connected. As part of their instruction in Latin, however, students had been required to translate "into a good English stile,"[47] and as late as the end of the nineteenth century proficiency in English was still tested by translation from Latin. Whether it was in Latin or English or Latin *and* English, medieval exercises in grammar and translation were an integral part of writing instruction. A master at

---

[46]Ian Michael, *The Teaching of English from the Sixteenth Century to 1870* (London: Cambridge University Press, 1987), 315.
[47]Ibid., 274.

Eton shared the common view that the only way to improve a student's English was through translation, but, in 1867, he urged that French or another modern language be substituted for Latin.[48] As the study of modern languages came into the curriculum, it was considered a viable method of improving English.

What we would now call Basic English was an important part of writing instruction, especially in the Scottish Universities. While the English Universities were elitist and exclusive, the more democratic Scottish Universities during the eighteenth century and well into the nineteenth century were dealing with a different student population and therefore saw as an important part of their purview the need to eradicate provincialisms. Consequently, particularly in the Scottish schools but in the English ones as well, elocution gained importance in the curriculum. With their early emphasis on training ministers, the Dissenting Academies also stressed elocution.

Rhetoric took on a new form under the influence of the Scottish Common Sense Philosophy and classical rhetoric was delegated to that part of the course that dealt with oral delivery. Written and oral skills and Latin and English were taught side by side, instruction in one reinforcing instruction in the other. The master often read a letter aloud, and the student then transposed it from Latin to Latin, then translated it from Latin to English, and finally transposed it from English to English.[49] It wasn't until late in the nineteenth century that oral and written skills were separated into different courses and different departments.

Just as there was a close association between the teaching of Latin and English, between oral and written skills, there was also a close association between reading and writing and between literature and composition. At first at the Scottish Universities and later at the University of London, works of literature, both classical and English, were introduced into the rhetoric course as models for good oratory and writing. Literature was a sort of "window display, to be taken in snippets...as illustrations for rhetorical techniques."[50] There was no attempt to analyze or

---

[48]Ibid., 311.
[49]Ibid., 308.
[50]McMurtry, 122.

critique, but literature served rhetoric in a very real way since students were often required to imitate the models. As the examples were drawn more and more from English literature, interest shifted during the nineteenth century from rhetoric to an emphasis on the literature itself, especially evident in the courses of Aytoun. Whenever rhetoric and literature are taught together, literature wins out with both instructors and students, and the nineteenth century was no exception. Nevertheless, the early professors of literature considered writing instruction their responsibility. Even though English literature came to dominate the newly formed English departments, writing instruction was an important part of not only the literature course but of all courses in the Scottish Universities and the Dissenting Academies during this period in British education. With its philosophically-based curriculum, Scotland saw communication skills, both spoken and written, as central to the entire educational endeavor. The Dissenting Academies and the Scottish Universities were dedicated to teaching their aspiring ministers facility in the use of language — through the media of written and spoken Latin and English, while Oxford and Cambridge maintained their emphasis on the classics.

The Lecture System and Writing

During this period there were important differences between the English tutorial system and the lecture system of the Scottish Universities and the Academies. In the Scottish system the lectures were augmented by the catechetical system whereby the professor lectured for one hour a day and spent an additional one or two hours questioning the students over the material covered in the lecture and responding to student essays. The lecture system differed from instructor to instructor and McLachlan describes methods employed at various Academies:

> Some of the later tutors dictated word for word. Others like Doddridge and Priestley read their lectures and then handed over the MSS. to be copied by their pupils at leisure. Belsham spoke from brief hints and imperfect notes. Pye Smith provided pupils with an outline of his principal course. Many lectures were printed for the use of students, and one course given by Priestley at Hackney College and previously at Warrington was printed in

order to save the students the trouble of transcribing them.[51]

Aided by their small size and in contrast to the English Universities, the Dissenting Academies had a tradition of free discussion. They departed from the traditional lecture course, which in their case usually consisted of comment on one text, and fashioned their courses to suit their own and their students' needs.[52]

After the medieval fashion, students often used their class notes as their text. Textbooks were expensive and students were often poor. The eighteenth-century published lectures of Blair and Campbell served as textbooks for almost a hundred years in the United States—one of the important ways that Scottish education influenced American education. Few of the Dissenting Academies had libraries, and students who often could not afford textbooks used their professors' personal libraries instead, but professors in the Academies were underpaid so books of all kinds were scarce.

The custom of "dictates," where the professor spoke slowly enough so that the student could take down the lecture word for word, provided accurate textbooks for the student, but there were abuses. The student notes from David Masson's course, for example, do not vary over thirty years by more than an occasional word or two. Robert Schmitz tells the story of students who were following Masson's lecture from sets of previous years' notes. They objected to changes in the lectures and when Masson deviated from their copies, they would shuffle their feet in protest, whereupon Masson, rising, would remark: "Gentlemen..., as I have been in the habit of saying" and would return to his previous years' notes.[53] J.D. Comrie writes about the lectures delivered by the three Munros— father, son, and grandson—who held the Chair of Anatomy at the University of Edinburgh for 150 years. The grandson, Monro Tertius, who held the chair in the nineteenth century, customarily read from his grandfather's lectures written about a century before; and even the shower of peas with which the expectant students greeted his annual reference, "When I was a student at Leyden in

---

[51]McLachlin, 23.
[52]Smith, 263.
[53]Cited in Robert Morell Schmitz, *Hugh Blair* (Morningside Heights, NY: King's Crown Press, 1948), 67.

1719," failed to induce him to alter the dates.[54]

Some students developed a shorthand in which they took notes (EUL Ms. Gen. 49D), while others used phonetic spellings, a popular movement in the nineteenth century (EUL Ms. Gen. 700). Professor Jardine at Glasgow objected to this procedure since the student "is constantly occupied with the mechanical operation of transferring the words of the lecture into his note-book." Consequently his mind is not engaged and "when he leaves college, accordingly, his port-folio, and not his memory, contains the chief part of the instruction which he carries away." He suggested instead that after leaving the classroom, students immediately review the lecture in their minds and "commit to writing in their own composition, whatever they judge to be of leading importance."[55] In this way, he asserts:

> The students have to remember,— to select and arrange the materials furnished to them, and to express, on the spur of the occasion, their ideas in plain and perspicuous language.[56]

This appears in fact to be the manner in which two students collaborated in taking the only set of notes that we have of Adam Smith's lectures on rhetoric.[57] Students often embellished their notes with drawings and bits of humor; one set contains scenes from Glasgow in the margins and a reference to Aristotle as the "Rev. J.G. Aristotle" (GUL BC 28-H.3.). In a moral philosophy course, one student complained that the professor was dictating "fast enough in all conscience to keep 20 persons writing" and that he "does not feel very morally philosophical" (EUL Ms. Gen. 850).

The reader of these notes is inclined to feel sympathy for these students, but the value in ridding students of their "Scottish rusticisms" and in training them in the mechanics of a written standard cannot be overestimated, and certainly Jardine's suggestion of summarizing the lectures in a written composition proved invaluable as a productive exercise in selecting and organizing a

---

[54]Comrie, 1927.

[55]Jardine, 278.

[56]Ibid., 289.

[57]J.C. Bryce, "Introduction" to *Adam Smith Lectures on Rhetoric and Belles Lettres,* gen. ed. A.S. Skinner (Indianapolis: Liberty Classics, 1985), 4.

body of information. These lectures with their various systems of notetaking were obviously used to supplement textbooks and instruction in writing. They were considered especially helpful for the student who was trying to eradicate traces of a northern dialect. In addition to their note taking, whatever form it might have taken, Scottish University students often continued with their preparatory school exercises, inherited from the medieval universities and the Latin tradition. While the English Universities restricted higher education to a small percentage of the population, Scotland still opened its doors to all able students who sought an education. Consequently, university courses were designed to supplement their preparatory training and to fill in deficiencies.

Grammar and Writing

Grammar was stressed at all levels and was considered a necessary part of instruction in composition, both Latin and English. Based on the assumption that there was a universal grammar common to all languages the Latin system was adapted without change to English. In the grammar schools, the students were often expected to know their grammar books by heart. Memorization of books and literary passages was a common practice even at the university level, since students were expected to have patterns of good writing in their heads. In addition, parsing and the correction of "false English" were widely used. Students were expected to correct sentences that had errors of spelling, syntax, or punctuation and give the rule that had been broken. The master then corrected the exercises orally, and returned them to the students who, with the help of their classmates, made their own corrections in writing. Since paper was expensive, students often wrote their first versions on slates and then copied the corrected versions into their notebooks.[58]

Grammar exercises associated with the old rhetoric were widely used by students at all levels: imitation; varying, which involved changing a sentence into all of its possible forms; paraphrasing; and prosing, turning verse into prose. Transposition, a common exercise, was "the placing of Words out of their natural

---

[58]Michael, 327.

Order, to render the Sound of them more agreeable to the Ear."[59]
Elliptical exercises were sentences with omitted words which the
student was expected to supply. Many of these exercises, closely
associated with the old rhetoric, began to die out by the nineteenth
century, but translation, from Latin to "correct English" and later
from a modern foreign language, continued to be used well into
the twentieth century.

Examinations and Themes

The catechetical system, whereby students were quizzed on the
material in the lecture, was, initially, largely oral. Toward the
middle of the nineteenth century the written examination began to
replace the oral question and answer format. In the description of
his course on Moral Philosophy, Professor Calderwood at the
University of Edinburgh asserts that class time is devoted "partly
to examinations, written and oral." He adds that "subjects are also
prescribed for elaborate Essays, as well as for briefer occasional
exercises" (EUL Calendar 1859-60). In the same calendar, Fraser,
professor of logic and metaphysics, wrote that class hours are
devoted to lectures and

> also to a Discipline, by means of Conversations, short Exercises,
> and Essays, meant to train the members to logical habits and a
> reflective life. General Examinations, at which answers are
> returned in writing to questions proposed by the Professor, are
> held at intervals in the course of the Session.[60]

In general the practice of writing instruction followed the
recommendation of the *1831 Report of the Royal Commission:* "In
addition to Examinations, Exercises and Essays should be required
from all the regular Students in each class, and ought to be
criticized by the professor."[61] Consequently, instruction in writing
was never confined to any single course.

Professor Scott, in giving evidence before that commission in
1827, describes the manner in which he conducted his class in

---

[59]Cited in Michael, 283.
[60]Ibid.
[61]*Royal Commission,* 35.

moral philosophy which met for two and a half hours during the day. The first half hour is spent in oral examination of the preceding day's lecture "with the students reading aloud their written answers to questions assigned the day before." He adds that a considerable part of the afternoon hour is spent "in the practice of composition" and that subjects are prescribed "and a time fixed, before which the essays must be left by the authors at the Professor's house."[62]

George Jardine at Glasgow in his 1825 *Outlines of a Philosophical Education* gives his procedure for assigning themes. The themes should be "prescribed frequently and regularly" and the subjects should be "numerous and various." In a four-ordered sequence, he describes his assignments. In the first order, during the first two months, there is a theme almost every day, "the subject proposed in the form of a question." The second order uses analysis and classification: "How may books in a library be arranged?" The third order of themes suggests a proposition that the student is to prove: "The hand of the diligent maketh rich," "Do holidays promote study?" or "Personal talents and virtues are the noblest acquisition." The fourth and final order engages the student "in the higher processes of investigation," which "may be said to constitute the envied endowment of genius."[63]

Responses to Writing

Edinburgh University Library has in its manuscript library a collection of twelve essays written by John Dick Peddies in 1844-45 in William Spalding's course in Rhetoric and Belles Letters (EUL Ms. Gen. 769D). Written in his last year at the university, these themes vary in length from 12 to 42 pages covering such subjects as "Remarks on Harris' Treatise on Music, Painting, and Poetry," and "Remarks on different points in the Association Theory of Beauty." Professor Spalding's comments are not lengthy and are generally complimentary and it may be assumed that they were augmented by oral comments. He corrects some errors like

---

[62]*Royal Commission,* 40.
[63]Jardine, 291-360.

agreement and the use of "will" for shall." The students' misspellings of *principle* for *principal* and *their* for *there* seem very much like those of the twentieth-century student. In notes from David Masson's class in 1881, the student jots down the professor's assignment and instructions on the last page of volume 4: "Attend to neatness of form, expression and pointing, as well as the matter" (EUL Ms. DK. 4.28-30).

Throughout the eighteenth and nineteenth century, with few exceptions, responding to student writing was a matter of correction rather than appraisal, and more often than not it was oral. In the lower schools it was largely correction of mechanical errors. Michael describes John Walker's "Hints for correcting and improving juvenile composition":

> The pupil writes a first draft on loose paper. Next day he copies it, with amendments, onto the lefthand page of an exercise book. He reads the theme, without interruption, to the teacher, who then takes it sentence by sentence and shows the pupil 'where he has erred, either in the thought, the structure of the sentence, the grammar of it, or the choice of words.'[64]

The pupil then makes a fair copy on the righthand page of his exercise book. Michael comments that Walker "understandably advises that classes for composition should be as small as possible."[65]

Often students read their work aloud and it was criticized publicly either by the professor or their classmates or both. In describing his course to the Royal Commission, Professor Robert Scott in 1831 describes such a method:

> After being examined in private by the Professor, and the inaccuracies, whether of thought or composition, carefully marked, they are returned to the authors, by whom they are read publicly in the class; their inaccuracies are pointed out, and commented on, and an opinion as to their merits or defects publicly expressed.[66]

Professor Scott adds that the first set of essays "is generally read by the Professor, without mentioning the names of the authors...to

---

[64]Cited in Michael, 222.
[65]Ibid.
[66]*Royal Commission,* 40.

save the feelings of individuals."[67]

Professor Jardine's method of responding to themes, outlined in a chapter titled "On the Method of Determining the Merits of the Themes," sounds remarkably modern. Faced with a class of nearly 200 students he contends that "experience and habit enable the teacher to execute this work more expeditiously than might at first be believed."[68] He urges that "the professor must touch their [students'] failings with a gentle hand."[69] He further suggests for large classes the use of "examinators," ten or twelve students from the class who read other students' written work with the professor selecting works that "abound with defects" for his own inspection, which he returns with remarks "most likely to encourage, and to direct future efforts."[70]

CONCLUSION

In summary, it is evident that at the eighteenth- and nineteenth-century Scottish Universities and at the Academies writing was taught by precept reinforced by intensive practice. The eighteenth-century published lectures, so full of precepts, might raise doubts on this issue, but there is ample evidence that students wrote frequently in all of their courses and at all levels. In the grammar and high schools, in addition to exercises, students wrote fables and stories and composed verse. At the university level, the students wrote essays on a variety of subjects in addition to summaries and responses to the lectures. George Davie gives the subjects of the essays of Professor Stevenson who taught Logic at Edinburgh from 1730 to 1772: "Of the Nature and Origin of Poetry," "Of Spartan Education," "Of the Differences between mathematical reasoning and philosophy."[71] The curriculum for the Arts program proposed by the Royal Commission of 1831 recommended that during the third and fourth years classes meet two hours each day—the first hour for lecturing and a second

---

[67]Ibid.
[68]Jardine, 364.
[69]Ibid., 365.
[70]Ibid., 371.
[71]Davie, 18.

hour for "Examination, Exercises, Themes, and Composition."[72]
This pattern was widely adopted in the Scottish Universities with
some professors, such as Jardine at Glasgow, adding an additional
hour "for the purpose of examining them on the subjects discussed
in the lecture, and of prescribing written exercises, on topics more
or less connected with these subjects."[73] Precept guided practice; it
did not preclude intense practice in the form of examinations,
exercises, and essays. Such instruction was never isolated in a
single course, but was considered a part of learning in any subject.
Instruction in writing and speech continued side by side within the
same courses; professors responded to essays and themes in much
the way that professors do today. Faced with large classes in
Scotland, they looked for new ways to lighten the load, as
professors do today. Since Oxford and Cambridge conserved the
classical tradition until nearly the end of the nineteenth century, it
is finally to the red-brick universities, to the Dissenting Academies,
and particularly to the Scottish Universities that we must look for
the roots of the modern tradition in English studies. Alexander
Bain of Aberdeen brought to writing instruction some of the
methods still used by instructors of basic writing. Edward Edmonstone Aytoun, through the popularity of his lectures, brought
English literature into the university. Finally, George Jardine
prefigured many of the reforms embraced in the last twenty years
in composition theory. There is abundant evidence that writing
instruction, whether in Latin or English, whether oral or written,
was an important part of education at all levels in the Britain of
the eighteenth and nineteenth centuries.

---

[72]*Royal Commission,* D 3.
[73]Jardine, 281.

CHAPTER SIX

FROM RHETORIC TO COMPOSITION: THE TEACHING OF WRITING IN AMERICA TO 1900

S. MICHAEL HALLORAN

Early in the seventeenth century, the Virginia Company of London commissioned a Puritan minister and schoolmaster named John Brinsley to develop a plan for a grammar school and college to be established in the new colony of Virginia. The project was halted by an Indian massacre, but not before Brinsley had published *A Consolation for Our Grammar Schools* (1662), a work that can serve as a guide to some important assumptions, purposes, and practices that would govern education in the New World well into the eighteenth century. In the book's elaborated title and dedicatory letter, Brinsley emphasizes the improvement of people in such "ruder" lands as Ireland, Wales, and Virginia through the establishment of "pure" English and the Christian religion. Among specific educational practices, Brinsley gives special emphasis to "grammatical translation," a refinement of the double translation method described by Roger Ascham in *The Schoolmaster,* a book he recommends highly. Among the 34 specific purposes Brinsley sets for the grammar school, here are a few that give a sense of how the teaching of "writing" was treated in the curriculum:

1. To teach scholars how to be able to read well, and write true orthographie in a short time.
4. In the severall Fourmes and Authors to construe truly, and in proprietie of words and sense, and also in pure phrase; to parse of themselves, and to give a right reason of everie word, why it must be so and not otherwise; and to deliver the English of the Lectures perfectly out of the Latine.

5. Out of an English Grammaticall translation of their Authors, to make and to construe anie part of the Latine which they have learned, or do presently learne; to prove that it must be so, and so to reade the Latine out of the English, first in the plaine Grammaticall order; after as the words are placed in the Author, or in other good composition. Also to parse in Latine, looking onely upon the translation; and in all their Poets which they so learne: to do all this without booke, which is farre the surest, viz. to repeate, construe, and parse with their booke under their arme.
20. To write Theames full of good matter, in pure Latin and with judgement, and how to invent matter of themselves.
22. So to imitate and expresse Ovid or Virgil, as you shall hardly discerne, unlesse you know the places, whether the verses be the Authors or the Scholars: and to write verses extempore of any ordinarie theame.
23. To translate forth of English or Latin into Greeke. Also to write theames or verses in Greeke.
23. To come to that facilitie and ripenesse, as not onely to translate leisurely and with some meditation, both into English and Latin... but more also, to reade anie easie Author forth of Latin into English, and out of English to reade it into Latin againe, as Corderiius, Terence, Tullies Offices, etc. To do this in Authors and places which they are not acquainted with, and almost as fast as they are able to reade the Author alone.
33. To grow in our owne English tongue, according to their ages, and growth in other learning: to utter their minds in the same both in propriety, and purity; and so to be fitted for divinity, law, or what other calling or faculty soever they shall be after employed in.[1]

What these purposes show is that the ability to write *in English* was clearly and consistently related to the ability to read and write *in the classical languages*—indeed, was subordinated to it. Growth in "our owne English tongue" was assumed to follow as a consequence of growth in the ability to read, analyze, and write Latin and Greek, and to a lesser degree Hebrew. (Among the numbered purposes not quoted here are a few dealing with Hebrew.) "Purity" in English was to be attained through the practice of emulating

---

[1]John Brinsley, *A Consolation for Our Grammar Schools* (London: Printed by Richard Field for Thomas Mann, 1622; New York: Scholars' Facsimilies & Reprints, 1943). Brinsley had previously written the *Ludus Literarius* referred to by Don Abbott in chapter four of this book.

classical models and internalizing the grammatical and rhetorical forms of the classical languages.

A less obvious but equally important point is that texts by both canonical authors and students were meant to be read aloud. The primary medium of instruction was speech, and the translation, imitation, or composition a student wrote, whether in English or in one of the classical tongues, was understood as a script for oral performance. This was so in part because the work for which students were assumed to be preparing would in most cases entail roughly the same sort of scripted oral performance; note that Brinsley mentions divinity and law, professions in which speech-making is crucial even today, as the paradigm callings in the paragraph numbered 33 above. While seventeenth century culture was highly literate, it still relied heavily on oral communication for day-to-day business and used writing and print as means of scripting and recording oral communication. Paper was relatively expensive, and would continue to be for at least two centuries. Books were likewise scarce and expensive. To reserve a written or printed text for a single, private reader was a considerable extravagance, so texts were commonly shared by the expedient of reading aloud.

The school and college Brinsley planned were never established, but his views were typical of English education in the early seventeenth century. Thus, when schools and colleges were established in the American colonies, they followed a pattern articulated in Brinsley's *Consolation.* Writing English was closely connected with study of the classical languages, and with oral performance. Translation, imitation of models, reading aloud, copying dictated material and printed texts, and recitation both catechetical and disputational were standard classroom activities. The primacy of the classical languages is ironically suggested by the fact that when Harvard students formed their first extracurricular literary and debate society near the end of the second decade of the eighteenth century, they established a rule *against* the use of Latin.[2] Such literary and debate societies would eventually play a role in supporting a curriculum of oratorical and literary studies in English. But for more than a century after the founding of the first

---

[2]David Potter, "The Literary Society," in Karl R. Wallace (ed.), *History of Speech Education in America: Background Studies* (New York: Appleton, 1954), 238-58.

American college, students learned to write English through learning to write and speak the classical languages. The methods of instruction had been in use since classical times (when the classical languages were vernacular), and have been described in previous chapters of this book.[3]

The shift from this classical, oratorical pedagogy to the vernacular, compositional writing pedagogy of the twentieth century took place in two steps. First, English replaced Latin as the primary medium of instruction, and writing pure and eloquent English consequently became an immediate goal of instruction rather than something supposed to happen as a consequence of work on the classical languages. Second, writing meant for silent reading only, and not as a script for oral performance, became more and more common in the schools (as in the society beyond), eventually becoming the primary focus of rhetorical instruction.

While the move from classical to vernacular can be placed roughly in the eighteenth century, and the move from oral scripting to silent prose in the nineteenth, it would nonetheless be a considerable oversimplification to characterize these as two discrete steps completed at fixed dates in the past. Writing in English was well established in American schools by the closing decades of the eighteenth century, yet as recently as the 1930s Bliss Perry could offer the opinion that the best way to learn to write English is to study the classical languages.[4] And while "composition," in the sense of a course in the writing of silent prose, was probably the sole common denominator in American colleges by the close of the nineteenth century, reading papers aloud has always been a more or less commonly used pedagogical practice, more common now than at the end of the nineteenth century, as it happens. And while they are overshadowed by courses in "English composition," meaning the writing of silent prose, courses in formal speech continue to flourish in many colleges today, particularly in the midwest.

The movements from classical to vernacular and from scripted

---

[3]For an excellent discussion of writing instruction in this period, see Porter Gale Perrin, "The Teaching of Rhetoric in the American Colleges before 1750," diss., The University of Chicago, 1936.

[4]Bliss Perry, *And Gladly Teach: Reminiscences* (Boston: Houghton Mifflin, 1935), 254-55.

speech to silent prose are nonetheless both sufficiently distinct in historical fact and sufficiently distinguishable in concept to be useful in organizing the history of writing instruction in America. In the remainder of this chapter, I will therefore consider first the oral-vernacular curriculum of the late eighteenth and early nineteenth centuries, then the development of a "compositional" curriculum, meaning a curriculum emphasizing the writing of prose meant for silent reading, in the nineteenth century. What I have to say throughout should be regarded as provisional. History is of course always subject to revision, since it is always written from the perspective of a particular moment in history. But in this case the provisionality of the story goes beyond the simple fact of being rooted in a historical perspective. What primary materials exist — textbooks, student manuscripts, diaries, lecture notes, college calendars and catalogs — have not been given the attention they deserve. Writing has been a virtually invisible topic in the material history of modern culture, and the teaching of writing has been similarly neglected in the history of education. Much scholarship remains to be done before we can be confident of the story of writing instruction in America.

THE ORAL-VERNACULAR CURRICULUM

During the course of the eighteenth century, the writing of formal English gradually established itself as a primary concern in American colleges. In the period immediately preceding the Revolution and extending into the early decades of the nineteenth century, writing instruction was governed by assumptions and methods drawn from the system of classical rhetoric. Oratory of the deliberative, forensic, and ceremonial kinds was assumed to be the most important mode of discourse. Students learned the conceptual material, the techne or "art" of rhetoric by transcribing dictated lectures and engaging in catechetical or disputational recitations, though topical invention and deductive argument were deemphasized, under the influence of the new empirical philosophy.[5]

The two most characteristic surviving examples of the art as

---

[5]Wilbur Samuel Howell, *Eighteenth-Century British Logic and Rhetoric* (Princeton, N.J.: Princeton University Press, 1971), 441-45 and passim.

taught in this period are John Witherspoon, "Lectures on Eloquence" and "Lectures on Moral Philosophy" (1802) and John
Quincy Adams, *Lectures on Rhetoric and Oratory* (1810).[6] Also
significant were John Ward's *A System of Oratory* (1759) and
Hugh Blair's *Lectures on Rhetoric and Belles Lettres* (1783).[7]
Ward's *System* was taught at Harvard and used there to draw the
statutes for the Boylston Professorship of Rhetoric and Oratory,
and by this means became a model for Adams' *Lectures*.[8] Blair's
Lectures eventually became the most widely used rhetoric text in
America, and I shall have more to say of its significance below.
Witherspoon's lectures were read at Princeton, where he served as
president from 1768 until his death in 1794. Adams presented his
lectures as the first Boylston Professor of Rhetoric and Oratory at
Harvard from 1805 to 1809. I call Witherspoon and Blair the two
most characteristic American rhetorics of the late eighteenth and
early nineteenth centuries because they represent deliberate efforts
to appropriate classical rhetoric for use in America. Ward and
Blair were British writers whose works happened to be used here.[9]

In addition to learning the art (or what we would call the

---

[6]Witherspoon's Lectures were first published in *The Works of the Rev. John
Witherspoon, D.D. L.L.D. Late President of the College at Princeton, New Jersey* III
(Philadelphia: William W. Woodward, 1802), 367-592; they were also published
separately under the title *Lectures on Eloquence and Moral Philosophy* (Philadelphia:
Woodward, 1810). A modern edition is forthcoming from Southern Illinois University
Press, under the editorship of Thomas Miller. For Adams lectures see John Quincy
Adams, *Lectures on Rhetoric and Oratory* (Cambridge, Mass.: Hilliard and Metcalf, 1810;
reprint New York: Russell & Russell, 1962).

[7]John Ward, *A System of Oratory* (London: printed for John Ward in Cornhill,
1759; fascimile reprint, Hildesheim & New York: Georg Olms Verlag, 1969). Hugh Blair,
Lectures on Rhetoric and Belles Lettres (London and Edinburgh: Strahan & Cadell and
Creech, 1783; Philadelphia: Robert Aitken, 1784; also numerous American editions
through the nineteenth century; and the Landmarks in Rhetoric and Public Address
edition ed. by Harold F. Harding, Carbondale: Southern Illinois University Press).

[8]Ronald F. Reid, "The Boylston Professorship of Rhetoric and Oratory, 1806-1904:
a Case Study in Changing Concepts of Rhetoric and Pedagogy," *Quarterly Journal of
Speech* 45 (Oct. 1959), 241.

[9]Warren Guthrie's series of articles under the collective title "The Development of
Rhetorical Theory in America" remains dependable as a bibliographical guide to the
rhetorical works used in America during the period through 1850. See *Speech
Monographs* 13 (1946), 14-22; 14 (1947), 38-54; 15 (1948), 61-71; 16 (1949), 98-113;
18 (1951), 17-30.

theory) of rhetoric, students wrote "compositions" of various kinds, including orations that were supposed to exhibit the full range of techniques described by the theory. Witherspoon prescribed the following sequence of compositional exercises, in ascending order of complexity: translation, narration, imitation of particular passages, description, argumentation, persuasion. (487) Note that his sequence *begins* with "translation." While he is directly concerned with teaching students to be eloquent in the vernacular (as teachers of the early part of the eighteenth century were not), he nonetheless assumes that students know the classical languages and that their command of formally composed English will be built upon that knowledge. In this he is in agreement with Quintilian, who prescribed translation as one means of making Roman students eloquent in Latin. Witherspoon also included the study of English grammar in the Princeton curriculum — an important innovation for the time — and took the relatively modern and non-prescriptive view that the grammar of a language is "fixed" by its best writers. Among models of English prose, he particularly recommends Addison, Swift, and Pope. He mentions Samuel Johnson only as a negative example, but recommends Shakespeare, Hume, Tillotson, Hervey's *Meditations,* and Mrs. Rowe's and Lady Mary W. Montague's Letters as stylistic models. He especially recommends imitation as a compositional exercise, but cautions against devoting too much time to the imitation of any one author.

In practice, the writing exercises done at Princeton during the period of Witherspoon's presidency seem to have fallen into two broad categories: compositions and orations. The former were relatively brief pieces done on the short notice of no more than a few days for presentation in a recitation period, during which the class tutor and sometimes the other students would offer critical comments. A student diary from 1786 reveals that writing "compositions" (which category probably included Witherspoon's translation, narration, imitation, and description) did not inspire much enthusiasm. The student diarist (identified in the Princeton Library catalogue, but not the diary itself, as John Rhea Smith) procrastinates and dithers over these assignments and not infrequently completes them after the due date. Yet this same student exhibits considerable enthusiasm and diligence in working on "orations." In an entry for Jan. 6, he records writing out an

oration due to be presented one week later, then going to bed
without having begun to write a composition due the next day.[10]
"Smith" is habitually tardy and uninterested when working on
compositions, yet seeks out opportunities to practice his orations
before tutors and fellow students. He worries when his good coat
may not be back from the tailor in time for his speech and is
jubilant when told that he has spoken much better than before.
(entry dated March 17). The difference may have been a matter of
audience, and may have been peculiar to this student. The primary
audience for his compositions was a class presided over by a tutor
named Greene (most likely Ashbel Greene, later president of
Princeton) for whom "Smith" obviously has neither respect nor
affection. The audience for orations was the entire college
assembled in the main hall.

In keeping with the emphasis of the current rhetorical theory
on civic life, the topics on which students wrote tended to be
political. Here is a list of some questions disputed at Harvard
College commencements in the decades leading to the Revolution,
illustrating the increasing focus on contemporary political affairs:

> Is unlimited obedience to rulers taught by Christ and his
> apostles? (1729)
> Is the voice of the people the voice of God? (1733)
> Is it lawful to resist the Supreme Magistrate, if the Common-
> wealth cannot otherwise be preserved? (1743)
> Does Civil Government originate from compact? (1743, 1747,
> 1761, and 1762)
> Is civil government absolutely necessary for men? (1758)
> Is an absolute and arbitrary monarchy contrary to right reason?
> (1759)
> Can the new prohibitary duties, which make it useless for the
> people to engage in commerce, be evaded by them as faithful
> subjects? (1765)
> Is a just government the only stable foundation of public peace?
> (1769)
> Are the people the sole judges of their rights and liberties?
> (1769)

---

[10][John Rhea Smith], *A Journal at Nassau Hall* photostatic copy of an unpublished
manuscript dated 1786, held in the Princeton University Library.

Is a government tyrannical in which the rulers consult their own
interest more than that of their subjects? (1770)
Is a government despotic in which the people have no check on
the legislative power? (1770)[11]

The period spanned by this list coincides with the shift at
Harvard from Latin to English as the primary focus of rhetorical
instruction. When they were first introduced, the English language
disputations and orations were assigned to the duller students, but
starting in the 1740's they were more and more often assigned to the
brighter ones. The question listed above for 1743 was argued in the
affirmative by Samuel Adams, that listed for 1758 by John Adams.

The appendix to this chapter illustrates the kind of speech a
student of the time would have composed in responding to such a
question. This one was delivered at the commencement of
Princeton (then called the College of New Jersey) in 1772 by
Philip Vickers Fithian, defending the thesis that "Political jealousy
is a laudable passion." Among other purposes, this example may
serve as evidence against the golden age myth, according to which
students of times past were uniformly better than those of today (a
myth which seems popular in an endless succession of todays).
This being a commencement oration, we can assume that Fithian
lavished his best efforts on it, yet it is somewhat murky in thought,
flat and pedantic in style, erratic in punctuation and other
mechanical elements. But for all its flaws, this oration has in it a
detectable hint of the persuasive logic that would characterize the
writings of Fithian's contemporary at Princeton, James Madison
(class of 1771), and of many others who studied the neo-classical
rhetoric taught during this period. It illustrates the traditional
rhetorical form characteristic of most of the student writing done
in this period, and likewise the concern with civic problems.

In addition to their assigned work, students spent considerable
effort on composing orations and debates for the student literary
societies. Originating with the Spy Club founded at Harvard in
1719, the movement for literary and debate societies gathered
momentum quickly around mid-century. By the closing decades,

---

[11]Samuel Eliot Morison, *Three Centuries of Harvard 1636-1936* (Cambridge:
Harvard University Press, 1936), 90-91.

the typical college had at least two, and rivalry between them was
a powerful motive for hard work on writing.[12] The Princeton
diarist "Smith" writes with obvious enthusiasm of his own
activities with the Cliosophic Society, including an episode in
which they discover a draft copy of a speech by a member of the
rival Whigs. There is much mirth over its being "shockingly spelt
& poorly written," and the Cliosophics use it to taunt and tease
the Whigs. (entries dated March 14-17) Anne Ruggles Gere
correctly notes that activities of the societies included a great deal
of what we now call "peer response": students would critique each
others' work within the society in preparation for a contest or
other public performance, then receive criticism of their public
performance from the college at large.

On the evidence of the "Smith" diary, peer response was
important for assigned work as well. "Smith" frequently seeks out
classmates as well as tutors to practice his assigned orations on,
and he clearly values the criticism of his peers equally with that of
the tutors. Indeed, the tutors seem to have stood in such a
relationship to the students that their criticism would have as much,
perhaps more in common with "peer response" than with a modern
composition teacher's critique of a student's paper. "Smith"
records, with no sense of its being a remarkable event, that the
tutor Greene "attempted an extempory discourse but did not shine
very brilliantly" in a meeting of the Cliosophic Society. (entry
dated March 19) The tutors participated more or less as equals
with the students in the rich oratorical activities of the college and
could expect the same sort of criticism of their own efforts as the
students received from the tutors and each other. Neither the tutors
nor anyone else "graded" students' work in the way we do today;
the work was not done in the context of courses and credit hours
and grade point averages. The audiences for which a student wrote
regularly were his own class, his literary society, and the entire
college assembled. It was the approval of these audiences that
mattered, and the critical response of the tutor was valuable
insofar as it helped a student achieve that end. Examination for

---

[12]Potter, op. cit. See also Anne Ruggles Gere, *Writing Groups: History, Theory, and
Implications* (Carbondale: Southern Illinois University Press, 1987), 9-16.

purposes comparable to what we call grading was done infrequently, usually in the form of oral disputation with the college president and perhaps the trustees judging the students' performance.

FROM SCRIPTED ORALITY TO SILENT PROSE

Gerald Graff writes of an "oratorical culture" that provided some rationale and support for literary study in colleges during the first half of the nineteenth century.[13] By an "oratorical culture," he means the activities of the literary and debate societies and the formally required speaking exercises in English that pervaded college life from roughly 1750 up to what he calls "the professional era" (starting at around 1875) in English studies. Equally important, and perhaps more clearly, this oratorical culture provided an appropriate and supportive context for writing instruction in a period when writing was primarily the scripting of an oral performance.

While students participated enthusiastically in this collegiate oratorical culture up through the opening decades of the nineteenth century, Graff shows that the system was beginning to seem archaic by the 1820s and gradually fell apart over the succeeding decades. Looking at the process from the viewpoint of modern vernacular literary studies, Graff is inclined to see it as the inevitable collapse of a weak system. But from the perspective of writing instruction, the old system had important virtues and its decay calls for an explanation. While a full explanation is beyond the scope of this chapter, I want to focus on three aspects of the change that can shed light on the nature of the new modes of writing instruction that came into use during this period. First, there was a new emphasis, both in the colleges and in the society at large, on belletristic forms of writing — poetry, fiction, drama, essay — that had occupied a less prominent place in the older oratorical culture. Second, the emergence of a middle-class and the professions altered the curriculum and student population in ways that placed new burdens on academic writing. Third, certain technological developments facilitated a heavier reliance on writing as an independent medium in both the society at large and the schools. I will take these three topics up in order.

---

[13]Gerald Graff, *Professing Literature: an Institutional History* (Chicago and London: The University of Chicago Press, 1987), 35-51.

Belletristic Rhetoric

The increased interest in belletristic writing is reflected in the textbooks used through the early decades of the nineteenth century. The most popular was Hugh Blair's *Lectures on Rhetoric and Belles Lettres,* published in Scotland in 1783 and adopted at Yale and other American colleges shortly thereafter, but the belletristic trend is equally evident in the first commercially successful American text, Samuel P. Newman's *A Practical System of Rhetoric* (1827).[14] Some belletristic notions are also present in John Witherspoon's primarily neo-classical *Lectures on Eloquence,* particularly in the final lecture which is devoted to principles of taste and criticism which Witherspoon no doubt learned as a classmate of Hugh Blair's at the University of Edinbergh. According to Warren Guthrie, Blair's *Lectures* had become the most popular work on rhetoric in American colleges by 1803, and its continuing influence is suggested by the numerous editions that appeared to and beyond the middle of the nineteenth century.[15] Guthrie records that it was in use at Yale and Williams as late as 1860. Another important Scottish belletristic rhetoric, Alexander Jamieson's *A Grammar of Rhetoric and Polite Literature* (1818), appeared regularly in American editions from 1820 until about 1880, and was established as a regular text for sophomores at Yale by Chauncey Allen Goodrich.[16] At Wesleyan and Amherst, Jamieson was used for a while and then replaced by Newman's *A Practical Stystem of Rhetoric.*[17] Belletristic rhetoric thus became popular at the peak of the oral-vernacular period in writing instruction, and the growth of its influence coincided with the decline of what

---

[14]Newman devotes two of his five chapters to the belletristic notion of "taste" and in other ways exhibits the belletrists' tendency to foreground aesthetic considerations in writing. *A Practical System of Rhetoric,* tenth edition (New York: Dayton and Newman, 1842).

[15]"The Development of Rhetorical Theory in America, 1635-1850, III," *Speech Monographs* 15 (1948), 62.

[16]A. Craig Baird, "Introduction" to *Essays from Select British Eloquence* by Chauncey Allen Goodrich (Carbondale: Southern Illinois University Press, Landmarks in Rhetoric and Public Address series, 1963), xvi.

[17]"The Development of Rhetorical Theory in America 1635-1850, IV," *Speech Monographs* 16 (1949), 102.

Graff calls the oratorical culture, and with a growing interest in the creation of an American national literature.

In Blair, Jamieson, and Newman, belletristic rhetoric incorporates some of the traditional concern for oratory in the classical genres, and includes a classical pedagogy based upon the use of models, imitation, and graded practice, including translation into English from other languages. But the emphasis shifts somewhat, from persuasive to poetic discourse, and from the rhetorical virtue of *eloquence* to a new ideal of *taste.* This in turn tends to shift standards of rhetorical judgment from a complex domain combining the moral, the aesthetic, and the pragmatic to a more purely aesthetic one. An eloquent speech is one that moves its audience to action because it is both aesthetically and morally appealing. A discourse appealing to taste may be simply beautiful or in some other way aesthetically pleasing, without accomplishing any practical end or having reference to any moral standard. A second implication of belletristic rhetoric's substitution of taste for eloquence is that it tends to make rhetoric an art of the audience more than of the speaker or writer. Taste is a quality that distinguishes readers of texts. Eloquence is a virtue of the speaker or writer who makes them. Belletristic rhetoric thus set the stage for the elevation of interpretation and reading over invention and writing that would characterize the discipline of English studies.

Perhaps owing to their elevation of aesthetic concerns and the role of the reader, belletristic rhetorics offered analyses of prose style more detailed and meticulous than anything in the neoclassical texts. Blair and Jamieson in particular are still worth reading for their stylistic analyses.[18] Conversely, the belletristic rhetorics had less to say about invention in the traditional sense, emphasizing instead the genius of the individual author as a source of the material of discourse. And in keeping with this emphasis on the individual, they presented a more individualistic view of style. Alongside the classical ideal of plain, middle, and grand styles, which in Cicero were treated not as distinct kinds but as stylistic

---

[18]Jamieson offers what I believe is the earliest published discussion of anticlimax as a deliberate rhetorical effect, giving an astute analysis of the sinking sound and sentiment in Horace's line, "Parturient montes, nascetur ridiculus mus." *A Grammar of Rhetoric and Polite Literature* (New York: A. C. Armstrong & Son, no date), 182 (book V, ch. 1).

registers that might all be present in the same speech,[19] belletristic
rhetoricians developed longer catalogues of stylistic characters that
distinguished the qualities of particular writers. Witherspoon, for
example, gives primary emphasis to the traditional categories of
plain, middle, and grand styles (calling them "plain," "mixed," and
"sublime"), but also describes "more personal" characters of
style — including the simple, smooth, sweet, concise, elegant,
ornate, just, nervous, chaste, and severe styles — and illustrates
each with one or more references to specific authors. The older
plain-middle-grand view was centripetal, tending to promote a
stylistic ideal assumed to be more or less the same for all writers.
The new belletristic practice of distinguishing multiple styles was
centrifugal; it suggested that there are many distinct stylistic ideals,
and it thus represents an early step toward our own emphasis on
the need for each writer to articulate a distinct personal "voice."

Robert Connors points to a more direct consequence of the
belletristic emphasis on the individual, realized in late nineteenth-
century composition pedagogy: a strong shift to more "personal"
topics for assigned writing.[20] While his argument is marred by a
surprising hostility toward rhetoric in the classical tradition and an
overstated opposition between the "personal" and the "abstract" or
"objective", Connors shows that many of the topics for writing
assignments advocated in late nineteenth-century composition texts
focussed more sharply on the students' personal experience and
feelings than had the writing assignments typical of earlier times.
In the traditional rhetoric students might have been asked to
develop a broad and general topic such as "patriotism;" a late
nineteenth-century text such as Reed and Kellogg's *Higher Lessons
in English*[21] would urge students to narrow the subject to
something like "How Can a Boy Be Patriotic?" and consult their

---

[19]For this reading of Cicero on the plain, middle, and grand styles, see S. Michael
Halloran & Merrill D. Whitburn, "Ciceronian Rhetoric and the Rise of Science: the Plain
Style Reconsidered" in James J. Murphy (ed.), *The Rhetorical Tradition and Modern
Writing* (New York: The Modern Language Association of America, 1982), 61.

[20]Robert J. Connors, "Personal Writing Assignments," *College Composition and
Communication* 38 (May 1987), 166-83.

[21]Alonzo Reed and Brainerd Kellogg, *Higher Lessons in English* (New York: Clark
& Maynard, 1878).

own experiences and feelings in developing it. This shift reflects the same concern with private, individual experience that marks imaginative literature, particularly that of the romantic and post-romantic period, in contrast to traditional oratory's focus on culturally sanctioned commonplaces. The shift to more personal writing assignments thus fits with the rise of literary study as the central focus of the new departments of English that were the locus of instruction in rhetoric.

The Rise of the Middle Class

The new emphasis on the individual was of course not peculiar to literature or the teaching of writing. The seventeenth and eighteenth centuries saw a growth of individualism that manifested itself, for example, in the American Declaration of Independence. Through the eighteenth century, individualism was in this country chiefly a matter of political rights, but during the nineteenth century the idea that everyone has a "right" to rise socially and economically took root. People came to see the socio-economic status of their birth not as a place they ought to occupy for life, but as a starting point from which to climb upward in competition with their fellows. As Burton Bledstein shows, this new middle-class ethos, which developed during the first half of the nineteenth century, was crucial to the emergence of the apparatus of professionalism during the second half of that century.[22] The middle-class spirit made people competitive strivers; professionalism created arenas for striving and a currency of exchange in the form of "professional expertise."

These developments had profound consequences for the place of writing and the teaching of writing in American colleges. The growth of the middle-class spirit placed a new burden on the colleges in both sheer numbers of students and new responsibilities. Students who came to college as a means of rising on the socio-economic ladder swelled classes far beyond anything known in the

---

[22]Burton J. Bledstein, *The Culture of Professionalism: the Middle Class and the Development of Higher Education in America* (New York and London: W. W. Norton & Company, 1976).

seventeenth and eighteenth centuries.[23] The increasingly competitive social spirit that brought these students to college imposed a "credentialing" function schools had perhaps always had in theory, but had never had to take quite so seriously before. The larger numbers of students made the old system of oral recitation and disputation unworkable, and writing was a means by which larger numbers of students could demonstrate whether they had learned what was being taught. The new competitive spirit of the society gave a much greater importance to the business of "sorting" students, of determining which ones were superior and which ones merely adequate, and here too writing recommended itself as a means. Because written work could be evaluated more precisely, it allowed for a more meticulous sorting of the students.[24]

One result was a growing emphasis on correctness of grammar and usage. As Sterling Andrus Leonard showed more than fifty years ago, the ideal of "correctness" in English was essentially an eighteenth-century invention.[25] Some evidence of this development can be seen in American colleges during the late eighteenth century, particularly in the views of John Witherspoon, who inveighed on aesthetic grounds against the use of contractions and invented the term "Americanism" as a pejorative for forms of expression peculiar to this side of the Atlantic.[26] But by the standards that would become current in the closing decades of the nineteenth century, Witherspoon was permissive, advising his students not to worry overmuch, for example, about punctuation.

---

[23]At Harvard, class size first reached 100 in 1860, then went to 200 in 1877, to 300 in 1892, to 400 in 1896, to 500 in 1904, and to 600 in 1906 and remained at about that level until shortly before World War I. Morrison, *Three Centuries of Harvard,* 415-16.

[24]Francis Wayland, then president of Brown, argued for a shift from oral to written examination in *Thoughts on the Present Collegiate System in the United States* (1842; rpt. New York: Arno Press and The New York Times, 1969) 99 ff.

[25]Sterling Andrus Leonard, *The Doctrine of Correctness in English Usage, 1700-1800* (Madison: University of Wisconsin Press, 1929; rpt. New York: Russell and Russell, 1962).

[26]Witherspoon's diatribe against contractions is contained in the "Lectures on Eloquence," lecture number three. According to H. L. Mencken, *The American Language: an Inquiry into the Development of English in the United States* (1919; fourth edn. New York: Alfred Knopf, 1960), Witherspoon invented the term "Americanism" in papers called "The Druid" which appear in Witherspoon's *Works,* vol. IV. (Mencken, 4-6).

Since eighteenth-century American society had offered little motive for upward striving, the dialect a person learned in childhood would in most cases serve for life.

In the competitive middle-class society of the nineteenth-century, speaking and writing "correct" English took on new importance as a sign of membership in the upper strata. The new reliance on writing as a medium of evaluation lent further importance to correctness, and such current-traditional rhetoricians as John Franklin Genung, Barrett Wendell, and Adams Sherman Hill consequently gave heavy emphasis to usage and grammar.[27] Many of them, Hill in particular, developed standards of correctness far more subtle than the actual practice of elite speakers and writers, and thus beyond anything requisite to give students the social mobility they sought. And by attempting to impose a "hyper-correct" dialect on the generally privileged students at Harvard and the other established liberal arts colleges, Hill and others may actually have strengthened the linguistic obstacles to upward mobility. The relationship between the middle-class ethos and the rhetoric of correctness was thus a complex one. The rhetoricians prepared students to leap social hurdles, while at the same time elevating the hurdles.

The coincidence of the middle-class ethos with advances in science, commerce, and industry produced a new cultural ideal: professionalism. According to Bledstein, at least two hundred learned societies were formed in this country during the 1870s and 1880s, formalizing a professional ethos in areas ranging from chemistry to folklore, political science to ornithology. Even sports began to take on the trappings of "professionalism" during this period, underscoring the power of the new ethos.[28] To be a professional was a new ideal representing what the culture most valued, as Quintilian's citizen orator had represented what classical culture most valued. Unlike the citizen orator, a version of which was central to the vernacular neo-classical rhetoric of the late

---

[27]A standard work on what happened to rhetoric during the move toward written composition is Albert Raymond Kitzhaber, "Rhetoric in American Colleges 1850-1900," diss., University of Washington, 1953. It is Kitzhaber who dubbed Genung, Wendell, Hill, and Fred Newton Scott "the big four."

[28]*The Culture of Professionalism,* 80 ff.

eighteenth century, the professional was a specialist whose service to society took the form of applying arcane, scientifically-based knowledge to "the common purposes of life."[29] In contrast to the communally sanctioned wisdom that had been the province of the citizen orator, the knowledge of the professional was morally neutral—in essence, a commodity that could be exchanged for money, and thus a means of advancing one's personal fortune while also serving the public good. Professional knowledge or "expertise" was rooted in methods of inquiry particular to the profession, a point which helps to account for the often noted decline of invention in nineteenth-century rhetoric.

The most appropriate rhetorical form for expression of the professional's expertise was clearly not the morally tinged persuasion of the old-style orator, but dispassionate exposition and argumentation. The new ideal of professionalism thus appears in rhetoric as a tendency to emphasize the last two of the four "modes of discourse"—description, narration, exposition, and argumentation. The modes, a prominent feature of late nineteenth-century current-traditional rhetoric, can be traced to the influence of faculty psychology, through the eighteenth-century Scottish rhetorician George Campbell.[30] In the current-traditional version of this scheme, persuasion became a minor aspect of argumentation, serving only to supplement substantive appeals with some appeal to the passions. Within the ethos of professionalism, passion would ideally be eliminated altogether, and so persuasion, once the overarching purpose of all rhetoric, became a concession to the weakness of the audience.

The ethos of professionalism is reflected also in the common organizational scheme for current-traditional textbooks: from words, to sentences, to paragraphs, and finally to the whole discourse. The

---

[29] I take this expression from a frequently quoted statement by Stephen Van Rensselaer of his purpose in founding what would eventually become Rensselaer Polytechnic Institute, one of the pioneer institutions in the development of the new profession of engineering: "the application of science to the common purposes of life." See Samuel Rezneck, *Education for a Technological Society: A Sequicentennial History of Rensselaer Polytechnic Institute* (Troy, N.Y.: RPI, 1968).

[30] See James A. Berlin, *Writing Instruction in Nineteenth-Century American Colleges* (Carbondale and Edwardsville: Southern Illinois University Press, 1984), 62 ff.

underlying metaphor is of the discourse as something constructed
carefully from parts, much as a machine is assembled from its
parts, or as science in the Baconian inductive mode assembles
discrete observations into general principles. Seen in this way,
discourse is not so much the moral and political engagement with
an audience of classical rhetoric, as the construction of a
knowledge-bearing object, a mechanism by which professional
expertise can be made available for use. A notable exception to the
tendency of nineteenth-century rhetoricians to treat discourse as a
mechanism is Fred Newton Scott, who preferred the organic view
developed by Plato in the *Phaedrus*.

Technological Developments

Discussions of the connection between technology and writing
usually focus on one or more of three "revolutions": the development of alphabetic literacy in ancient Greece; the invention and
diffusion of the printing press during the Renaissance; and the
development of electronic media, the word-processing computer
especially, in our own time. But another revolution in writing
technology occurred during the nineteenth century, one less
dramatic perhaps than these three, but nonetheless important in its
consequences for writing and writing instruction. Pens, ink, and
pencils improved significantly, making it possible for people to
write with less fuss and mess, and fewer pauses for blotting the ink
and sharpening pens. Paper decreased substantially in cost, making
it economically feasible for people to write more, to use writing
freely as a medium of exploration, to discard drafts and revise
more extensively. Book and periodical production increased dramatically, making printed material available to everyone. The postal
system improved, making it easier to conduct both business and
personal affairs in writing.

This nineteenth-century "revolution" is of course none other
than the Industrial Revolution, seen from the perspective of
writing and written communication. Its consequence was a society
more radically literate in the sense that public and private affairs
could rely on prose meant for silent reading only rather than as a
script for oral performance. Curiously, this aspect of the Industrial
Revolution seems not to have been very much commented on,
perhaps because it has been so successful. We find it difficult to

recall that the physical act of writing, of inscribing words on a surface, was once hard and costly work quite apart from the intellectual effort of inventing the words to inscribe. Yet for medieval monks copying manuscripts, it was exactly that. Elizabeth Larson notes, in an excellent brief study of the relationship between writing implements and the composing process, that scribal work was for monks considered a "reasonable substitute for physical labor," and that analogies between writing and such work as ditch digging were common in the medieval period. She notes further that the clumsy implements used by medieval scribes were not significantly improved until the nineteenth century.[31] The late eighteenth-century Princeton diarist quoted above most likely wrote with a quill pen that needed constant mending.

The physical recalcitrance of old-style writing tools necessitated a two stage composing process: first think out very carefully what to say, then write it down, ideally getting it exactly right the first time. Within this framework, "invention" occurs entirely in the mind rather than "at the point of utterance," and memory becomes a key inventive resource. Larson shows how our own very different view of writing as "a continuing process of revision" depends radically on the convenient writing implements and relatively cheap paper first developed during the nineteenth century. With pens that do not require constant sharpening, ink that requires little or no blotting, and cheap yet serviceable paper, it becomes possible to write in the free, exploratory manner advocated by Peter Elbow, for example. But while the potential for such a composing process was developed during the nineteenth century, it remained for later generations of teachers to exploit it. Current-traditional texts continued to treat thinking and inscription as distinct acts. And what little advice the nineteenth-century texts have to offer on the subject of revision remains grounded in the old two-stage composing process. G.P. Quackenbos, for example, tells the student to write a draft, then let sufficient time pass "so that the writer may, in a measure, forget the expressions he has used, and criticise his work as severely and impartially as if it were

---

[31]Elizabeth Larson, "The Effect of Technology on the Composing Process," *Rhetoric Society Quarterly* 16 (1986), 43-58.

the production of another."[32] The criticism is to be accomplished through reading the draft carefully aloud, after which another clean copy is written with full attention to "neatness of chirography." Like the rhetoricians of the eighteenth century, Quackenbos assumes a sharp distinction between the acts of thinking and inscription.

The current-traditional rhetoricians did exploit the potential of the new writing tools to some extent by having students write often and much. Barrett Wendell, who was first hired by Harvard to assist Adams Sherman Hill in reading the growing number of themes, required his own students to write "dailies"—short pieces of observation or reflection that would, as Wendell himself put it, "tell something that makes the day on which it is made differ from the day before." Wallace Douglas dismisses the dailies as "merely exercises in fluency and specificity and also a means of encouraging originality of perception," and he claims that they go "counter to all that is supposed to have been learned about the 'writing process' in the last few years."[33] I am not so sure that "exercises in fluency," if they really do make students fluent, should be characterized as "mere," nor am I convinced that daily themes as assigned by Wendell and others violate what we are supposed to have learned more recently about the composing process. In fact, they bear a noticeable resemblance to the practice of journal-keeping: they are supposed to be spontaneous and ephemeral, and are not subject to revision of any kind. They are a good instance of the move toward "more personal" writing assignments noted by Robert Connors.

VISUALIZING DISCOURSE

Douglas notes that Barrett Wendell gave considerable attention to the appearance of words on a page, advising students, for example, to place their "chief ideas" in the beginnings and endings of paragraphs, since "the human eye cannot help dwelling

---

[32]G. P. Quackenbos, *Advanced Course of Composition and Rhetoric* (New York: D. Appleton and Company, 1859), 334.

[33]Wallace Douglas, "Barrett Wendell" in John Brereton (ed.), *Traditions of Inquiry* (New York and Oxford: Oxford University Press, 1985), 14.

instinctively a little longer" at these points in a text. For Douglas, this emphasis on the physical appearance of words is yet another sign of simple-mindedness. "I have sometimes thought," he says, "that the doctrines and dogmas of [Wendell's] *English Composition* can all be explained by the pedagogical need to simplify, to develop a composing process that will produce themes that can be given 'a hasty categorical analysis' rather than be the means whereby young people can use their language toward growth in their thought."[34] This harsh verdict represents a fairly wide consensus among historians of rhetoric on Wendell and most of his contemporaries. With the exceptions of Fred Newton Scott and his student Gertrude Buck, the late nineteenth-century American rhetoricians have been uniformly regarded as simplistic, derivative, and in general worthy of attention only as examples of how not to teach writing.[35]

Without attempting to overturn the verdict, I want to speak in extenuation. Wendell's focus on the physical placement of words and sentences on the page, while simplistic and overstated, suggests an important new development in the art of rhetoric, a development that responds directly to the cultural, social, and technological changes sketched above. As Gerald Graff shows, the academic culture of the early 1800s was an oratorical culture, and while he does not say so, the larger culture was oratorical as well. It depended on formal speech as a medium for doing both public and private business, and it used writing as a means of scripting oral performance. What Northrop Frye would call the "radical of presentation" for academic writing was the orator on a podium, and so the traditional auditory metaphors for style remained useful. The culture in which Barrett Wendell and the other current-traditional rhetoricians taught had become literary and professional. It used writing as a medium in which to convey experience and information silently. The voice of the orator was not supposed to

---

[34]Douglas, 21.

[35]See for example Donald C. Stewart's "Two Model Teachers and the Harvardization of English Departments" in James J. Murphy (ed.), *The Rhetorical Tradition and Modern Writing* (New York: MLA, 1982), 118-29. This position is also taken in Kitzhaber, "Rhetoric in American Colleges 1850-1900" and Berlin, *Writing Instruction in Nineteenth-Century American Colleges.*

be present in the dailies Wendell's students wrote for class or in the business letters and professional reports they would write in post-collegiate life. This writing communicated through the eyes of readers rather than through the ears of an audience, and so visual metaphors had to be invented for understanding style and structure. Important among these were words, sentences, and paragraphs understood as "elements" of discourse; the outline format (which was an inheritance of Peter Ramus's earlier move in the direction of a visualized rhetoric); and the very notion of "structure," which suggests a quasi-architectural three-dimensional ordering of parts.

An influential effort to elaborate this notion of structure in discourse was the sentence diagramming system invented by Alonzo Reed and Brainerd Kellogg and established as a standard element of pre-college work in English through their *Graded Lessons in English* (1875) and *Higher Lessons in English* (1878). These two texts remained in print into the second decade of the twentieth century, and the Reed & Kellogg method of diagramming sentences endured for decades beyond. It was essentially a representation in abstract spatial terms of the grammatical relationships among words, phrases, and clauses in a sentence, and as such a step in the direction of modern linguistic techniques of representing syntactic relations, such as Chomskyan and immediate constituent diagramming. Unlike these later developments, the Reed & Kellogg system failed to preserve the natural order of words in the sentence, but it nonetheless represented an advance in the effort to understand the structure of discourse at the sentence level, and an important response to the shift from an oratorical to a literary and professional culture.

The inclination to represent discourse visually is likewise evident in Kellogg's independently authored *A Text-Book on Rhetoric* (1880). Though less frequently mentioned today than the works of Albert Kitzhaber's "big four" (Hill, Genung, Wendell, and Fred Newton Scott), Kellogg's *Text-Book* was widely used, going through frequent reprintings into the first decade of the twentieth century. It did not make use of the diagramming system, which was regarded as too elementary for the *Text-Book's* upper high-school, lower college level audience. It did present numerous exercises based on close analysis of syntactic structure, some of which would be fully at home in a modern sentence-combining text. In one instance, Kellogg also extended the approach of spatial diagramming to semantic relationships as well as syntax:

> To exhibit the relation of synonyms to each other let us draw the parallelogram 1-4,

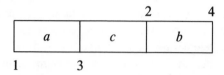

> and divide it into the two parallelograms 1-2 and 3-4, with 3-2 forming part of each. Now let us suppose the area 1-2 to represent the ground of meaning covered by one synonym, and 3-4 that covered by the other. 3-2, or the space marked c, will then picture that shared by the two synonyms; a, that which belongs exclusively to the first synonym; and b, that which belongs exclusively to the second. When then, below, we use the letters a, c, b, it will be understood for what parts of the synonyms they stand.
>
> Bear in mind that a and b do not give the full meaning of the synonyms. Add c to a for the meaning of the first synonym, add c to b for that of the second.
>
> If there are more than two in the group, conceive the parallelogram c to be extended upwards and downwards. Each extension plus c will then symbolize another synonym, and the complete figure will represent a group of four with the common meaning c.[36]

As in the example of sentence diagramming, which anticipates in crude form an important aspect of modern work in syntax, here Kellogg seems to be groping toward a modern view—which is to say a "visualized" view—of semantics. Yet he seems unaware that he is operating at a frontier in a developing field of knowledge. He treats rhetoric as a body of common knowledge to be recorded in a text-book for high-school and college students.

THE STATUS OF RHETORIC AS "COMPOSITION"

In the example of Kellogg attempting to create visual models of language structure can be seen the great and ironic failing of

---

[36]Brainerd Kellogg, *A Text-Book on Rhetoric* (New York: Maynard, Merrill, & Co., 1896), 97-8.

current-traditional rhetoric. The course in English composition that evolved in the late nineteenth century was an attempt to adapt rhetoric to dramatically changed conditions both inside and outside the academy, conditions produced by the industrial revolution and the new middle-class and professional mores. The task facing Kellogg and others was thus an opportunity for scholarly work of the highest order. But with few exceptions they showed no awareness of the potential seriousness of their work, and indeed little regard for the importance of the contributions they did make. Though some of them were serious and productive scholars of literature, they treated rhetoric as a set of low level skills worthy at best of half-hearted treatment in text-books addressed to children and undergraduates. While their text-books show flashes of originality, as in the example from Kellogg above, there is little effort to develop a historical context or probe underlying principles, and no sense that the subject is intellectually challenging and socially important.

Donald Stewart attributes this unfortunate limitation of late nineteenth-century rhetoric to the influence of Francis James Child, fourth Boylston Professor of Rhetoric and Oratory at Harvard.[37] Child held a largely undisguised contempt for rhetoric in both its traditional and more purely literate modes throughout his 25 year tenure as Boylston Professor, and when relieved by A.S. Hill in 1876 he became a driving force in establishing literary study as the central focus of the Harvard Department of English. Stewart contrasts Child's view of the emerging profession of English studies with that of Fred Newton Scott of the University of Michigan, one of the few late nineteenth-century scholars who saw rhetoric as an intellectually challenging subject and took a more balanced view of the English department as comprising scholarly work in rhetoric and linguistics as well as literary study. Stewart sees in the origin of professional English studies a struggle between the Harvard model of Child and the broader model advocated by Scott, a struggle in which the view of Child prevailed and the new discipline was effectively "Harvardized" by the early years of the twentieth century.

---

[37]Stewart, "Two Model Teachers and the Harvardization of English Departments."

Documentary evidence assembled by Gerald Graff and Michael Warner shows that the notion of a two-sided struggle between Harvard literati and Michigan rhetoricians giving shape to the profession of English studies is oversimplified.[38] Harvard and Michigan were by no means the only influential schools, nor were they necessarily the most influential ones. Further, among the early advocates of English literary study, there were numerous sharp differences, for example between the scientifically oriented philologists and proponents of an older belletristic approach. And of course the importance of a "belletristic" view should remind us that the shift of emphasis from writing to reading, and the consequent demotion of "rhetoric" to the status of a low-level service course, has roots in the rhetorical tradition itself. Stewart is nonetheless correct in his conclusion that *something like* Francis Child's vision came to dominate English studies, and the term "Harvardization" can perhaps serve as a useful synechdoche for what happened in the closing years of the nineteenth century. The discipline of English became primarily the study of literary texts, not in Stewart's catholic sense of "includ[ing] everything from a seventh grader's paragraph on fishing, to a graduate student's term paper on Chaucer's Pardoner, to *Moby Dick,*"[39] but in the narrow sense of classics understood to be fundamentally different from anything the student might write. Rhetoric became a secondary concern, largely unrelated to the study of literature and thus free to lay down "rules" for composition in total disregard and sometimes direct violation of the example set by those classic texts.

CONCLUDING REMARKS:
A SOCIAL PURPOSE FOR WRITING INSTRUCTION

Much of great value was lost in the evolution from the neo-classical rhetoric of the late eighteenth century to the composition course of the late nineteenth. Heuristic theory and procedures virtually disappeared, and the sense of audience was narrowed. In place of a rich array of stylistic forms and techniques was the flat

---

[38]Gerald Graff and Michael Warner (eds.), *The Origins of Literary Studies in America* (New York & London: Routledge, 1989).

[39]"Two Model Teachers," 125-6.

voice of mechanical correctness. The greatest loss was of the sense of a large social purpose for writing, a social role for which rhetorical art was necessary equipment. Neo-classical rhetoric had focussed on an updated version of Quintilian's citizen orator as the role for which students were being educated. They were supposed to become virtuous leaders of their communities, and effective writing was one of the key abilities they would need to fulfill this responsibility. The new course offered little in place of this ideal. Composition "skills" were important for success in the new middle-class, professional culture, but there is no evidence that even this somewhat narrow and functionary purpose was made clear to students. And the larger purpose of social leadership through discourse that had been both central to and explicit in neo-classical rhetoric had no equivalent in the rhetoric of English composition.

One can question whether the Quintilianic ideal or anything like it could or should have survived. For one thing, it was aristocratic, perhaps fundamentally so. It assumed as audience a *mobile vulgus* needing the intelligent and moral leadership of a skilled orator. For another, it assumed a stable and readily compassable body of common knowledge. The first assumption was in conflict with the ideology of populist democracy, the second with the rapid advance of specialized, arcane knowledge and its applications to "the common purposes of life."

My own view is that aristocratic assumptions about speaker and audience were accidental to the theory and practice of classical rhetoric, and that it could have been adapted quite readily to the needs of a widening democracy. Frederick Antczak shows persuasively that there was a need, and it was not fulfilled by the schools. The new "democratic" political campaign methods developed in post Jacksonian times—when neo-classical rhetoric was on the decline in American higher education—were at least as manipulative as anything the patrician Federalists had attempted, and far less rational.[40] Classical rhetoric might have been adapted to the needs of the changing American culture and served as an art

---

[40]Frederick Antczak, *Thought and Character: the Rhetoric of Democratic Education* (Ames: The Iowa State University Press, 1965), 12-54. Antczak's primary focus is on non-academic efforts, particularly the lyceum and chautauqua movements, to "reconstitute" the democratic audience as politically competent.

of political competency for the widening enfranchised public. Instead, it was virtually abandoned by the colleges in favor of a socially and politically unaware rhetoric of composition. Simultaneously, and perhaps in consequence, our political discourse grew increasingly artless and irrational.

The second point—traditional rhetoric's assumption that knowledge is stable and compassable by the individual—is more problematic. We continue to wrestle with it, for example in the extraordinary debate, both academic and public, that has surrounded such books as E.D. Hirsch's *Cultural Literacy* and Allen Bloom's *The Closing of the American Mind.* The growth of specialized knowledge in the nineteenth century was directly related to the development of English composition. The new disciplines and professions left a smaller and smaller place in the curriculum for "rhetoric," which at the beginning of the nineteenth century had occupied as much of the students' time as the major discipline does for most of our students today. "Composition," as understood by Hill, Genung, Wendell, Kellogg, and Scott was simply a course in our sense of that term, competing for the students' time and attention with an ever growing array of other courses, some of which bore ironic traces of the rhetorical tradition they were displacing. The much maligned current-traditional rhetoricians had to adapt to the new reliance on silent prose, and yet accomplish their work in a narrow corner of the curriculum.

Perhaps they deserve more credit than they have had. The social and technological changes of the nineteenth century were profound. The new course in English composition, which by the turn of the twentieth century was probably the sole common element in American college education, was itself an important invention, an educational "technology" to deal with dramatically changed circumstances and problems. If not giants on whose shoulders we now stand, the current-traditional rhetoricians are nonetheless significant contributors to the tradition of writing instruction. Seen in the context of the time, their accomplishments are deserving of some attention and respect.

APPENDIX

AN EXAMPLE OF STUDENT WRITING
IN THE REVOLUTIONARY PERIOD

September 10th 1772
Nassau Hall
Princeton University

An Exercise at the Public Commencement

It is altogether needless, to detain this respectable assembly only for two or three minutes, with any introduction to the following Subject, further than by just telling them it is my design to prove that *"political jealousy* is a laudable passion."

Jealousy is a strange temper in the human mind, & like several other of our passions, it has various effects when its subjects are different; it is also of many kinds, as political, domestic, & ecclesiastic Jealousies, Jealousy in Friendship, and between the Sexes; each of which has a different effect on the mind from all the others, & several of them, if carried to any considerable length, are generally attended with dangerous consequences: especially the two kinds last mentioned, Jealousy in Friendship, & between the Sexes; for in friendship when two persons of agreeable tempers, have by long acquaintance proved each others fidelity, so as to communicate all their secret intentions to each other, & have contracted a particular esteem between themselves, if by any means, whether false or true, the one becomes suspicious that the regard, or the faithfulness of the other is diminished, he is then watchful of every action, & misapplies every unmeaning expression, which at once destroys their quiet, & is seldom removed, but most usually terminates in open hatred. But it is said by some that a small degree of Jealousy between those of different Sexes improves, & increases mutual Esteem, because esteem is said to be the foundation of Jealousy; but when it arrives at a certain pitch, it then turns the other way, & rages with ungovernable violence; like attraction in small bodies, which ceases to act at a certain distance, & then repulsion separates them with a double force; I am, however, quite unable to comprehend what can be a cause for this mysterious limitation, & as no valid reasons have been brought to support it, but innumerable Examples which operate against it, we conclude that wherever Jealousy between the sexes takes place, it destroys the comfort & happiness of the parties, in proportion to its Strength, & Duration. It is therefore mischievous in its nature in both these kinds, & neither desirable, nor laudable; perhaps the same things or worse might be said of domestic & eclesiastic Jealousies, but I pass them by, & proceed to observe that *political Jealousy* differs from them all in these respects; it is rational, & uniform, & necessary.

Any person who considers the importance of a free State, of how great value the lives the liberties, & the property of a nation are, & considers that the surrounding nations are envious of their neighbours happiness, & therefore always desirous of reducing them to subjection, will see at once & readily confess, that it is most just, that those who have the ruling power, should keep a watchful eye upon the whole conduct of those in whose power it is to disturb & injure them; & this observation is Jealousy of their designs, which is the first & surest step to self-preservation, because it is the simplest, & most safe method that can be taken to preserve the state, as it does not suffer mischief to take place & the safety of every individual in a state depends entirely upon the Security of the whole, consequently this kind of Jealousy is a first principle of Nature, which never goes contrary to reason; & which always directs to something needful & for our good, political Jealousy is therefore rational & founded in unerring nature.

It is like wise uniform, for it only excites politicians to a constant attention to those things which are likely to keep the state in safety, but when public hostilities are committed against the state there is nothing then that can be called Jealousy for the resentment is open and common: Political Jealousy, then in this view, is of great importance in two respects, it is first the most easy and effectual way to keep a nation in peace, or make them successful in war, as it urges to constant readiness for the greatest danger; & likewise its natural tendency is to unite the people; for when they see the Rulers of the nation inattentive to the national welfare, they immediately become dissatisfied, because their own lives and property are in danger, & often in this case they rebel against the government, & unite among themselves to defend their own lives & secure their property; but when a people see their Rulers watchful over the state, & always forward to detect & chastise intruders, if the nation is in peace they are quiet & at ease, and when war commences they cheerfully, & couragiously join

with their rulers, to scourge, & subdue the common enemy; now
seeing Jealousy of this kind never grows to be a tumultuous, &
dangerous passion, it certainly cannot be deny'd but that it is
useful; & it is besides a necessary passion for it is the spring that
gives life and motion to government, & its force is so powerful
that its influence extends throughout the largest State, & so mild
that it never injures the weakest subject.

It seems, finally to have been a particular passion, implanted
by the supreme God in certain Men, which assists them to rule a
state in equity, & to make use of all necessary, & possible means
to preserve it in safety; & when those who are destitute of it are
set over a nation they seem placed there by providence to chastise
the people, & for their own destruction; when private interest is
prefered by Politicians to the National welfare, or when *discord* &
mischievous factions enter among them, these show at once that
instead of being directed by the genuine gentle temper above
described they are *possessed* with a spurious, selfish, helborn
passion.

Now seeing it has been made appear that this kind of Jealousy
tends in general to the good of a Nation; seeing it never promotes
feuds, & factions, nor ever grows to be turbulent & excessive;
seeing its tendency is to unite a people in friendship among
themselves, and make them powerful against their enemies; &
seeing its influence is as extensive as the most populous state, & at
the same time mild & gentle, who can deny; I ask, who can deny
but that it is laudable, lovely, desirable, & most excellent? did I ask
who can deny? It is a confessed truth, & admitted by all; ⎯⎯⎯⎯
It therefore only remains that I implore the great *Genius* which
presides over our nation, to inspire our *king* & his *council,* & all
our *Rulers* with this noble spirit. Oh! inspire them mighty
Goddess, with a temper like to thine; suffer them not we first
intreat thee to be swayed from their duty by sordid interest; make
them always consider that upon their consultations depends the
safety of a vast empire! let them therefore be all men of integrity,
& unquestionable sincerity; take from them all malice, & revenge-
ful inclinations, & fill them with love & harmony among one
another, so that our happy government may be established &
flourish, so long as the Sun & Moon endure ⎯⎯⎯⎯ But, if it is
written in the books of *Fate* that a change in the Government must
take place; Oh! transfer it to this *western World,* set up *here* thy

royal standard, where ignorance & barbarity lately reigned; may virtue & learning, & Arts be always the subjects of thy particular attention; establish a Government, & set over it such men as shall be ever watchful for the common good, that they may forever rule a brave, a free, & a happy People.

                                               - Philip V. Fithian

From Philip Vickers Fithian, Journal and Letters, 1767-1774. *ed. John Rogers Williams, Princeton, New Jersey: The University Library, 1900.*

CHAPTER SEVEN

WRITING INSTRUCTION IN SCHOOL AND COLLEGE ENGLISH, 1890-1985

JAMES A. BERLIN

English studies in public schools and colleges in the U.S. during the last hundred years or so has organized itself around the teaching of literature and composition—more specifically stated, the interpretation of literary texts and the production of rhetorical texts. Of the two, the attention to literary texts is more recent, constituting a revolutionary development in language studies in the U.S. In the nineteenth-century high school and college, by contrast, the literature studied was more likely to be Roman or Greek while the focus in the study of the vernacular was rhetoric, both oral and written. Despite their recent appearance on the scene, however, literary texts have received more than an equal share of attention from those who have traced the history of English studies in this country. Both Arthur N. Applebee and Gerald Graff,[1] for example, have presented accounts that intentionally exclude a consideration of composition in school and college English programs. One unfortunate consequence of this omission is the suggestion that the teaching of text production was at some point banished from English studies. This essay is intended to demonstrate that no assertion could be further from the truth. The teaching of writing, and to a lesser extent speaking, in the school and college English course has been an uninterrupted pursuit in English studies throughout the last century, and I would like to sketch an outline of the trajectory it has followed.

---

[1]Arthur N. Applebee, *Tradition and Reform in the Teaching of English: A History* (Urbana: NCTE, 1974); Gerald R. Graff, *Professing Literature: An Institutional History* (Chicago: University of Chicago Press, 1987).

English studies in its various manifestations has been at the center of the educational experience in this country, constituting one of the few requirements for all students in the grades, in high school, and even in college (in the case of the last, most commonly in the form of composition). The teaching of literature and composition has figured prominently in the formation of educational curricula at all levels. Curricular decisions are, however, often negotiated responses to larger economic, social, political, and cultural events in a society. As Joel Spring in *The American School 1642-1985*[2] has convincingly argued, the curriculum in the U.S. school and college has been a terrain of conflict among competing groups, groups representing shifting alliances of politicians, government agencies, labor unions, business concerns, education experts of various stripes, and parents, each itself divided along lines of class, race, gender, and other loyalties. In other words, education in a democratic society is invariably a scene of contesting over the kind of economic, social, and politial formations the schools ought to endorse. It is no wonder then that English studies with its concern for the literary texts that students will be required to read and the rhetorical texts they will be required to produce is always near the very center of curricular decisions. Even before the poststructuralist contention that language constitutes and creates much more than it reflects our experience, those who turned their attention to shaping education realized that the study of literature and language was an integral part of the content of learning, not a mere mechanical acquirement.

Applebee has impressively traced the ways the study of literature in the U.S. school was from the start considered an extension of ethical and social training. In this essay I plan to show that writing instruction has been a comparable scene of struggle over competing claims about the purposes of education, more specifically about the society the school and college should advocate and the kind of individuals they should encourage. The composition course will be examined in its response to major curricular statements. These curricular programs in turn will be seen as the responses to larger economic, social, and political debates during the past century. The argument over the contents and methods of writing instruction will then be regarded as reflections

---

[2](New York: Longman, 1986).

and refractions of larger conflicts, with the curriculum the mediator between the two realms. This does not mean that writing instruction was a simple mechanical response to the curriculum or to larger historical events. It does mean that no classroom pedagogy can long survive without in some way responding to its historical conditions, and considering these various responses will be at the center of this study.

THE NEW SCHOOL AND COLLEGE

The last two decades of the nineteenth century inaugurated both the modern high school and the modern comprehensive university. The two were a part of a larger shift in capitalism from a *laissez-faire* market economy of unbridled individual competition to a managed economy of corporate and government alliances and planning. Education played a central part in this transition. For most of the nineteenth century, the college experience was primarily restricted to a prosperous elite. Its purpose was to prepare the leadership class to take its rightful place in society. The three major career choices were law, medicine, and the ministry, but the undergraduate curriculum was nearly identical for all students, emphasizing rhetoric, classical languages and literature, moral philosophy, and a few rudiments of mathematics and science.[3] Specialized training in the professions was carried out primarily through apprenticeship programs after college, although a few professional schools were available. The new comprehensive university was signalled by the passing of the Morrill Federal Land Grant of 1862, establishing state institutions designed to apply the findings of science to the managing of economic affairs. Even schools far removed from the land-grant model — Harvard, for example — responded to the demand for this new institution. The curriculum was to be elective, not prescribed, and its purpose was to train certified experts in the new sciences, experts who could turn their knowledge to the management of the production, distribution, exchange, and consumption activities of society for profit. Colleges, especially state institutions, were to open up their doors to people of talent — women as well as men, black as well as white, although

---

[3]Ibid., 65.

genuine equality was an unattained ideal rather than a reality. This
change in higher education was closely related to changes in the
high school. While virtually all states by the time of the Civil War
provided some form of common school for the elementary grades,
most secondary schools were private and were designed as places
for college preparation. The same sort of political pressures that
encouraged colleges to become places of scientific training for a
more productive work force were effective in arguing that high
schools should serve the same purposes. Thus, in 1890, 202,963
students attended 2,562 public high schools; in 1900, the figure
doubled with 519,251 students in 6005 public high schools; and by
1912, enrollment reached 1,000,000. Attendance among fourteen-to-
seventeen year olds continued to increase with 28 percent of this
age group in school by 1920 (2,200,389 students), 47 percent by
1930 (4,399,422 students), and two-thirds of this population by
1940 (6,545,991 students).[4] Increased attendance in colleges was
almost as dramatic: 597,880 students in 1920; 1,100,737 by 1930;
and 1,494,203 in 1940.[5] Today, nearly 12,000,000 students are in
college, representing over 30 percent of the available population.
     The role of gender in these revised educational arrangements is
crucial. In the new profession of teaching, women dominated at the
elementary and junior high levels, demonstrated a clear majority at
the secondary level, and fell significantly in numbers to a small
minority at the college level. As Sue Ellen Holbrook has indicated,
the percentage of women in public school teaching was 75 percent
in 1900, 84 percent in 1930, 72 percent in 1960, 70 percent in
1970, and 68 percent in 1981. By comparison, men represented 94
percent of college teachers in 1900, 68 percent in 1930, 78.5
percent in 1960, 75 percent in 1970, and 76 percent in 1981.[6] The
salaries for women at both levels, furthermore, were less than men's
for the same work. This pattern of discrimination should be kept in
mind in discussing the activity of a profession in which women
played so prominent and successful a role.

---

[4]Ibid., 194.

[5]James A. Berlin, *Rhetoric and Reality, Writing Instruction in American Colleges,
1900-1985* (Carbondale: Southern Illinois University Press, 1987), 59.

[6]Sue Ellen Holbrook, "Women's Work: the Feminizing of Composition," (Paper
presented at CCCC, St. Louis, March 18, 1988), 23.

THE REPORT OF THE COMMITTEE OF TEN

This growth in accessibility to education occasioned the first debate over the composition course in the high school. As mentioned earlier, the secondary school had previously been committed to preparing students for colleges, a preparation that emphasized classical languages and literature. Language study in the new high school and college was to be organized around the study of English. In the earlier school and college only the rhetoric course had focused on the vernacular. As a result, the original courses in the emerging English department at the college level, most conspicuously at Harvard, were in composition. Harvard had indeed been the first to introduce the new entrance exam in writing, an exam destined to replace the classical language requirement, although it would be some time before this objective would be attained. In 1873-74, Harvard announced that each candidate for admission was required to write an essay on "such works or standard authors as shall be announced from time to time."[7] The essay, as Applebee has indicated, was designed to test writing ability, not knowledge of literature. The prestige of Harvard, the fact that secondary schools had previously based the curriculum on college preparation, and the absence of any new curricular model for the new high school all conspired to make the new entrance policy decisive in shaping secondary English courses. However, since Harvard's reading list—as well as the lists of those colleges emulating its example—changed from year to year, it was difficult for the high school teachers to know what literary works to teach. As a result, regional organizations were established to provide uniform reading lists, and these groups were finally replaced in 1894 by the National Conference on Uniform Entrance Requirements. In addition, in 1892 the National Education Association appointed a group known as the Committee of Ten with Harvard president Charles W. Eliot as chair. Its purpose was to examine the entire curriculum on secondary schools.

The Conference on English appointed by The Committee of Ten was chaired by Samuel Thurber, master at Girls' High School Boston, and its secretary was George Lyman Kittredge of Harvard's

---

[7]Applebee, 30.

new English department. Its mission was to formulate the purposes of English studies in the high school, its final report beginning with an important policy statement:

> The main objective of the teaching of English in the schools seems to be two: (1) to enable the pupil to understand the expressed thoughts of others and to give expression to thoughts of his own; and (2) to cultivate a taste for reading, to give the pupil some acquaintance with good literature, and to furnish him with the means of extending that acquaintance.[8]

For our purposes, the elaboration of the first is crucial. The document encouraged the student in the elementary school "to furnish his own material, expressing his own thoughts in a natural way" and relying on his own "observation or personal experience."[9] This represented a consession to student interest and innovation, however, that was to be abandoned by the secondary school where the emphasis was to be "training in expression of thought."[10] Here the orientation was provided by the tenets of mental discipline and faculty psychology, now offered in the service of the scientific values of precision, clarity, and conciseness — in short, of efficiency. Indeed, given that the members of the Conference on English were appointed by Eliot and that it included Kittredge, it is not unexpected to discover that the method of writing instruction for high schools recommended was the one now characterized as current-traditional rhetoric, the very method rigorously pursued in Harvard's English department.

Harvard was one of the founding centers of current-traditional rhetoric during the last century, particularly through the textbooks of A.S. Hill and Barrett Wendell (although those of John Genung of Amherst sold as well). Its epistemological base is positivistic and rational, offering writing as an extension of the scientific method. Since the basis of all reliable knowledge is sense impression, the writer is to use inductively-derived data whenever possible.

---

[8]Alvina Treut Burrows, "Composition: Prospect and Retrospect," *Reading and Writing Instruction in the United States: Historical Trends,* ed. H. Alan Robinson (Urbana: International Reading Association, and ERIC, 1977), 24.

[9]Ibid., 25.

[10]Kenneth Kantor, "Creative Expression in the English Curriculum," *Research in the Teaching of English 9* (Spring, 1975), 5-29.

Language is a sign system that serves to stand in place of concrete experience. The mind is composed of a set of faculties that correspond so perfectly to the external world that these faculties inevitably give rise to the invariable forms of rhetorical discourse: description and persuasion corresponding to the emotions and will. The last is particularly suspect since it involves the ordinarily distortive feelings. In this scheme, knowledge is always prior to the act of writing, to be discovered through the appropriate inductive method of one's scientific area of expertise. As a result, invention as the discovery of the available means of persuasion is excluded from rhetoric and attention is shifted to arrangement—the modes of discourse—and style, now conceived as superficial correctness.

This epistemology is complicit with a politics designed to preserve the interests of corporate capitalism and the university-trained experts who serve it. For this rhetoric, the inductive method of science is as effective in addressing questions of social, political, and ethical value as it is in responding to scientific problems. Indeed, all social problems are reduced to technical problems. Thus, the engineer who determines the best location and the best method for building a bridge is regarded as possessing equal expertise in deciding whether or not the bridge ought to be built in the first place. Questions in the realm of public discourse which in a democracy are commonly considered to be the responsibility of all citizens to decide are now relegated to the recently created class of professional experts. These experts, in addition, usually find through their scientific decision-making process the solutions to problems that best serve their own class interests. The new high school and college then were part of the creation of a meritocracy, a hierarchical class structure in which the certified professional is given an inordinate amount of power and rewards for solving the problems considered worth solving by the demands or corporate capitalism. The objective, disinterested, and mechanical rhetoric they were learning in school was thus meant to reinforce their authority and to conceal the economic and political sources of power on which their claims to privilege were based.

Current-traditional rhetoric did not go unchallenged in the new college and university. Its most important opponent was situated at Yale and other established prestigious Atlantic seaboard colleges. These schools came to stand for an ideal of English studies which has been labelled "liberal culture." It was Yale, after all, which in 1892 opposed Harvard's use of literature to teach composition, arguing that literature ought to be studied for its own sake. The proponents of liberal culture argued that the literary text was the expression of the highest potential of human nature, representing the perfect fusion of truth, goodness, and beauty. From this perspective, the claims of current-traditional rhetoric were altogether too democratic, arguing mistakenly that writing, like engineering or farming or pharmacy, could be taught.

A summary of the disagreement between Harvard and Yale was found in a 1912 essay by Glenn E. Palmer entitled "Culture and Efficiency through Composition." For Yale, if writing was to be taught at all in college, it ought to be taught to the few who were gifted, and then in order to encourage the creation of literature, not rhetoric. The Harvard method insisted all should be required to undergo writing instruction in order to cultivate "good language habits."[11] Yale was instead concerned with providing all its students "the inspiration of literature, recognizing that there can be no literary production without culture." This production, however, had as its chief objective the encouragement of a "few geniuses." The only way to learn to write for the liberal culturist was to read literature and to talk and write about literature under the direction of an expert in literature.

Liberal culture represented the reaction of the old, elite colleges to the new meritocratic university. While it did not openly oppose democracy, it argued that the business of higher education was to train the leaders of society, unquestionably men, not women, with the innate gifts for leadership, and that the only way to offer such training was to rely on a literary education. Liberal culture embraced the Arnoldian notion that literature represented the best thought of the best minds and was the appropriate basis for educating each new generation. Most proponents argued for the inevitability of class, gender, and race distinctions as a matter of genetic transmission and aspired to the status of an educated aristocracy of leadership and privilege, both to be granted on the basis of a spiritual superiority that was a result of birth and breeding.

---

[11]Glenn Palmer, "Culture and Efficiency Through Composition" *English Journal* 1 (1912), 488.

The divisions in these two conceptions of writing instruction are fairly transparent in the debates taking place at the college level during this time. When we turn to the practices of high school teachers, however, the methods called upon in teaching writing are not nearly so clear-cut. Despite the fact that as high school enrollments increased the absolute numbers of students not going on to college increased, the curriculum remained tied to the needs of the college-bound. This meant that most of the writing a student attempted focused on literary texts. This writing, however, varied greatly depending on the nature of the literary study undertaken. The philological method that emphasized responding to the text as an historical artifact to be studied scientifically lent itself to the composing process of current-traditional rhetoric. Thus, the text could be used to demonstrate certain rhetorical principles, or the student could be asked to write about certain historical features of the text's production. A reading, on the other hand, that insisted on the unique ability of the literary text to provide a rare experience of truth and beauty would be more inclined to use the rhetoric of liberal culture. This classroom encouraged students to offer an appreciative reading of the text, sometimes a unique response to the text in unique language or occasionally an original literary production. The point was to develop literary taste in students which would equip them for a better life both morally and aesthetically, and to discover those with the talent for creative effort, if any were in fact in the classroom. This method, as will be seen later, often merged with the attempt to address the psychological needs and interests of the student, in this way moving against the elitist stance of the liberal culture ideal. As is indicated by some of the high school textbooks at the turn of the century, sometimes the two methods appeared in the same classroom.[12] In general, the high school English class at this early stage of its history was marked by uncertainty and experimentation, the only constant being the reading of literary texts and some sort of writing in response to them.

---

[12]Nancy McCoy, "The Relationship Between Rhetoric and Poetics in the Nineteenth Century" (Dissertation Prospectus, Purdue University, 1988).

1900-1917

During the first two decades of this century, the teaching of English in the high school and college attained professional standing. English teachers now were more confident about the special materials of their domain and of the methods for teaching them. It is important to note, however, that there were still large disagreements. These, however, tended to take place among competing groups, each of whose members were themselves in agreement about their endeavors. A number of social and political developments at this time encouraged the new stability and status of English studies.

The attempts to control the vagaries of competitive capitalism through a planned economy managed by corporations and government resulted in extending to the public schools the concept of "social efficiency." As Joel Spring explains, schools were to provide curricula that met "the future social needs of the student," taught "cooperation as preparation for future social activities," and provided for "the future social destination of the student."[13] Students were now to be prepared for life in the large-scale organizations where cooperation (as well as conformity) was valued over competition. This also included, however, some attention to the individual differences and needs of students being encouraged by the now flourishing child-study effort of such pioneers as G.K. Hall, an effort that argued for considering a student's stage of psychological development in planning instruction. Schools were also to become attentive to the needs of the work place so that even high school students were expected to undertake some specialized study. These programs were especially important to the parents of working class students intent on upward mobility, as well as to their employers. Finally, school and work were regarded as places of equal opportunity where the best, the brightest, and the hardest working were to be rewarded in accordance with strictest meritocratic principles, another ideal never quite realized.

High school teachers played an important role in working out the consequences of these developments for students. They were

---

[13]Spring, 98.

now freed of the obligation to groom all students for college. Young people were to be prepared for the economic and social roles they chose for themselves, not for the college education which at this time only four percent pursued.[14] Teachers of English were especially conspicuous in supporting this change. In fact, the National Council of Teachers of English was formed in 1911 in protest to the Uniform Reading Lists. A coalition made up primarily of teachers from the Midwest and New York City argued that teachers, not the colleges, should set reading and writing requirements for their students, taking into account their special needs. Their resolve was intensified by their concern for the learning problems of the many students not going on to college, particularly the increasing number of immigrant students. Another effect of the move for social efficiency was the development of the comprehensive high school, offering a wide variety of curricula for students. One strong objection to these specialized curricula in the high school was that they brought about social fragmentation in the student community. Attempts to overcome the worst effects of this fragmentation included the formation of extracurricular activities for all—such as student government, social occasions, and athletic events—and the teaching of the "mother tongue."[15] English teachers were to provide through literature and composition the means for a common culture that would increase social cohesion. After World War I this function was further encouraged through the "Americanization" programs provided for the new wave of immigrants. Finally, the efforts of secondary teachers to determine their own curricula led to support for separating the teaching of literature from the teaching of composition. If each was to be given its fair share of attention, each must be treated alone.

The effects of the social efficiency movement on classroom teaching practices in high school English courses were in no way monolithic. The new emphasis on vocational education often led to English courses that ignored literature altogether, offering instruction in current-traditional rhetoric. As Applebee points out, these often included "units in salesmanship, advertising, and

---

[14]Frederick Rudolph, *The American College and University: A History* (New York: Vintage, 1962).

[15]Spring, 203.

printing added for variety and breadth."[16] In other words, the emphasis on the high school as a place of training for work could restrict writing instruction to the strictly utilitarian and vocational, without regard for the personal or political life of the student. At its best, however, the drive for social efficiency promoted a democratic rhetoric that responded to the progressive agenda of John Dewey's full educational experience: self development within a democratic environment, a concern for social reform and harmony, and the preparation for economic integration. This rhetoric is seen in the work of Fred Newton Scott of the University of Michigan, Joseph Villiers Denney of Ohio State, and Gertrude Buck of Vassar. Others who shared this perspective were George Pattee of Pennsylvania State, Katherine Stewart Worthington of Columbia, and Sterling Andrus Leonard of Wisconsin. Scott is particularly worth examining as an example it this social rhetoric because of his considerable influence in both public schools and colleges.

Scott's rhetoric was consciously formulated as an alternative to current-traditional rhetoric with its emphasis on the scientific and practical, and to the rhetoric of liberal culture with its privatization of experience and elitism. Reality for Scott was neither exclusively sensory nor exclusively subjective, but was a product of the interaction of the private and public in a social setting. Scott's rhetoric was thus intent on providing for public discourse in a democratic and heterogeneous society. The writing course should not provide students exclusively with the means for presenting scientific truths or private visions or even persuasive appeals. It should enable students to undertake all of these tasks and others. The important consideration is that "any piece of discourse, or mode of communication, is to be measured by its effect upon the welfare of the community."[17] Scott thus proposes a rhetoric of public service, a commitment to using discourse for the public good. Like Dewey, Scott argued that the first consideration of schools and colleges should be the preparation of citizens for a democracy who are trained to use their specialized knowledge for

---

[16]Applebee, 14.
[17]Fred Newton Scott, "Rhetoric Rediviva," Reprinted in *College Composition and Communication* 31 (1980), 413-19.

the welfare of the community as a whole. The subjects for writing Scott proposes in *Elementary English Composition,* a textbook for the schools written with Denney, accordingly emphasizes the relation of the writer or speaker to the entire rhetorical context — the audience and larger community, the subject from these perspectives, and the role of language in each and all. As Denney explained elsewhere, in leading students to topics it is necessary to choose "a typical situation in real life," express the topic so as to suggest to the student "a personal relationship to the situation," and provide "a particular reader or set of readers who are to be brought into vital relationship with the situation."[18] Thus Scott and Denney taught writing within a complete rhetorical situation, a situation that was thoroughly social without denying the importance of the individual.

The larger effects of the social efficiency effort on English studies were presented in a report entitled *Reorganization of English in the Secondary Schools,* published by the United States Office of Education in 1917. It argued that English courses should emphasize personal and social needs rather than college require-ments. They were to be "social in content and social in method of acquirement," to be attained by organizing them around "expres-sional and interpretive experiences of the greatest possible social value to the given class."[19] As for writing, there was to be, as in The Committee of Ten report, a progression from creative and individual activities at the lowest grades to social and more practical activities at the upper levels. Thus students in the seventh, eighth, and ninth grades were to engage in creative writing, such as stories about their experiences, sensory descriptions of memorable scenes, accounts of imaginary journeys, and fictional conversations. This creative effort was also to include oral expression, now returned to the English course. Imaginative work, however, was to appear less frequently in the upper grades except for those who display a special talent in this direction. Here the writing should be functional. It should grow out of the experiences of the students, but it should focus on social exigencies. Thus, the report recom-

---

[18]Joseph Villiers Denny, *Two Problems in Composition Teaching,* Contributions to Rhetorical Theory, 3rd ed., Fred Newton Scott, editor (Ann Arbor: n.p., n.d.), 173.

[19]Applebee, 66.

mended that writing should have a purpose, giving as an example the use of a school newspaper to publish student work. The student should write for a clearly designated audience, not "with the vision of a teacher, blue pencil in hand, looking over his shoulder." Thus the content and the form of the essay should be determined by "the purpose in view and the audience for whom the composition is prepared,"[20] and the same is true of the oral presentation. Finally, it should be mentioned that the report was in general a conservative document, emphasizing the utilitarian and social nature of mature discourse but saying little about the uses of writing in preparing students for citizenship in a democracy, or in enabling them to arrive at personal fulfillment. The strongest impulse for writing instruction is to prepare the student to be an efficient worker, as indicted by the opening paragraph of the report on the senior high school:

> The purpose of teaching composition is to enable the pupil to speak and write correctly, convincingly, and interestingly. The first step in the use of language is the cultivation of earnestness and sincerity; the second is the development of accuracy and correctness; the third is the arousing of individuality and artistic consciousness.[21]

As already indicated, the third step receives little attention while the social dimension of discourse is subsumed under efficiency.

THE PERIOD BETWEEN THE WARS

World War I served to establish beyond doubt the value of English studies to the nation as a whole. While English teachers in the schools organized courses around patriotic themes, their counterparts in the universities turned their pre-war training in German universities to the national interest, especially in the post-war occupation. The following years were a time of relative prosperity and optimism for the schools. In English studies, the most notable turn was the concern for the unique individuality and creative potential of each student. The center of composition

---

[20]Burrows, 30.
[21]Ibid., 27.

activities for an increasing number of school and college teachers became expressive writing about personal experience and occasionally creative writing. As I have argued in *Rhetoric and Reality,* the insistence of liberal culturists on genius as the essential element of writing at its best was now given a democratic application. Each and every individual was seen to possess creative potential, a potential the proper classroom environment could unlock and promote. This was the result of a number of forces. The child study movement represented by G. Stanley Hall had taken hold at the new schools of education. In addition, as Lawrence Cremin explains, after the war there arose "a polyglot system of ideas that combined the doctrine of self-expression, liberty, and psychological adjustment into a confident, iconoclastic individuality that fought the constraints of Babbitry and the discipline of social reform as well."[22] This resistance to social efficiency in the name of the individual was also aided by a bowdlerized version of Freud that depicted the innate impulses of children as innately good. The classroom was to unlock these virtuous and creative springs of feeling and conduct by providing a free and uninhibited environment. Finally, the example of aesthetic expressionism in dance, music, and poetry — particularly among the surrealists — was invoked as the paradigm for genuine writing.

For expressionist rhetoric, writing — all writing — is accordingly art. This means that it can be learned, and learned by all, but not taught. The work of the teacher is to provide an environment in which students can learn what cannot be directly imparted in instruction. The expression of the writer is the product of a private and personal vision that cannot be expressed in normal, everyday parlance. This language, after all, refers to the public world of sense data and social experience. The writer must instead learn to use metaphor to express meaning that is separate and above this limited realm. Sensory experience, on the other hand, is also very important since it provides experiences that can be used as materials for metaphor. Writing from this perspective enables students to get in touch with the private and the personal, the source of all that is meaningful. It thus empowers the student to

---

[22]Lawrence Cresmin, *The Transformation of the School: Progressivism in American Education, 1876-1957* (New York: Vintage, 1961).

shape a newly uncovered and better self—that is, half creating and half discovering the source of all truth and value. Furthermore, this product of the authentic writing experience—the truly personal—is organic, representing the perfect fusion of form and content. Finally, this method of teaching writing is concerned with power and politics, sometimes by implication and at other times openly in its critique of the dehumanizing effects of industrial capitalism. Its response is to enable each individual to realize his or her true self in order to bring about a better society. In other words, the private and personal is always prior to the public and social, the latter being an effect of the former.

In his historical perspective of creative expression in the school English curriculum, Kenneth Kantor offers the best overview of the various features of the expressive movement between the two wars.[23] One form it took was to argue that English is an art subject—like painting or music—not preparation for the more efficient uses of language. Proponents such as Hugh Mearns and Harold Rugg argued that traditional English courses had encouraged conformity and imitation rather than self-expression, Mearns maintaining that "children speak naturally in a form that we adults are accustomed to call poetry, and without any searching for appropriate use of the medium."[24] Rugg emphasized that the teacher must focus on the process of composing, not merely the product. John T. Frederick argued that creative writing enables the student to recognize the dignity of his own experience. Writing, like art, becomes concerned with intrinsic rewards, rewards that are available to all, not just the creative few. Numerous claims for the benefits of expressive writing were also made. This writing can be therapeutic, "doing away with maladjustments of personality."[25] It can advance cultural values, although, as Kantor points out, these values were most commonly those of the comfortable middle class, ignoring, for example, the experiences of African Americans and other minorities. Expressive writing, others argued, can improve the mechanical elements of writing as students strive to communicate a message that really matters to them. It can also enhance

[23]Kantor, 12-21.
[24]Ibid., 13.
[25]Ibid., 18.

students' enjoyment of literature since they can discover for themselves the values of literary discourse through their attempts to produce it. (Notice that this is the reverse of the earlier argument that reading literature will improve writing: here writing improves reading.) Finally, many argued that expressive and creative writing would enhance students' pleasure in writing of all kinds, encouraging an enjoyment of composing regardless of its purpose.

This enthusiasm for expressive writing did not go unchallenged. One contrary consequence of the turn to the methods of psychology in studying the development of children was found in the quantitative method of Edward L. Thorndike. Thorndike argued that whatever exists, exists in some quantity and so could be measured. His research sponsored a behavioristic approach in which teaching objectives were stated in measurable terms and the learning then measured through the appropriate testing device. In English studies this rage for quantification produced a variety of activities, some salutary, others unfortunate. The testing of student abilities led to tracking in English courses at both the high school and college levels, the latter in composition courses. This tracking on the basis of culturally-biased tests tended to reinforce class, race, and gender relations at both levels. In another area, the drive for efficiency in business and industry that came to be called Taylorism (after Frederick W. Taylor, one of the leaders in scientific management) combined with the influence of Thorndike to produce studies of the efficiency of high school and college writing courses. A joint survey conducted by MLA and NCTE found that high school students wrote on average 400 words per week while college freshmen averaged 650. The study revealed just how "efficient" English studies was, the course clearly overworking teachers to an appalling degree. The report argued convincingly for reform,[26] although none was forthcoming. A less useful application of this drive for quantitatively demonstrated efficiency came in the evaluation scales developed by Thorndike and Milo Burdette Hillegas, a device used to measure the quality of student essays in the secondary schools. The test itself had considerable merit,

---

[26]John Michael Wozniak, *English Composition in Eastern Colleges, 1850-1940* (Washington: University Press of America, 1978), 169-170.

requiring the teacher to evaluate student work by comparing it to nationally-normed models of varying degrees of excellence. Its pitfall was that it encouraged mechanistic approaches to writing instruction, teaching for the test and stressing matters of superficial form and correctness. The fact that results of the test were occasionally used to evaluate teacher effectiveness without regard for the ability level of students added to its destructive potential.

Another challenge to the dominance of expressive writing came in the form of socially-based rhetorics. These were found in courses inspired by Dewey and Scott, and were especially apparent during the Depression years. The insistence that writing is a social act performed through a complex interaction of writer, audience, subject, and language appeared at colleges in every geographical region.[27] These offerings tended to be specifically political in their orientation, addressing the economic crisis at home and the international crises abroad as failures of the total community, not of the individual. As we have seen, those supporting the value of expressive writing looked to private and personal resolutions to the economic and social catastrophes of the day. Those in the camp of social rhetoric, on the other hand, lay the blame for these disorders at the feet of the social and political arrangements generated by capitalism, a diagnosis in which they were led by strong factions in the American Historical Society and the Progressive Education Association.[28] While the expressionists looked to the individual to address the horrors of the thirties and forties, the sponsors of social reform looked to collective solutions, beginning with a critique of the excesses of the free enterprise system.

All of these conflicting positions on the most effective method for teaching writing are reflected in the NCTE sponsored *An Experience Curriculum in English,* published in 1935. This is not unexpected considering that the shapers of the report, numbering over 100, conceded the pluralistic nature of the document, explaining that any "attempt to create a single curriculum suited to pupils in environments so different as are to be found in the United States would be folly". Beginning with an assumption

[27]Berlin, *Rhetoric,* 81-90.
[28]Applebee, 115-116.

encouraged by the social efficiency movement as well as by certain strands of progressive education, the report asserted that "Experience is the best of all schools. ... *The ideal curriculum consists of well-selected experiences*" (italics in original). The experiences selected for students were those that were part of adults' daily lives as well as "desirable possible experiences they miss."[29] As far as writing is concerned, the report distinguished creative and expressive writing from social communication, providing experiences for each while favoring neither. The report implied that both privatized expression and public discourse were to be encouraged in the classroom and were not in any way incompatible. Finally, the report came out against the mechanistic and formulaic methods of current-traditional approaches, most controversially in its recommendation that formal grammar training be abandoned in favor of teaching grammar as a part of composing. In this the report reflected the influences of such enlightened linguists as Sterling Andrus Leonard, Robert C. Pooley, A.H. Marckwardt, Fred G. Walcott, and Charles Fries, all of whom argued for the social basis of language and the need for teachers to consider the importance of class relations and political contexts in teaching writing.[30]

1945-1960

During World War II, the Progressive Education Association sponsored a report entitled *Education for All American Youth* (1944), a document that became the major statement of what came to be called "life adjustment" in the schools. As Kantor explains, "Personal and social adjustment became the great concern of post war education," providing "a new security for those whose lives had been disrupted."[31] This effort was concerned with preparing students for the experiences they would encounter outside of school, including those associated with "civic competence." Unfortunately, the report contained excessive emphasis on "functional experiences in the areas of practical arts, home and

---

[29]Ibid., 119.
[30]Berlin, *Rhetoric,* 88-89.
[31]Kantor, 21.

family, health and physical fitness"[32] as well. The result in the composition course was a concern for the narrowly utilitarian, such as conversation, letter writing, and interviewing. Applebee's judgment of the life-adjustment effort is probably accurate: "In spite of occasional disclaimers, the emphasis in both name and activities was on 'adjustment,' 'conformity,' and a stable system of values. The traditional concern of progressive education with the continuing improvement of both the individual and his society was submerged and ultimately lost in the formulation."[33]

While life adjustment became the dominant influence in secondary school writing instruction, the communications course offered an alternative that was especially influential in colleges and to a lesser extent in high schools. The communications course was a combination of writing, reading, speaking, and listening activities. It was strongly influenced by the General Education movement during the thirties and by the General Semantics school of linguistics. It became a strong force in education, however, only after the army adopted it in its officer training programs during the war. As I have explained in *Rhetoric and Reality,* the communications course was varied in the form it assumed in colleges during the late forties and the fifties, even including attempts to introduce life adjustment into the college. Most of these courses, however, were conservative, offering a current-traditional approach that presented communications in the service of the democratic ideals recently challenged from abroad. The assumption was that a rhetoric committed to a disinterested objectivity would inevitably discover the validity of U.S. economic, social, and political arrangements. In other words, these courses were unaware of the ideological predispositions of the rhetoric they were forwarding. The communications course declined during the fifties. It did, however, for a brief time bring members of speech departments and English departments together, leading to an enrichment of rhetorical studies among English teachers. It also helped bring about the formation of the College Composition and Communication Conference (CCCC) in 1949.

---

[32]Applebee, 144.
[33]Ibid.

Writing in the secondary schools during this time was pursuing the path of life adjustment or of communications, although both occasionally led, as I have noted, to the use of expressive and creative writing. The formation of the CCCC, however, signaled a renewed interest in composition at the college level, motivated in part by the large number of veterans attending college on the G.I. Bill. The pages of *College Composition and Communication* and *College English* during this time attest to this new activity. Three areas are especially worth noting: literature and composition, linguistics and composition, and the revival of rhetoric.

Using literature texts as materials for analysis in order to teach writing had of course been a commonplace throughout the century. Despite the claims of college professors that students ought to come to college with mastery of the composing process, no generation of college students has ever in fact done so. Twentieth-century U.S. colleges, like their more elite counterparts in the nineteenth century, have continued to provide courses in writing, and there is obviously something perverse in labelling as remedial a course which is necessary for nearly all students. Those colleges most opposed to this course have often concealed their admission of its necessity by offering a "Freshman English" course devoted to literature, a course which is in fact a class in rhetoric, albeit of a belletristic variety. The distinguishing feature of the fifties in considering the relation of literature to composition is that, for the first time since the Uniform Lists, college professors were in large numbers insisting that the best way to teach composition is through reading literature and writing about it. This was in large part a result of a sense of professional identity achieved by teachers of literature following the war, a development described in Richard Ohmann's *English in America: A Radical View of the Profession.*[34]

As I have indicated elsewhere,[35] the arguments offered in defense of this view came directly from the tradition of liberal culture, still alive in literary studies. Students, it was charged, had nothing to say and literature provided them with rich subject matter. Writing about themselves required "a flair amounting to

---

[34](New York: Oxford University Press, 1976).
[35]Berlin, *Rhetoric,* 107-111.

genius," and most were certainly "not geniuses."[36] Reading literary texts and writing about them provided the knowledge and stimulation that the student needed to become liberally educated and enabled the teacher (almost certainly at this time a male) to keep his career alive and vital. The communications course, this argument went on, failed to provide for the individual while literature preserved the integrity of the individual against the tyranny of the mob. In fact, the liberal culturist notion of the uses of literature in the writing class is offered in the name of democracy. College is to prepare the leaders of a democratic society, and literature is the best means for doing so. Writing about literature was also offered in the interests of the college teachers themselves: after all, it was literature that they knew best and, if they were to be forced to teach writing, they ought certainly to do so by focusing on their own area of expertise. That this might mean serving the professional interests of the teachers more than the instructional needs of the students was not considered. It should finally be noted that these arguments for placing literature at the center of English studies and marginalizing writing instruction were to prove extremely successful during the sixties and the seventies when, as Applebee explains, "an academic revival...wrested the initiative in educational reform away from progressive education and returned it to college faculties of liberal arts."[37] This influence of college English teachers in curriculum formation will eventually have serious consequences for writing instruction in the schools.

Structural linguistics during the fifties seemed for many to offer a panacea for the difficulties of learning to write. Learning about the structure of language would enable students to learn about the structure of discourse, not to mention master grammar, making them better writers. In the sixties and seventies this would give rise to research in sentence combining in the work of Donald Batemen and Frank Zidonis, Kellogg Hunt and R.C. O'Donnell, John C. Mellon, Frank O'Hare, Lester Faigley and Stephen Witte, and others, and to the classroom techniques based on their work,

---

[36]Randall Stewart, "The Freshman Course Needs a Current of Ideas," *College English* 17 (1955), 16-19.
[37]Applebee, 32.

particularly those of Francis Christensen and the team of Donald Daiker, Andrew Kerek, and Max Morenberg. The interest in linguistics also encouraged the important statement on the CCCC's position statement entitled "Students' Right to Their Own Language," in which James Sledd played so important a part, a document that resisted dialectal imperialism as class and race discrimination. This attention to linguistics has also been a part of the poststructuralist turn to language as constitutive rather than merely reflective of reality, a matter that will be taken up later.

The attention to historical rhetorics, like that paid to linguistics, was part of the rediscovery of the complexity of language in all its manifestations, a complexity which many in English studies restricted to literary texts, seeing all other discourse as a simple signal system. The revival of rhetoric studies was undertaken with special rigor by the Neo-Aristotelians at the University of Chicago, most notably Henry Sams, Richard McKeon, and Richard Weaver. A similar concern for rhetoric in the history of literature was also undertaken at this time in the work of M.W. Croll, George Williamson, Sister Miriam Joseph, Rosemond Tuve, and others. A number of voices heard at this time have continued to be influential in rhetoric and composition studies, particularly James J. Murphy and Edward P.J. Corbett.[38] This recovery of historical rhetorics reminded English teachers of the central place that text production had occupied in the educational institutions of the past, serving in many ages as the organizing element of the entire curriculum. In addition to uncovering valuable information about the history of language and of its place in larger cultural formations, these studies contributed to a sense of the importance of composition teaching at all levels of schooling.

1960-1975

Joel Spring argues that after World War II the "corporate liberal state" — that is, the combined resources of private corporations and various government agencies — had increased its effort to bring education in the U.S. in line with national economic and

---

[38]Berlin, *Rhetoric,* 115-119.

social policy. As he explains, "selective service, the NSF, the NDEA, and the War on Poverty are considered part of the general trend in the twentieth century to use the schools as a means of cultivating human resources for the benefit of industrial and corporate leaders."[39] One of the major concerns after the war was the continued provision of talented and trained workers to serve the economic growth of the nation as a means to prosperity and national security. Indeed, the introduction of selective service deferment for those who attended college and graduate school was motivated by this consideration as were the establishment of the National Science Foundation and later the National Defense Education Act. As we have seen, life adjustment in the schools had originally begun as an attempt to provide for the socially efficient use of the nation's pool of talent. During the fifties, however, the almost exclusively practical and excessively student-centered orientation of life adjustment came under attack from a variety of politically conservative critics of the schools. The major charge made was anti-intellectualism, the results of which were a failure to provide the educated experts needed for a strong economy and a strong nation. The public schools, this argument went, should be subject-centered, not student-centered, emphasizing the scientific and scholarly disciplines around which the college is organized. This note was sounded in the popular critiques offered by Arthur Bestor, Hyman G. Rickover, Robert M. Hutchins, Mortimer Adler, James B. Conant, Mark Van Doren, and Paul Woodring. The Russian launch of Sputnik in 1957 gave instant credibility to these charges, providing concrete evidence to many that the U.S.'s technological dominance was being eclipsed.

A number of measures by government agencies and by private foundations to address this crisis — the extent of which we now know was grossly exaggerated — were taken immediately. The important role of the schools in providing the expertise to address this perceived national threat were underscored by the passage of the National Defense Education Act in 1958. This measure was at first designed to improve school instruction in math and the sciences, but by 1964 it also included the study of literature,

---

[39]Spring, 282.

language, and composition—particularly the latter two. Efforts to consider English studies itself at this time included the "Basic Issues" conference of 1958. A meeting of representatives from the MLA, NCTE, American Studies Association, and the College English Association, funded by the Ford Foundation, the conference was designed to address the English curriculum of the public schools. The College Entrance Examination Board in 1959 appointed a Commission on English to "propose standards of achievement" and "to suggest ways of achieving them"[40] for the schools, resulting in the report entitled *Freedom and Discipline in English* (1965). The most important of the curricular efforts for composition, however, was, interestingly enough, the Wood Hole Conference sponsored by the National Academy of Science under the direction of Jerome Bruner. The result was reported in *The Process of Education,* a document that served as an account of the new spiral curriculum. This plan organized the school curriculum around the structure of an established academic discipline which was then to be presented sequentially to students according to their level of cognitive development. Bruner's thought as found here and in several other of his essays from this period was highly influential. Its recommendation for the organization of a sequenced curriculum was influential in other curriculum studies, including *Freedom and Discipline in English,* and was central in the policies of Project English, a program for funding research founded in 1962 by the U.S. Office of Education. It was also important in the funding policies of the NDEA when it began granting money to English studies in 1964.

Bruner encouraged the use of cognitive psychology in discussions of educational matters. His emphasis was on learning as "process," a concept that had been an important part of the progressive educationist's program. Bruner, however, conceived of the learning process in terms of the cognitive level of the student and its relation to the structure of the academic discipline being studied. He was not interested in relating knowledge to society. Instead, he argued that each academic discipline had a structure determined by the experts within its confines, and that students

---

[40]Applebee, 196.

should learn this structure at a level of complexity appropriate to their ages. Bruner relied on Piaget's thinking in determining levels of cognitive development. The crucial element, however, was the student's mode of behavior. Bruner emphasized the role of discovery in learning, arguing that students should use an inductive approach in order to discover on their own the structure of the discipline under consideration. This did not mean merely pursuing the scientific method in a slavish and mechanical fashion. Instead, Bruner placed a premium on intuitive methods, approaches that enabled the student to go from creative guesses to verification in the more orthodox manner. The student was to engage in the act of *doing* physics or math or literary criticism, and was not simply to rely on the reports of experts. Bruner believed that students learned the structure of a discipline through engaging in research as a practitioner of the discipline.

The implications of Bruner's thought for writing instruction are not difficult to deduce. Students should engage in the process of composing, not in the study of someone else's process of composing. Teachers may supply information about writing or direct students in its structural stages, but their main job is to create an environment in which students can learn for themselves the behavior appropriate to successful writing. The product of student writing, moreover, is not as important as engaging in the process of writing. Writing involves discovery, a practice requiring intuition and pursuing hunches — in short, acting in the way mature writers do. The emphasis in the classroom should be on individuals coming to terms with the nature of composing — its inherent structure — on their own, without regard for social processes. The individual must arrive at a unique, personal sense of the knowledge of the discipline concerned, and only through this private perception is learning to compose possible.

Teaching writing as a cognitive process was immediately encouraged by a number of researchers and teachers. Janet Emig's *The Composing Process of Twelfth Graders* (1971) was especially important since it provided research evidence supporting the description of composing being forwarded by cognitivists. Emig also provided a great many of the terms which were to mark discussions of cognitive rhetoric. James Britton's *The Development of Writing Abilities (11-18)* (1975), the results of research conducted in England, furthered the cognitivist agenda. Emig and Britton were probably the two most respected empirical researchers in composing among school and college teachers in the seventies, and both provided suggestions for organizing a writing curriculum in the schools. The most detailed curricular recommendation along cognitive lines, however, was provided by James Moffett's *Teaching the Universe of Discourse* (1968). Moffett presented a series of activities sequenced to correspond to the four developmental stages of students as they passed from elementary school to high school—the stages being interior dialogue, conversation, correspondence, and public narrative. The use of the cognitive model of composing was also found at the numerous summer workshops for high school teachers sponsored by the College Entrance Examination Board's Commission on English in the sixties. And at the college level, the cognitivists during this time were represented by Janice Lauer, Richard Larson, and Frank D'Angelo.

The cognitive version of the composing process was not the only alternative to be forwarded at this time. A related paradigm that is finally much different was endorsed by the Dartmouth Conference of 1966. This meeting brought together approximately fifty English teachers from Britain and the U.S. to consider their common problems. The result was a revelation to the U.S. representatives. Contrary to the emphasis on English as an academic discipline which emerged in this country after the rejection of the child-centered approaches of the progressives, the British offered, as Applebee explains, "a model for English instruction which focuses not on the 'demands' of the discipline but on the personal and linguistic growth of the child."[41] For the British, the emphasis was not on subject matter, as had been the focus of recent discussions of the curriculum, but on providing "experiences through which the child could experiment, testing and strengthening his linguistic and intellectual skills by using them in a variety of contexts." Once again, explains Applebee, process was the guiding concept: "it was process or activity rather than content which defined the English curriculum for the British teacher."[42] This process, however, was different from that of the cognitivists since its primary objective was, in the words of John Dixon, a major

---

[41]Ibid., 229.
[42]Ibid., 230.

voice at the conference, "sets of choices from which we must choose one way or another of building our inner world."[43] Here the emphasis was not on mastering the composing process because of its value in solving writing problems, but experiencing it because of its value to the personal development of the student. As Kantor has argued, the difference between the cognitivist process of Bruner and the expressionist process of the Dartmouth Conference can be stated in a number of clear-cut oppositions: cognitive learning and intellectual development against affective response; a process of knowing "a body of material in a 'spiralling' fashion" against a "process of personal development"; communication for practical purposes against symbolic expression for self fulfillment; discovery through induction against creation through intuition.[44]

The result of the Dartmouth Conference was to reassert for U.S. teachers the value of the expressive model of writing. Writing is to be pursued in a free and supportive environment in which the student is encouraged to engage in an art of self discovery. This method had never altogether faded from the public schools, and had even been recommended by Albert Kitzhaber in a report on a Commission on English summer workshop in writing.[45] It had, however, been de-emphasized in most curricular recommendations in the early sixties. The political activism of the late sixties and early seventies, on the other hand, gave it new life. A major feature of the counter culture response to the Vietnam War, racial injustice, and environmental disasters had been based on the politics endorsed by expressionist rhetoric. The highly personal, private, and individual process of composing once again became conspicuous at the high school level, most notably in the recommendations of Ken Macrorie. It was also at the center of the influential study among college students of Gordon Rohmann and Albert Wlecke, entitled *Pre-Writing: the Construction and Application of Models for Concept Formation in Writing,* published in 1964. Other college English teachers who employed this method were Donald Murray, Walker Gibson, William Coles, Jr., and Peter Elbow. It should finally be noted that the cognitivist process

---

[43]Ibid., 230.

[44]Kantor, 24-26.

[45]Berlin, *Rhetoric,* 127.

and the expressionist process were most often called upon to
support divergent political perspectives. The expressionist process
was frequently taught in classes organized around resistance to
dominant political formations, particularly during the sixties, in the
interest of preserving the integrity of the individual. The cognitive
process, on the other hand, most commonly adopted the stance of
disinterested rationality, either avoiding political conflicts or addressing them as rational problems to be addressed in the terms of one
academic discipline or another. The result was a tendency to
reduce social, political, and personal problems to problems in
technical management.

   Both cognitivists and expressionists emphasized the private and
psychological elements of composing, the first the rational and the
second the emotional. Conceptions of composing that placed
writing in a social context were most commonly found in college
classrooms rather than in the public schools. These took two
dominant forms: revivals of classical rhetoric and new formulations
that came to be called "epistemic." The first, especially encouraged
by the likes of Edward P.J. Corbett and James Kinneavy,
emphasized writing as a response to public discourse politically
conceived. The text is a product of the interaction of the writer,
the particular audience addressed, the community at large, and the
subject considered. Decisions about language then arise out of this
complex network in a process that involves invention, arrangement,
and style. This rhetoric was criticized by the second group of
social rhetorics because it privileges the rational over the pathetic
and ethical appeals and because it regards language as an
unproblematic part of the rhetorical act. (Kinneavy's position on
this last matter later changed.) The central place of language in
rhetoric is the distinguishing feature of those in the epistemic
camp, a group including Richard Ohmann, Harold Martin, the
team of Kenneth L. Pike, Alton Becker, and Richard Young, Ann
E. Berthoff, Kenneth Bruffee, and W. Ross Winterowd. These
diverse approaches agree that language is constitutive rather than
simply reflective of material and social realities. This means that
the writer, the audience, the larger community, and the subject
addressed are all at least partly constructed by their verbal
formulations. From this perspective, we never know things in
themselves, but only linguistic mediations which refract as much as
they reflect signifiers. These rhetorics then are preeminently social

in their orientation since they argue for the public and communal nature of language, a system of differences which is formed not by individuals or even by the system as a whole but by interaction among people. At its most extreme form, this rhetoric argues that we exist in a prison house of language, never reaching contact with any externally verifiable realities. More commonly, however, these rhetorics, as among those figures already mentioned, argue for a dialectical relationship among the elements of the rhetorical context. Their differences reside in how they conceive this dialectic and are especially apparent in their political positions — for example, in the liberalism of Bruffee versus the Marxism of Ohmann.

1975-1985

The attempt to focus curricula on serving the needs of the liberal corporate state which began in the sixties reached new extremes in the late seventies and under the Reagan administration in the eighties. Part of the success of this conservative turn was a national backlash engineered by the Nixon administration against what was portrayed as the political and personal excesses of the protest movements of the sixties and seventies.[46] During this period, corporate management models of profitability came to prevail in the organization of public institutions. Schools everywhere were charged with being "accountable" for the "products" they were producing. Students were now considered a commodity to be weighed and measured, and nationally normed achievement tests were introduced in virtually all of the states. As Daniel Koretz has demonstrated, the proliferation of these tests resulted in the decline of writing instruction in the public schools.[47] After all, machine graded, fill-in-the-blank tests do not require writing ability. Ordered to improve the scores of their pupils, teachers taught to the tests — indeed, so successfully that scores continued to improve in the eighties. Unfortunately, since writing ability was commonly not measured in these tests, writing was often simply not taught at all.

---

[46]Spring, 312-327.

[47]Daniel Koretz, "Arriving in Lake Woebegone: Are Standardized Tests Exaggerating Achievement and Distorting Instruction?" *American Education* 12.2 (Summer 1988), 8-16, 44-52.

There is still another important reason for the reduction of classroom time given to writing in the schools during this period. As was earlier indicated, in the sixties college English teachers became responsible for guiding school curricula, a result of the spiral curriculum concept. College English studies, however, was then just beginning to develop rhetoric as a disciplinary formation. Indeed, the spiral curriculum can be partly credited with providing a hospitable, environment for this development, arguing as it did that the college expert in an academic subject was to determine its structure. Thus when college teachers formulated the structure of English studies for the schools, their emphasis was understandably on their area of greatest expertise, the literary text. Writing instruction thus received short shrift in these curricular guides. The irony, of course, was that many college teachers of literature continued to insist that writing instruction was the sole business of the schools, yet were unable to advise these schools on the methods for carrying out their mission. In short, those who did not know how to teach writing were responsible for guiding those who did not know how to teach writing. Indeed, the Squire and Applebee survey of successful high schools in 1966 discovered that while students were writing in the advanced tracks of schools, virtually no instruction in writing in these classrooms was taking place. Students in the tracks provided for those not going to college were writing little, if at all, and likewise receiving no instruction. The impoverished program provided these non-college-bound students was another unfortunate result of curricular thinking at this time, one for which neither the spiral curriculum nor English teachers can be held responsible. Since the emphasis in the fifties and sixties was on locating and training the best and the brightest for a time of national emergency, surprisingly little thought was given to appropriate instruction for average and below average students. Thus, the 1966 Squire and Applebee survey found that while advanced English classes were focusing on the study of literary tests, other tracks revealed "material of lower quality; the teaching technique less varied; the amount of time spent on worksheet and seat-work greater."[48] And as already

---

[48] James R. Squire and Roger K. Applebee, *High School English Instruction Today: The National Study of High School English Programs* (New York: Appleton-Century-Crofts, 1968), 78.

mentioned, writing instruction in the composing process was virtually non-existent at all levels, and writing itself found only at the highest tracks and in connection with the reading of literature. Finally, the decline of writing and writing instruction throughout the high schools during the seventies was further confirmed in Arthur Applebee's *Writing in the Schools in the Content Areas,* published in 1981.

In 1975 this failure of the schools to teach writing received national attention in a *Newsweek* cover story. As Lester Faigley and Thomas P. Miller[49] have pointed out, at a time when the demand for workers who could write was increasing, the attention to writing in the public schools and even in the colleges, where many mistakenly argued that the best and the brightest did not need this instruction, was on the decline. Since that time, a re-assessment of the role of writing in English studies has taken place, despite the baneful effects of accountability testing and the resistance of some college professors. Teachers in the schools, sometimes allied with university education departments, have led the way in re-introducing lessons in the composing process to their students, often without the encouragement of the official curriculum with its emphasis on test scores. Writing programs in colleges have meanwhile been dramatically strengthened during this time. In this last section of the essay, I would like to focus on the most prominent forms this instruction in the schools has taken and then turn to a brief consideration of its counterpart in the colleges.

Unlike virtually every earlier period in the century, national leadership in the form of government and foundation support has recently been all but nonexistent. National education policy under Reagan was to blame the schools for the nation's economic failures while giving the administration credit for its successes. The numerous complaints levelled at the schools during the eighties, furthermore, share the assumption that the sole business of education is to prepare a trained and disciplined work force. These discussions have said little or nothing about readying students for citizenship or for providing them with means for personal fulfillment that go beyond mere commodity consumption. The

---

[49]Lester Faigley and Thomas P. Miller, "What We Learn from Writing on the Job," *College English* 44 (1982), 557-69.

making of money in order to be a bigger consumer has been considered the sole end of education.

It is gratifying to report that teachers themselves have taken the initiative in filling this leadership vacuum. Three efforts are particularly worth noting: the National Writing Project, the teacher-as-researcher phenomenon, and the whole language movement.

The National Writing Project (NWP) was organized in 1974 as the Bay Area Writing Project. Under the direction of James Gray, the NWP has established teacher-training centers to improve the teaching of writing in the schools in virtually every state. The unique feature of this effort is that its work is almost exclusively conducted by teachers in the schools. Although each site is usually situated at a university, the training programs are run by teachers and for teachers. Indeed, the major purpose of the university is to house and administer the program. Successful teachers of writing from all levels themselves design the instructional materials during a summer workshop, and then share them with other teachers in inservice workshops throughout the school year. Both activities, furthermore, provide financial compensation. The NWP sites reached more than 70,000 teachers in 1984, and Anne Ruggles Gere has estimated that it may have affected some 300,000 by 1987.[50] It should also be noted that the NWP has no hard party line insofar as theory is concerned. It can, however, best be characterized as student-centered and expressive in its orientation.

The teacher-as-researcher phenomenon is described in a collection of essays entitled *Reclaiming the Classroom: Teacher Research as an Agency of Change,* published in 1987.[51] Its proponents are working to return the control of the classroom to the teacher. Partly an attempt to resist narrow state and district-mandated curricula, this approach to pedagogy encourages teachers to study the unique features of their students in order to design the learning and teaching strategies best suited to their students' situations. The Bread Loaf School of English has been a leader in forwarding these methods, calling on the work of a broad range of established

---

[50]Anne Ruggles Gere, *Writing Groups: History, Theory and Implications* (Carbondale: Southern Illinois University Press, 1987).

[51]Dixie Goswami and Peter R. Stillman, eds., *Reclaiming The Classroom: Teacher Research as an Agency for Change* (Portsmouth, NH: Boynton/Cook Heinemann), 1987.

and new researchers, including Garth Boomer, James Britton, Anne E. Berthoff, Donald Graves, Shirley Brice Heath, Ken Macrorie, Janet Emig, Mina Shaughnessy, Nancie Atwell, Lucy Calkins, and others. The attention to ethnographic techniques in studying cultural contexts has made this approach to writing instruction sensitive to the social dimensions of learning and writing, particularly to issues of class, race, and gender. This social concern, furthermore, is present despite the fact that, as the above list indicates, a number of the research studies invoked start from expressive or cognitive premises, especially the latter. One of the best applications of the pedagogical possibilities of the union of cognitive psychology and ethnographic study is seen in Nancy Atwell's *In the Middle: Writing, Reading and Learning with Adolescents.* This book won the MLA's Mina Shaughnessy Award for 1987, representing the first work by someone other than a college teacher to be so honored. A collection of essays representing the products of a teacher-as-researcher conference at Miami University (Ohio), edited by Don Dalker and Max Morenberg, is scheduled for publication in 1990.

The whole language approach to English studies in the schools is closely related to the teacher-as-researcher phenomenon in that a number of the same researchers and techniques are often invoked. Whole language teachers, however, might be characterized as less interested in cognitive and emotional processes and more interested in the social nature of learning. They also insist on the integrated nature of reading, writing, speaking and listening in all experience, and argue for the need to create learning activities that bring them together in social environment. Judith M. Newman has outlined the main features of whole language learning:

> Language and language learning are social activities: they occur best in a situation which encourages discussion and a sharing of knowledge and ideas.

> Language learning necessarily involves the risk of trying new strategies: error is inherent in the process.

> Reading and writing are context-specific: what is learned about reading and writing is a reflection of the particular situation in which the learning is occurring.

> Choice is an essential element for learning; there must be

opportunities for students to choose what to read and what to write about.

"Whole language" activities are those which support students in their use of all aspects of language; students learn about reading and writing while listening; they learn about writing from reading and gain insights about reading from writing. Our role as teachers is best seen as "leading from behind" by supporting the language learning capabilities of students indirectly through the activities we offer them.[52]

The democratic nature of this method is unmistakable. Whole language theory is an international phenomenon, appearing in New Zealand, Great Britain, and Canada, as well as the U.S. Among the leaders in this country are Yetta and Ken Goodman.

Finally, I would like to add a short comment on the course of rhetoric and composition studies at the college level between 1975 and 1985. The field has clearly arrived at disciplinary status, complete with graduate programs, undergraduate majors, major conferences, and journals. The trajectory of its development has been chronicled in Stephen North's *The Making of Knowledge in Composition,*[53] Lester Faigley, et al.'s *Assessing Writer's Knowledge and Processes of Composing,*[54] and my own *Rhetoric and Reality.* The encouragement of composition studies by college administrations is obviously a response to the demands of the work place, where complicated bureaucratic decision-making requires writing ability to an extent greater than ever before. As a discipline, however, rhetoric and composition studies is as much a response to its own problematic, its own "internal organization," to cite Bruner, as it is to its uses outside the academy. There is no question that professional writing courses and programs motivate much that goes on in the field. The discipline has also, however, formulated a research program responsive to its own agenda rather than that of the economic needs of students and employers, although, as will be seen, this agenda is not without its relationship

---

[52]Judith Newman, *Whole Language Theory in Use* (Portsmouth, NH: Heinemann, 1985), 5.

[53](New Jersey: Boynton/Cook, 1987).

[54]Lester Faigley and Roger D. Cherry, David Jolliffe, and Anna M. Skinner, *Assessing Writers' Knowledge and Processes of Composing* (New Jersey: Ablex, 1985).

to the economic. Today there are three major paradigms or problematics competing for attention in college rhetoric and composition programs, and I would like to close with a brief sketch of each. I should also mention that some of the figures mentioned will have already figured in the discussion of writing research in the schools, an indication of the rich interchange between school and college researchers now taking place.

Perhaps the most influential of the three paradigms is that of cognitive rhetoric. This paradigm argues for the primacy of cognitive structures in composing, arguing that any study of the process must begin with an analysis of these structures. Relying on the methods of qualitative research, especially protocol analysis, such researchers as Linda Flower and John Hayes, Sondra Perl, Nancy Sommers, Thomas Newkirk, and Carl Bereiter and Marlene Scardemalia have offered empirical data toward understanding composing behavior. Other workers in this area have applied findings of research in cognitive psychology as well as cognitive rhetoric in discussing the composing process, among them being Joseph Williams, Lee Odell, and Charles Cooper. As I mentioned earlier, however, cognitivist researchers are also moving in the direction of ethnographic studies, examining group behavior as well as cognitive processes, as seen, for example, in the recent work of Flower and Hayes, Carol Berkenkotter, Anne Ruggles Gere,[55] Lucy Calkins, Donald Graves, Thomas Newkirk, Barry Kroll, Kenneth Kantor, and others. The results of combining research in the privatized cognitive with research in group processes is certainly promising. Finally, it should be mentioned that it is the cognitivists who are most often called upon by those interested in the intersections of writing and the work place—for example, in composing and the computer. Cognitive rhetoric's reluctance to explore the ethical or political dimensions of writing in favor of the disinterested scientific stance lends its conclusions about composing to indiscriminate application in the economic setting, as I have argued in a recent *College English* essay.

The expressionists remain a force in rhetoric and composition studies. Such figures as Peter Elbow, Donald Murray, Ken Macrorie,

---

[55]See *Writing in Groups,* note 50, above.

William Coles, Jr., Walker Gibson, and others continue to explore writing as a private and personal act. It is this group that continues to insist on the importance of the individual against the demands of institutional conformity, staunchly holding out for the personal as the source of all value. Expressionists are most concerned with the individual studying her own composing process, regarding language as a probe for the discovery and formation of the self. Interestingly enough, while expressionists usually resist cognitivist methods and pedagogy, cognitivists often cite expressionists as providing intuitive observations about composing that empirical research has verified. The ideological loyalties of expressionists, however, are with the individual and against corporate activities, whether scientific, political, or economic.

Finally, the group of rhetorics that are being variously labelled social constructionist or social epistemic constitute a third paradigm. These start with the social as the foundation of subject formation and so tend to call on neo-pragmatist, Marxist, or poststructuralist formulations in presenting their case. All emphasize to a greater or lesser degree the constitutive power of language in human activity. Sometimes the focus is on collaborative writing, as in Kenneth Bruffee, Elaine Maimon, and Andrea Lunsford and Lisa Ede. Others have emphasized the social nature of composing, seeing the writer as always already socially situated—such as W. Ross Winterowd, Ann E. Berthoff, George Dillon, Charles Bazerman, and Carolyn Miller. Still another group bears marks of poststructuralist and Marxist elements, arguing for composing as political critique, moving in the direction of cultural studies—among whom are Ira Shor, Nan Elsasser, Greg Myers, Patricia Bizzell, Linda Brodkey, David Bartholomae, and John Trimbur. A number of efforts employing a feminist orientation fit into this category—for example, certain of the essays in two recent collections, one by E.A. Flynn and P.P. Schweickart[56] and the other by C.L. Caywood and G.R. Overing.[57]

Writing instruction will continue to occupy a central place in

---

[56]*Gender and Reading: Essays on Readers, Texts and Contexts* (Baltimore: Johns Hopkins, 1986).
[57]*Teaching Writing: Pedagogy, Gender, and Equity* (Albany: SUNY, 1987).

the school and college classroom, if only because more writing is required of skilled workers than ever before. As this survey has indicated, however, there are other compelling reasons for teaching people to write. The work of French poststructuralist language theory, of American neo-progmatist philosophy, and of epistemic rhetorical theory has argued that language is at the center of the formation of consciousness. From this perspective, culture is made up of an assortment of competing linguistic codes that "write" individual subjects. What this means is that each of us is a product of a variety of cultural codes or languages—class codes and gender codes, for example. The purpose of English studies can then be seen as an attempt to learn the way these codes operate, to learn to read and write them. It is important to note, however, that reading in this scheme becomes very close to writing since both are constructive acts requiring code formation as well as interpretation—both now being interchangable. In the end then, writing and reading in the English class may enable us to understand the central processes in forming culture, the self, and their relationship.

APPENDIX
AND
BIBLIOGRAPHY

APPENDIX

GLOSSARY OF KEY TERMS
IN THE
HISTORY OF WRITING INSTRUCTION

Abbreviation. Compression of a given long text into a few lines of verse or prose. The reverse of Amplification.

After-lecture Summary. Proposal of George Jardine at Glasgow that students not take notes in class but instead write an abstract of the lecture's main points afterward.

Amplification. The dilation or verbal expansion of an idea or text. As an exercise in the "development" of concepts through additional detail, the main purpose is to give the student practice in handling multiple aspects of a given subject. See also *copia, progymnasmata,* and Topics.

Amplification of Outlines. Assignment of speech outlines prepared by the teacher for students to develop into complete orations for oral delivery in the classroom.

Analysis of a Text (praelectio). Detailed oral dissection of a text to evaluate the author's style and structure. The second stage in Imitation. This micro-analysis as used in English schools led to the term "parsing" (from the Latin question *pars orationis?* — that is, "what part of speech is this word?").

Analysis of Authorial Choices. Detailed discussion of an author's rhetorical choices in a given text, with reasons proposed for authorial decisions at each point. A part of the Imitation process.

Analysis of Structure. Discussion of a work as a whole, with particular attention to Arrangement (e.g. arrangement of parts, methods of begining and ending, or proportion of the work devoted to a particular theme).

Anthologies of Standard Texts. Conscious retention of certain texts as best for exemplifying both stylistic form and moral content. The *Liber Catonianus,* Virgil's *Aeneid* and Lincoln's *Gettysburg Address* provide three examples.

Apprenticeship. The practice of sending a student to live with and emulate a practicing professional. The method was used into the nineteenth century, especially in law, and continues in a modified form in modern medical internships.

Artificial Order. Artistic alteration of normal chronological order in a narrative, to achieve a rhetorical effect. Medieval commentators for example saw a double order in Virgil's *Aeneid:* artificial because it begins *in media res,* natural because the first six books illustrate the six stages of a man's life.

Belletristic Writing. Writing with "taste" and aesthetic principles as the main features; greatly influenced by British and Scottish textbooks like Hugh Blair's *Lectures on Rhetoric and Belles Lettres* (1783).

Catechetical System. Lecture followed by a period in which the lecturer questions the students over the material covered in the lecture.

Chreia. Amplification of what a person said or did. One of the *progymnasmata.*

Cognitive Model of Writing. Writing instruction based on cognitive psychology, which analyzes learning as a process susceptible to empirical investigation.

Commonplace. Casting a favorable or unfavorable light — "coloring" — on something admitted. One of the *progymnasmata.*

Communications Course. A course combining writing, speaking, reading, and listening activities. Popular during the 1940's and 1950's.

Comparison. Treating two subjects in one composition, praising or dispraising both or praising one and dispraising the other ("contrast"). One of the *progymnasmata.*

Composition Based on Classical Rhetoric. Composition in this sequence occurs in four chronological interior steps—Invention
(discovery) of ideas, their Arrangement, their wording (Style),
and their retention in Memory—followed by one exterior step:
for oral language the step of Delivery (through Voice, facial
Expression, and Gesture), and for written language through the
step of physical inscription (Orthography) of words on some
receptor like papyrus, wax tablet, or paper.

Conference on College Composition and Communication (CCCC).
Association of writing teachers formed in 1949.

Continuity of Method. Re-use of proven teaching methods from one
period to the next, even as conditions change.

Copia. Term used by Desiderius Erasmus to denote the ability to
express oneself in different ways; analogous to Amplification.
The term includes variation, abundance, and eloquence. The
term is not original with Erasmus, being a major feature of
Cicero's rhetorical theory.

Copy Book. Book of blank pages in which English grammar school
students were expected to write commonplaces gleaned from
the texts they read. Also called "Commonplace Book."

Correct Language as Social Status. The favorable effect, from
Roman antiquity to present-day America, of the capacity to compose oral and written language according to accepted usage; the
corollary has often been a heightened emphasis on grammatical
"rules," and determined efforts to eliminate "dialects."

Correction. Public oral evaluation of student performance by the
master and at times by the other students as well. The seventh
stage in Imitation.

Courses in Composition. Separate courses in composition appear
only in late nineteenth- and twentieth-century America, though
(as Berlin points out in chapter seven), they are the one element common to every level of education in America.

Current-Traditional Rhetoric. Writing as an extension of scientific
method, with emphasis on inductive method. Prominent at
Harvard in the late nineteenth century.

Curriculum. A systematic educational program designed to achieve a particular objective. (The word literally means "little course," from the latin *currus*—"racecourse"—to which the diminutive —*ulum* has been added.) As Professor Welch points out, the itinerant Sophists of ancient Greece could have little opportunity for systematic development of their ideas before they moved on; Isocrates on the other hand developed a purposeful curriculum over many years in one place, greatly influencing the Romans in their systematizing of education.

Declamation. Classroom speeches on assigned issues, either political *(suasoriae)* or judicial *(controversiae)*. Generally regarded as the most difficult of all the Roman exercises since it included all the others. During the Roman Empire Declamation also became a popular form of public entertainment, with adult speakers performing.

Description. Dilation of detail in vivid description, "bringing before the eyes what is to be shown." One of the *progymnasmata.*

Dictation. Oral reading of a text for the purpose of student transcription. It was used in the Roman system for early training in sentence structure, but in early modern Scottish universities in the absence of textbooks some "lectures" were delivered slowly enough to allow verbatim copying.

Dominance of Latin. The Assumption, from Roman times into the late eighteenth century, that Latin was the language of literacy.

Dominance of the Oration. The assumption, common into the nineteenth century, that oral discourse—and, therefore, the rhetoric that underlay it—was the highest form of language use, and should therefore serve as a model for all types of discourse.

Eight Parts of Speech. A Taxonomy of Latin words popularized by Aelius Donatus (c. A.D. 350) in his *Ars Minor* and applied thereafter to large numbers of vernaculars as well.

Elliptical Exercise. Sentences with omitted words for students to supply.

Encomium. The praise of virtue or dispraise of vice in a person or a thing. One of the *progymnasmata.*

Epistemic Rhetoric. Writing instruction based on language itself rather than social or audience-reaction elements.

Examinators. Selected students in George Jardine's classes at Glasgow who would read and correct other students' written work.

Exemplification of Figures. Two forms: (1) short composition giving an example of one figure; (2) composition consisting entirely of examples of a standard set of figures of thought and figures of speech, in the order given by a standard source. A famous one is in Geoffrey of Vinsauf's *New Poetics* (Poetica nova), using the 64 figures from the *Rhetorica ad Herennium.*

Exercise Book. Book of blank pages for student compositions; a draft is written on the left-hand pages, then a final copy is written on the right-hand pages after the instructor has commented on the draft.

Expressionist Rhetoric. Writing as art, which can be learned by the student but cannot be taught directly. Thus the work of the teacher is to provide an environment in which students can learn what cannot be directly imparted in instruction. "Creative" and "expressive" writing are forms of this method.

Fable. Re-telling of a fable from Aesop, either shorter or longer than the original. One of the *progymnasmata.*

Facility (facilitas). The term used by Quintilian to describe the ultimate objective of the Roman educational system — that is, the ability to improvise appropriate and effective language in any situation. See Habit.

Faults in Language Use. Deliberate study of imperfect texts to illustrate defects to be avoided.

Forms. Student groupings or classes in English grammar schools, with specific curricula and timetables laid out for each form.

Grammar. In antiquity, "the art of speaking correctly and the interpretation of the poets" (i.e. literature). In modern times, standards of correctness based on well-known textbooks. In Renaissance English grammar schools, however, the term denotes as integrated curriculum of oral and written composition combined with literary criticism.

Habit. The deep-rooted capacity *(facilitas)* to produce appropriate and effective language under any circumstances; in Roman theory habit is the result of long practice in a carefully-planned set of incremental exercises like Imitation and the *progymnasmata.*

Imitation. A sequence of interpretive and re-constitutive activities using pre-existing texts to teach students how to create their own texts. One of the most pervasive and long-lasting methods of teaching writing and speaking, it appears in Greece in the fifth century before Christ, was systematized by the Romans, had continuing influence through the middle ages, the Renaissance, and early America, and continues in an altered form in many current textbooks. The complete Roman system has seven steps: reading aloud, analysis of text, memorization of model, paraphrase of model, transliteration of model, recitation of paraphrase or transliteration, and correction of the recited text.

Impersonation. Composition of an imaginary monologue that would fit an assigned person in certain circumstances. One of the *progymnasmata.*

Interactive Classroom. A Roman learning situation in which both students and teacher evaluated not only the model texts chosen for study, but each other's performance in recitation, in analysis, and in Declamation.

Language Acquisition. The natural process by which a child learns oral language on his own by listening to and imitating his elders; by contrast, writing requires external instruction, and cannot be learned on one's own.

Laws. Composition of arguments either for or against a proposed law. One of the *progymnasmata.*

Lecture. The direct, uninterrupted oral transmission of information by a teacher to a group of students. This method became popular only in early modern times, and was greatly spurred by the democratization of education that enlarged class sizes. See also Dictation.

Letteraturizzazione. Term used by George A. Kennedy to denote a movement from oral rhetoric ("primary rhetoric") toward written forms of discourse ("secondary rhetoric").

Letter-writing. A basic mode of writing practice from the early middle ages into the nineteenth century.

Liberal Culture. Writing based on literary works, with emphasis on appreciation of literature as the best thoughts of the best minds. Prominent at Yale in the latter part of the nineteenth century.

Life Adjustment. A movement begun in the 1940's to use writing as a means to prepare students for specific real-life experiences they would encounter outside of school.

Memorization. Verbatim memorization of a text for either (1) oral recitation in the classroom or (2) analysis of the text as a part of Imitation.

Modes of Discourse. Types of composition stressed by Alexander Bain at Aberdeen: narration, description, exposition, argument, and poetry. Bain also urged frequent and sequenced writing assignments. Some others attribute the "modes" to the influence of faculty psychology, through the Scottish rhetorician George Campbell.

Multi-purpose Exercises. A basic tenet of the Roman program, in which writing, speaking, listening, and reading are purposely combined wherever possible. Memorization for recitation was a common way to accomplish several ends in one exercise.

Narration as the Primary Step. Story-telling, and story re-telling (as in Imitation), as prior to any instruction in persuasion; exercises in Vivid Description *(ecphrasis)* accentuate the details of a narration.

National Council of Teachers of English (NCTE). Association of teachers founded in 1911 in protest to uniform reading lists. The NCTE argued that teachers rather than the colleges should set reading and writing requirements for their students.

National Writing Project. A teacher-organized program of teacher-training centers in virtually every state, organized initially as the Bay Area Writing Project in 1974.

'Old Education.' The family-tutorship-apprenticeship mode of education common in ancient Greece and in Republican Rome up to the time of Cicero before the prevalence of rhetorical schools.

Orthography. The physical act of writing words on a page. By late antiquity Orthography was a standard part of treatises on Grammar. Quintilian and other authors as late as the nineteenth century comment on the effects that writing instruments and writing surfaces could have on the thinking aspects of writing. Until very recently the sheer labor of transcription with stylus or quill pens encouraged writers to think their texts through very carefully before starting the difficult process.

Paraphrase of models. Re-telling of something in the student's own words. The fourth stage in Imitation.

Precept. The author of the *Rhetorica ad Herennium* (86 B.C.) defines Precept as "a set of rules that provide a definite method and system of speaking." In Roman education, Precept included both rhetoric and grammar, and was linked in the pedagogical triad with Imitation and Practice.

Progymnasmata. A set of graded incremental composition exercises; each exercise builds on the ones before it but adds a new element to create a higher level of difficulty for the student. The twelve common in antiquity are described by Hermogenes, whose revival in Renaissance Europe transmitted them to America as well. They are: Fable, Tales, *chreia,* Proverb, Refutation/Confirmation, Commonplace, Encomium, Comparison, Impersonation, Description, Thesis, and Laws. See also Modes of Discourse.

Proverb. Amplification of an aphorism *(sententia).* One of the *progymnasmata.*

Reading Aloud (lectio). Oral reading of a model as the first step in Imitation. Also used with a student's own composition as prelude for evaluation by the master and his fellow students.

Recitation of Paraphrase or Transliteration. Oral presentation by student of his version of the text; sometimes recited from memory, sometimes read aloud from a written text. The sixth stage in Imitation.

Refutation and Confirmation. Disproving or proving a narrative. One of the *progymnasmata.*

Regent System. System in eighteenth-century Scottish universities in which one professor taught all the subjects and stayed with one group of students during their entire education. Writing instruction was connected with every course.

Rhetoric. Precepts concerning the "art of speaking," though many of its doctrines have been and continue to be applied to writing as well. The subject was central in Western education from the first century before Christ until the late nineteenth century in America. Its traditional parts are Invention, Arrangement, Memory, Style, and Delivery.

School. A system of group education under a dominant teaching master who follows a plan of learning experiences designed to produce certain results in the knowledge-level and behavior of his students. The school in this sense is a Greek invention. Isocrates is the most influential Greek schoolmaster, being a major influence on Roman practice; his contemporaries Plato and Aristotle, on the other hand, operated schools devoted more to philosophical inquiry than to student development.

Self-correction. Quintilian urges that adults continue throughout their whole lives to use the methods learned in school to evaluate their own writing, to determine what to add, to take away, or to alter.

Sentence Diagramming. A process of visualizing syntactic relationships, begun by Alonzo Reed and Brainerd Kellogg in the 1870's.

Sequencing. The systematic ordering of classroom exercises to accomplish two goals: Movement from simple to complex, and Reinforcement by reiterating each element of preceding exercise as each new one appears.

Short Compositions. Student writings, as short as one sentence, or a pair of opposing sentences, to provide practice in the use of particular techniques (e.g. a rhetorical figure, a contrast, or a description.)

Silent Reading. The dominant form of reading after the spread of printing, so that eventually writing became the medium for silent reading rather than the script for oral performance.

Social Efficiency. Writing instruction aimed at preparing students to be competent members of society.

Student Literary and Debate Societies. Self-organized student groups begun in eighteenth-century America which evaluated each others' work and held oral and written competitions.

Structural Linguistics. Analysis of language structure, such as sentence combination, as an aid to learning how to write.

Tales. Recounting of something that happened or may have happened. One of the *progymnasmata.*

Theme. A prose composition as distinguished from a composition in verse.

Thesis. Composition of an answer to a General Question, that is, a question not involving individuals. One of the *progymnasmata.*

Topics. A method of discovering ideas (Invention) through designated "places" or "regions of argument" (to use Cicero's term). Aristotle names 28 in his *Rhetoric* II.23, though he discusses more than 200 in his book titled *Topics.* Cicero's *Topica* treats 14, divided into those inherent in the subject at hand, and those extrinsic to it. Each Topic is a mental process which directs the mind toward a certain activity which will recall pre-existent knowledge so that it may be used in composition. Common examples still used in modern textbooks (usually without acknowledgement) are definition, comparison and contrast, cause and effect, division, circumstances, and testimony.

Translation. The exercise of reproducing a text in another language. It was prominent in Roman times with Greek, and, beginning with the late middle ages, with vernaculars. It is a form of Transliteration in the process of Imitation.

Transliteration of Models. Student re-casting of a text in a different form: prose to verse, or verse to prose, or from one language to another. The fifth stage in Imitation.

Tutorial System. One-on-one teaching program in which the tutor assigns theme topics then evaluates the written text orally with the student; especially prevalent at Oxford and Cambridge universities.

Universal Grammar. Assumption that there is a grammar common to all languages, permitting Latin grammar to be applied to the English language.

Whole Language Learning. Modern learning environment which stresses the integrated nature of reading, writing, speaking, and listening.

Word-play as First Exercise. Medieval practice of introducing students to tropes and figures, complemented by memorization and recitation, before taking up Arrangement and finally Invention.

Writing as Academic Sorting. An effect of middle-class expansion in nineteenth-century America as increasing class sizes made oral recitation and oral disputation unworkable, making writing a useful means of assessing student ability.

BIBLIOGRAPHY
FOR FURTHER STUDY

Adams, John Quincy. *Lectures on Rhetoric and Oratory.* (Cambridge, MA: Hilliard and Metcalf, 1810). (Reprinted New York: Russell and Russell, 1962.)

Applebee, Arthur N. *Tradition and Reform in the Teaching of English: A History.* (Urbana, IL: NCTE, 1974).

Archer, R.L. *Secondary Education in the Nineteenth Century.* (Cambridge: Cambridge Univ. Press, 1921).

Ascham, Roger. *The Scholemaster.* Ed. John E.B. Mayor. (London: Bell and Daldy, 1863). (Reprinted New York: AMS Press, 1967.)

Bain, Alexander. *English Composition and Rhetoric: A Manual.* (London: Longmans, 1866).

Baldwin, T.W. *William Shakespere's Small Latine and Less Greek.* (Urbana, IL: Univ. of Illinois Press, 1944).

Barnard, H.C. *A History of English Education From 1760.* 2nd ed. (London: London Univ. Press, 1961).

Beck, Frederick A.B. *Album of Greek Education: The Greeks at School and Play.* (Sydney: Cheiron Press, 1975).

Beck, Frederick A.B. *Greek Education, 450-350 B.C.* (New York: Barnes and Noble, 1964).

Berlin, James A. *Rhetoric and Reality: Writing Instruction in American Colleges, 1900-1985.* (Carbondale, IL: Southern Illinois Univ. Press, 1987).

Blair, Hugh. *Lectures on Rhetoric and Belles Lettres.* (London and Edinburgh: Strahan and Cadell and Creech, 1783; Philadelphia: Robert Aitken, 1784).

Bledstein, Burton J. *The Culture of Professionalism: the Middle Class and the Development of Higher Education in America.* (New York and London: W.W. Norton, 1976).

Bonner, S.F. *Education in Ancient Rome from the Elder Cato to the Younger Pliny.* (Berkeley: Univ. of California Press, 1977).

Brinsley, John. *A Consolation for Our Grammar Schools.* (London: Printed by Richard Field of Thomas Mann, 1622). (Reprinted New York: Scholar's Facsimiles, 1943.)

Brinsley, John. *Ludus literarius.* English Linguistics 1500-1800, 62. (Menston, England: Scolar Press, 1968).

Clark, Donald Lemen. *John Milton at St. Paul's School: A Study of Ancient Rhetoric in English Renaissance Education.* (New York: Columbia Univ. Press, 1948).

Clark, Donald Lemen. *Rhetoric in Greco-Roman Education.* (New York: Columbia Univ. Press, 1957).

Curtis, S.J. *History of Education in Great Britain.* 4th ed. (London: University Tutorial Press, 1957).

Davie, George Elder. *The Democratic Intellect: Scotland and Her Universities in the Nineteenth Century.* (Edinburgh: Edinburgh Univ. Press, 1961).

Day, Angel. *English Secretorie.* English Linguistics 1500-1800, 29. (Menston, England: Scolar Press, 1967).

Diringer, David. *Writing.* (London: Thames and Hudson, 1962).

Enos, Richard Leo. *The Literate Mode of Cicero's Legal Rhetoric.* (Carbondale, IL: Southern Illinois Univ. Press, 1988).

Erasmus. *Adages.* Trans. Margaret Mann Phillips. Vol. 31 of *Collected Works of Erasmus.* Ed. Craig R. Thompson. (Toronto: Univ. of Toronto Press, 1978).

Erasmus. *Literary and Educational Writings: De copia/De ratione studii.* Trans. Betty I. Knott. Vol. 24 of *Collected Works of Erasmus.* Ed. Craig R. Thompson. (Toronto: Univ. of Toronto Press, 1978).

Erasmus. *The Ciceronian: A Dialogue on the Ideal Latin Style.* Trans. Betty I. Knott. Vol. 28 of *Collected Works of Erasmus.* Ed. Craig R. Thompson. (Toronto: Univ. of Toronto Press, 1978).

Freeman, Kenneth J. *Schools of Hellas.* (New York: Teachers College Press, 1969).

Frykman, Erik. *W.E. Aytoun, Pioneer Professor of English at Edinburgh.* Ed. Frank Behre. Gothenburg Studies in English, 17. (Gothenburg, 1963).

Gaff, Gerard. *Professing Literature: an Institutional History.* (Chicago and London: The Univ. of Chicago Press, 1987).

Gaur, Christine. *A History of Writing.* (London: British Library, 1984).

Gelb, I.J. *A Study of Writing.* (Chicago: Univ. of Chicago Press, 1963).

Gere, Anne Ruggles. *Writing Groups: History, Theory and Implications.* (Carbondale, IL: Southern Illinois Univ. Press, 1987).

Golden, James L., and Edward P.J. Corbett. *The Rhetoric of Blair, Cambell, and Whatley.* (New York: Holt, Rinehart and Winston, 1968).

Grafton, Anthony and Lisa Jardine. *From Humanism to the Humanities.* (Cambridge, MA: Harvard Univ. Press, 1986).

Gwynn, Aubrey. *Roman Education from Cicero to Quintilian.* (Oxford: The Clarendon Press, 1926).

Hans, Nicholas. *New Trends in Education in the Eighteenth Century.* (London: Routledge and Keegan Paul, 1955).

Harris, Roy. *The Origin of Writing.* (London: Duckworth, 1986).

Hoole, Charles. *A New Discovery of an Old Art of Teaching Schoole.* English Linguistics 1500-1800, 133. Ed. R.C. Alston. (Menston, England: Scolar Press, 1969).

Howell, Wilbur Samuel. *Eighteenth-Century British Logic and Rhetoric.* (Princeton: Princeton Univ. Press, 1971).

Humes, Walter M. and Hamish M. Paterson, eds. *Scottish Culture and Scottish Education: 1800-1980.* (Edinburgh: John Donald, 1983).

Jamieson, Alexander. *A Grammar of Rhetoric and Polite Literature.* (New York: A.C. Armstrong and Son, [1818]).

Jardine, George. *Outlines of Philosophical Education Illustrated By the Method of Teaching Logic, or First Class of Philosophy in the University of Glasgow.* (Glasgow: Andrew and James Duncan, 1818).

John of Salisbury. *The Metalogicon of John of Salisbury: A Twelfth-Century Defense of the Verbal and Logical Arts of the Trivium.* Trans. Daniel D. McGarry. (Berkeley: Univ. of California Press, 1955). (Reprinted Gloucester, MA: Peter Smith, 1971.)

Kaster, Robert A. *The Guardians of Language: The Grammarian and Society in Late Antiquity.* (Berkeley: Univ. of California Press, 1988).

Kellogg, Brainerd. *A Text-Book on Rhetoric.* (New York: Maynard, Merrill, 1896).

Kelly, Louis G. *25 Centuries of Language Teaching: An Inquiry into the Science, Art, and Development of Language Teaching Methodology, 500 B.C. — 1969.* (Rowley, MA: Newbury House, 1969).

Kennedy, George. *Classical Rhetoric and Its Christian and Secular Tradition from Ancient to Modern Times.* (Chapel Hill, NC: Univ. of North Carolina Press, 1980).

Kimball, Bruce A. *Orators and Philosophers: A History of the Idea of Liberal Education.* (New York: Teachers College Press, 1986).

Lentz, Tony M. *Orality and Literacy in Hellenic Greece.* (Carbondale, IL: Southern Illinois Univ. Press, 1989).

Leonard, Sterling Andrus. *The Doctrine of Correctness in English Usage, 1700-1800.* (Madison: Univ. of Wisconsin Press, 1929). (Reprinted New York: Russell and Russell, 1962.)

Little, Charles E. *Quintilian the Schoolmaster.* 2 vols. (Nashville, TN: George Peabody College for Teachers, 1951).

Marrou, H.I. *A History of Education in Antiquity.* Trans. George Lamb. (Madison: Univ. of Wisconsin Press, 1982).

McLachlan, Herbert. *English Education under the Test Acts: Being the History of Non-Conformist Academies 1662-1820.* (Manchester: Manchester Univ. Press, 1931).

McMurty, Jo. *English Language, English Literature: The Creation of an Academic Discipline.* (Hamden, CT: Archon, 1985).

Michael, Ian. *The Teaching of English from the Sixteenth Century to 1870.* (London: Cambridge Univ. Press, 1987).

Morgan, Alexander. *Scottish University Studies.* (London: Oxford Univ. Press, 1933).

Mulcaster, Richard. *Mulcaster's Elementarie.* Ed. E.T. Campagnac. (Oxford: The Clarendon Press, 1925).

Murphy, James J. *Medieval Rhetoric: A Select Bibliography.* 2nd ed. (Toronto: Univ. of Toronto Press, 1989).

Murphy, James J. *Renaissance Eloquence: Studies in the Theory and Practice of Renaissance Rhetoric.* (Berkeley: Univ. of California Press, 1983).

Murphy, James J. *Rhetoric in the Middle Ages: A History of Rhetorical Theory from St. Augustine to the Renaissance.* (Berkeley and Los Angeles: Univ. of California Press, 1974).

Murphy, James J. "The Modern Value of Roman Methods of Teaching Writing, with Answers to Twelve Current Fallacies." *Writing on the Edge* 1 (1989): 28-37.

Murphy, James J. "The Teaching of Latin as a Foreign Language in the Twelfth Century." *Historiographia Linguistica* 7 (1980): 159-75.

Murphy, James J., ed. *A Synoptic History of Classical Rhetoric.* (Davis, CA: Hermagoras Press, 1983).

Murphy, James J., ed. *Quintilian On the Teaching of Speaking and Writing: Translations from Books One, Two and Ten of the Institutio oratoria.* (Carbondale, IL: Southern Illinois Univ. Press, 1987).

Murphy, James J., ed. *The Rhetorical Tradition and Modern Writing.* (New York: The Modern Language Association, 1982).

Newman, Samuel B. *A Practical System of Rhetoric.* 10th ed. (New York: Dayton and Newman, 1842).

Ong, Walter. *Ramus, Method, and the Decay of Dialogue.* (Cambridge, MA: Harvard Univ. Press, 1958).

Ong, Walter J. *Orality and Literacy: The Technologizing of the Word.* (London: Methuen, 1982).

Palmer, D.J. *The Rise of English Studies: An Account of the Study of English Language and Literature from its Origins to the Making of the Oxford English School.* (London: Oxford Univ. Press, 1965).

Parks, E. Patrick. *The Roman Rhetorical Schools as a Preparation for the Courts Under the Early Empire.* (Baltimore, MD: The Johns Hopkins Press, 1945).

Pattison, Robert. *On Literacy: The Politics of the Word from Homer to the Age of Rock.* (Oxford: Oxford Univ. Press, 1982).

Quintilian. *The Institutio oratoria.* Trans. H.E. Butler. Leob Classical Library. 4 vols. (Cambridge, MA: Harvard Univ. Press, 1921-22).

Rainolde, Richard. *The Foundation of Rhetoric.* English Linguistics 1500-1800, 347. Ed. R.C. Alston. (Menston, England: Scolar Press, 1972).

Ramus, Peter. *Arguments in Rhetoric Against Quintilian: Translation and Text of Peter Ramus's Rhetoricae Distinctiones in Quintilianum (1549).* Trans. Carole Newlands. (DeKalb, IL: Northern Illinois Univ. Press, 1986).

Reed, Alonzo and Brainerd Kellogg. *Higher Lessons in English.* New York: Clark and Maynard, 1878).

Riché, Pierre. *Education and Culture in the Barbarian West, Sixth Through Eighth Centuries.* Trans. John J. Contreni. (Columbia, SC: Univ. of South Carolina Press, 1976).

Rudolph, Frederick. *The American College and University: A History.* (New York: Vintage, 1962).

Scholes, Robert. *Textual Power: Literary Theory and the Teaching of English.* (New Haven: Yale Univ. Press, 1985).

Scott, Izora. *Controversies Over the Imitation of Cicero as a Model for Style and Some Phases of Their Influence on the Schools of the Renaissance.* (New York: Columbia University Teachers College Press, 1910).

Smith, Adam. *Adam Smith Lectures on Rhetoric and Belles Lettres.* Ed. J.C. Bryce. (Indianapolis, IN: Liberty Classics, 1985).

Spring, Joel. *The American School 1642-1985.* (New York: Longman, 1986).

Stowe, A. Monroe. *English Grammar Schools in the Reign of Elizabeth.* (New York: Teachers College Press, 1908).

Vives, Juan Luis. *On Education [De tradendis disciplinis].* Ed. and trans. Foster Watson. (1913). (Reprinted Totowa, NJ: Rowman and Littlefield, 1971.)

Wagner, David L., ed. *The Seven Liberal Arts in the Middle Ages.* (Bloomington, IN: Indiana Univ. Press, 1983).

Ward, John. *A System of Oratory.* (London: Printed for John Ward in Cornhill, 1759). (Reprinted Hildesheim and New York: Georg Olms Verlag, 1969.)

Watson, Foster. *The English Grammar Schools to 1660.* (Cambridge: Cambridge Univ. Press, 1908). (Reprinted London: Frank Cass, 1968.)

Witherspoon, John. *Lectures on Eloquence and Moral Philosophy.* (Philadelphia: Woodward, 1810).

Woods, Marjorie Curry, ed. *An Early Commentary on the "Poetria nova" of Geoffrey of Vinsauf.* Garland Medieval Texts, 12. (New York: Garland, 1985).

Wozniak, John Michael. *English Composition in Eastern Colleges, 1850-1940.* (Washington, DC: University Press of America, 1978).